tides

For my closest of friends; without you
I could not have maintained this way of life and because of this
I am sincerely grateful.

tides

a climber's voyage

nick bullock

Vertebrate Publishing, Sheffield
www.v-publishing.co.uk

First published in 2018 by Vertebrate Publishing.

Vertebrate Publishing
Crescent House, 228 Psalter Lane, Sheffield S11 8UT United Kingdom.
www.v-publishing.co.uk

Cover and chapter heading illustrations: Tessa Lyons.
Photography by Nick Bullock unless otherwise credited.

A CIP catalogue record for this book is available from the British Library.

ISBN: 978-1-911342-53-3 (Hardback)
ISBN: 978-1-911342-54-0 (Paperback)
ISBN: 978-1-911342-89-2 (Ebook)

10 9 8 7 6 5 4 3 2 1

Design and production by Jane Beagley.
www.v-publishing.co.uk

Vertebrate Publishing is committed to printing on paper from sustainable sources.

Printed and bound in the UK by T.J. International Ltd, Padstow, Cornwall.

contents

prologue
living scared

December 2014
Stoke Bruerne, England

'I've lived too long.'

My parents, now retired, live on a canal boat moored permanently at Stoke Bruerne, Northamptonshire. When I visited on my way south from Llanberis to Chamonix for the winter, I walked the towpath. The day was washed out. Grit clung to the soles of my shoes, rotting leaves floated on the dark surface of the canal. The canal museum was closed for the winter. A mallard stirred the water. I bent and stepped into the crouch of the boat. It rocked as I opened one of the small wooden doors leading into the overheated living room.

'I've lived too long' were my dad's opening words. Paddy, the Jack Russell terrier, skittered across the wooden floor to jump and claw at me. I pushed him away. Dad sat in his wooden-framed chair with a cup of tea in one hand and a roll-up clamped between yellow-stained fingers of the other. The oil from years of manual labour that used to line Dad's crevassed finger skin had long gone. Wisps of smoke belly-danced toward the discoloured ceiling. I sat surrounded by paperback books, china figurines, glass paperweights and photographs of my sister's grown-up children. A birdcage stood on an old oak table. Barney, the African Grey parrot, was perched on top of the cage, pulling out her feathers.

It's easy to listen to something like my dad's statement and not fully take it in.

'I've lived too long.'

What's too long? Do many of us take life for granted, treat it as something that may be frittered away? Is there really such a thing as *'I've lived too long'*?

Recently, I've been waking up at 4 a.m. The wind shakes my van, and the rain plays a xylophone on the metal roof. I turn on the light. Perfect almonds of condensation have formed on the red ceiling. The wind grasps the van and an individual drop clings – clings and hangs, hangs and stretches. Stretches ... and finally lets go ... falling, falling, stretching, falling ... the drop holds together. Until after just a second ... it thuds on to my sleeping bag. I lie and worry about not having a fixed abode, a career, a partner or enough money to last until I die. As I lie staring, I see homeless people sleeping in doorways. I see buskers, beggars, the unemployed, the lonely.

Later, walking through the long grass of the clifftop, I watch shafts of sunlight penetrate the cumulus, illuminating the dark sea and embracing an oystercatcher that silently skims the waves. I see the wind catch the curling leaves of an ash tree and the trickle of water weaving a course along the dusty surface of yellow limestone. And all this reminds me that life, at whatever level, whatever frailty, has to be worth living.

The sun dips for another day, quenched by the green Irish Sea. High in the distance, a pair of gannets rise on a spiralling thermal.

1
love and hate

October 2003
Leicester, England

I stepped out through the small prison door and every sound changed. There was the distant rumble of a lorry, a snatch of a faraway police siren. Cars swished down Leicester city centre's Welford Road. I could hear the dull whine of planes descending into East Midlands Airport. A few pigeons huddled in the shadow of a prison turret were briefly mumbling to each other. I turned my face upward to feel the rain, and imagined the stars beyond the sodium street lights. The acidity of the rain felt cleansing. The exhaust fumes in the air smelled of freedom. I inhaled deeply. I listened to the air enter my body.

I breathed out, turned, and walked away.

Fifteen years. Fifteen years of aggression, violence and stress. Fifteen years of learning bitterness, prejudice, loneliness. Fifteen years of building walls. Fifteen years. The prison service had given me all of these things, but in some way it also had given me parole: I now had health, fitness and climbing. It had given me the money to pay off my mortgage. I was grateful for these things.

Looking over my shoulder, I followed the straight line of red brick. The prison wall stretched above with a thousand uniform bricks. Rain soaked my shoulders. High-level lights lit the street. Shadows hid, clinging to the corners as though scared.

I had done it. I was thirty-seven years old and I had resigned from my job as a PE instructor in the prison service. I had walked away from a job guaranteed for life. The job which earlier in my life was everything I desired: security, pension, stability, a regular wage, a profession. I had walked. And as I walked, the water beneath my feet squelched, and the stars – hidden behind the clouds – were burning bright. They were close enough to grab and take hold of. Close enough for me to grab and lock away. Lock away like some of the people that were no longer a part of my life, some of the people still serving a sentence: Reggie Kray, Hate-Em-All Harry Roberts, Bobby Dew, Rookie Lee, Houston, Charlie Bronson. I felt free.

Almost.

At the age of sixteen, I had taken out a loan to buy a motorbike. Each time I stamped on the kick-start, the engine screamed and my nose filled with the unburned tang of an oily two-stroke; the inches became miles. Cheadle, the town in Staffordshire where I was born and where I grew up, with its red brick, factories and fumes, gave way to verges stuffed with wildflower blurs. Red, green, yellow, pink; hedgerows that were home to pink-breasted bullfinch, greenfinch, goldfinch, chaffinch. In those boundless times, the miles turned to days and the days to weeks. That 50cc engine was a time machine, and our time was infinite.

Now, at the age of thirty-seven, I was sitting on the brand new carpet in the empty and newly decorated living room of my beloved house in the village of Burton Overy, in Leicestershire. Burton Overy had been my bolthole for fifteen years; it had been my escape, sanctuary and therapist. My treasured place. Mature oak and horse chestnut, tawny owls, the thatched post office, the pub, the house with warped walls and a tin roof, the grazing sheep, the telephone box, the humble medieval church built from ironstone, and the rabbits, rooks and lapwings. I didn't feel at all like a focused projectile, I felt more like a piece of wood careering down a river. *What had I done?* I was scared of what the future held, but the excitement of not really knowing where or how my life would move forward was simultaneously intoxicating.

Since walking from the prison I had felt my heart beat. Tomorrow I would leave Leicestershire, the day after catch a plane heading east for Nepal, and the day after that someone would move in to my home and start paying rent.

December 2003
Kathmandu, Nepal

The motorbike accelerated over the Kathmandu cobbles, speeding through dust and shit. White knuckles, wide eyes, hair on the back of my neck standing erect. It was going to be close. Why did I repeatedly find myself in these life-threatening situations? One move was hopefully all it would take to get us into a position of safety. One move, that was all, but the constriction we were now aiming to squeeze through was getting smaller by the second. Gripping hard. Squeezing. Knuckles white. The situation was out of my control.

All swinging hip bones, a black cow nearly finished us as she lurched into the gap. A passer-by whacked it, shooing it away. The atmosphere was overflowing with heat and dust and humanity. I could almost feel the warmth of the brightly clothed, sweating bodies packed into the narrow street as we passed. The gap grew bigger. Dawa twisted the throttle, and we hurtled through a human corridor of arms, legs, jeans, rags, robes. Silver-coloured metal boxes, stacked and shining; barking dogs; green, blue, red, a pile of blurred plastic buckets. Leaning to the right, to the left, the Nepali climbing agent handled the Honda with the skill of someone used to dealing with the chaos of daily life in Kathmandu. I, on the other hand, had only just returned from a month in the mountains, and it had been a long time since I had owned that white Yamaha.

It had been six weeks since leaving my home and my job, and it had been about six hours since the stomach-stressing flight from Lukla – famous for its terrifying runway and plane crashes. When I walked away from the prison, I had left behind everything that I grew up believing would make my life solid. This still had not sunk in, because if it had, I would have found it almost as terrifying as the flight.

Five weeks earlier, Al Powell, Jules Cartwright and I had landed and walked down the steps of the plane together in Nepal. We were stubborn, determined and ambitious. Powell was laid-back, stoic, quiet, gaunt and rangy, super fit with a reputation for going lightweight and speed in the hills. He was also down to earth, working class, straight talking, no frills. Cartwright was blonde, good looking, and the up-and-coming superstar of British alpinism. He was also the youngster at twenty-eight. On the surface Jules was very sure of himself – chain smoking, hard drinking, hard climbing, no nonsense, no bullshit. To the point and then straight to the pub. I had always surmised that his confidence, or at least some of it, came from being brought up in a relatively privileged, close-knit family. He appeared to ooze self-assurance, strength, immortality – the type of confidence that people without money or a private education often have difficulty expressing.

I felt old and intolerant. Intolerance was a hand-me-down from the prison service and my dad, but as we landed in a country new to me, a country with vibrancy, I could feel the shadows begin to lighten a little. I had begun climbing late in life at twenty-eight, after discovering the activity as part of PE officer training in the service. Finding climbing was an epiphany, and for most of the time, a life-enhancing activity that had almost immediately made me a better person and given me focus; climbing tested me both physically and mentally. Since becoming a climber, everything in my life had been steered towards becoming better and more experienced. I wanted to see how far I could take the activity and where it would lead me. Rock, ice, mountains; climbing had become my sole focus and I knew at some point I would have to dedicate myself completely, no matter the perceived risks and the sacrifice, and at times the physical and mental bruising that come as part of that package.

Landing in a tiny plane on that very steep, short runway in Lukla for the first time was shocking. The air – thin of oxygen but thick with glacial dust – scratched at my lungs. Wood smoke lingered in the streets above the heads of men and women with strings and hessian sacking hanging around their necks – tools of the trade for porters, people who appeared to live a life of punishing hardship. Lukla reminded me of a ramshackle frontier town from a cowboy film, a town catering to the needs of thousands of trekkers and climbers. Transients: guides, porters, boxes of beer, climbers, building materials, trekkers. On the move daylight or darkness, dry or wet, snow or heatwave. Fabled Lukla, the town and airport I had often read about and, until now, only imagined. Chickens and cows. Steam rising from the thick, tangled coats of yaks. People with almond eyes, red robes, shaved heads. Engraved golden prayer wheels, men and women bent over, weighed with loads to be carried up the valley.

I sat in a white plastic chair alongside Powell. We both sipped sweet milky tea while sunbathing on the veranda of Paradise Lodge near the airport. I had been transported to a different life, a parallel life to the one of walls and hate and oppression. The wildflower hedgerow blur from my teenage years felt almost within reach.

We had no official guide or helper. Loben Sherpa, a smiling, larger-than-life character and friend of Cartwright's – who lived in Kathmandu in the climbing and trekking season, but whose family and home were still in Darjeeling – sorted the bureaucratic details of the trip, between regular beers after cigarettes. I could see why he and Jules hit it off. Loben had fingers and thumbs in pies all over the place, and appeared to be able to fix problems with just a smile. I had realised the greasing of palms was an everyday part of bureaucracy in Kathmandu.

Jules had already visited Nepal nine times and had arranged the employment of three porters. As I revelled in the sun, the realisation that I was never returning to the prison service made me glow.

The three of us began walking, heading for Namche Bazaar. For some reason Cartwright was insistent we complete the walk in one day. The altitude of Kathmandu – where we had been in the morning – is 1,440 metres; Lukla is 2,860 metres. Namche is 3,440 metres. Why we had to get to Namche in a day baffled and surprised both Al and me. Around 9 p.m. the three of us, dehydrated and with thumping headaches, staggered into Namche Bazaar in the dark.

We were in Nepal to attempt a new route on the 1,600-metre north-west face of Teng Kang Poche above Thame, a small Sherpa village higher up the valley from Namche and the childhood home of Tenzing Norgay. It came as no surprise this face was unclimbed: ice streaked with loose limestone and threatening séracs made up the most part of it. Cartwright pushed for the big-bag, seven-day-up-three-day-off-the-back approach. I suspected that his ten-day epic on Ama Dablam in 2001 had affected his mental state. I, on the other hand, plumped for a slightly different line and a slightly different approach: four days up, one day down. Down the same side, reasonably fast and light, but not without suffering and risk. Having known Cartwright for a long time, I knew I was on to a loser trying to persuade him of the virtues of my approach, even though the trip was my brainchild from the beginning and he had jumped on board last minute. Cartwright had a lifetime of experience packed into his twenty-eight-year-old head, and I had an almost reverential belief in him. But I wondered what was driving my friend's decisions. Something different was happening inside that blonde head. My guess was self-induced pressure to perform and please sponsors. He was also attempting to become a mountain guide and everything this involves, and to keep his relationship in Sheffield going. Basically, life and the complexities of life that come from being successful and driven but still wanting more were starting to shake my friend and his once carefree attitude.

Leaving the half-built lodge at Thyangboche, a three-house settlement beneath our cliff, I struggled under the weight of my huge rucksack.

As Cartwright forced the pace again, I was forced to keep quiet. Due to the other two's late arrival at Thame we had missed our chance the previous afternoon to stash kit beneath the face. I had walked up to the hamlet a day earlier. In an attempt at an explanation for their late arrival, Powell complained about feeling 'powered down'. I substituted 'powered down' for 'pissed up'. Partying in Namche the evening before had been too good an opportunity for the pair to miss; Powell's strong and gnarly temperament was no match for Cartwright's thirst.

With a huge sigh of relief, we realised the initial snow cone at the base of the face was solid. Solid enough to support bag and bodyweight. Cartwright set the pace, Powell followed and I moaned. The giant, compact north pillar to the left twisted airily into the sky. A massive crumbling wall of rock running from the pillar hemmed the three of us in, teetering blocks threatened, séracs miles above intimidated. Easier-angled fields of loose rock, ice and snow were spread out in front of us. More bands of séracs stretched across the wall to the right. A Droites north wall on top of a Droites north wall.

Free from the constrictions and concerns of people, bills, work, worries and rope, we slowly left behind the daily grind; the unknown concerns affecting Cartwright and his decisions just beneath the surface were simmering away and in turn affecting my mood. The runnel walls drew in around us. The face steepened and we continued to solo. Occasionally the heavy rucksack stuffed with seven days' food and gear twisted and lurched, but still we soloed. Cartwright was in front, powering through unconsolidated snow. Powell was behind, competitive, refusing to compromise, refusing to give in by allowing the gap between himself and Cartwright to grow. I was at the rear and, recognising my weakness in this big-bag approach, I allowed the gap to grow. Guilt coursed through my mind: Cartwright had been breaking trail for so long, but my bag was so heavy because of his estimate of time and his choice of line and his refusal to return down the north side of the mountain. So it was with a sense of justice that I clung to my dignity.

'What the hell is this?!' I yelled.

The first roped climbing came as a shock as Cartwright and Powell were a lot taller than me and had been able to step down to reach a horizontal crack, ready to accept a crampon point easily. I, on the other hand, found the whole procedure desperate. I needed an intermediate placement, but none was forthcoming. Gently lowering myself, the parasitic sack drained my strength. I used a pick placement in a blob of ice to support myself.

The ropes running horizontally left around a corner rubbed on a sharp edge of rock. What if I fell now? Would just one rope fail, or would both ropes cut? Powell, out of sight, pulled. The rope drag left no feeling for sensitive belaying. I swayed. Powell pulled. I resisted and carefully pulled against the rope. A tug of war was not in my script. I stretched, full body length hanging from the pick hooked in the blob of ice. I was straight-arm hanging and still I was six inches short. 'Commit, come on! Decide to commit!' The ice blob made the decision for me as it broke off. Ice splinters spun into the thin air. My left front point screeched as it slid and then snagged in the crack. I stopped. Powell tugged again. This time I moved with tenacity. More projectile-like, not just driftwood. I moved and left behind my thoughts of 'what if?' We had too far to go to waste time on 'what ifs'.

It was only day one and already I detested the rucksack, the soft snow, Cartwright's drive and determination, his fitness, and his lack of years. At that moment I hated him … but I hated myself more. I hated that I was getting old. At one time I would have been fighting for the front, fighting to break trail. The competitive, driven streak running through my veins wouldn't have allowed anyone else to do all the work.

Reaching the top of the snowfield, a perfect tent spot presented itself and Powell volunteered to stay and dig. Ahead, the runnel had turned into a perfect two-pitch, seventy-five-degree ice gully. Cartwright asked if I wanted to lead it, and to address the balance in some way, and to ease my evening of self-doubt, I jumped at the chance. The rucksack could be left behind, as the plan was to climb two pitches, fix the rope and return to the tent spot ready for the following day.

Climbing the first pitch, the old feeling of being engaged in the ebb and flow of the vertical returned. Cartwright joined me and I set off again to lead the second pitch of the Himalayan Ben Nevis Green Gully. At the top I fixed the ropes ready for a session of jumaring in the morning and slid back to the yellow tent 120 metres below. The mountains across the valley from us turned into huge vermilion Victorian ladies' dresses and in the far distance, Everest, Lhotse and Cho Oyu blushed with their girth.

While Cartwright and Powell attempted to make a tiny two-man, single-skin tent into a home big enough for three, I patiently sat on my rucksack and leant against the overhanging rock the tent was beneath, contemplating the day.

I remember Dad, covered in dust and sweat, appearing from the side exit of the Cheadle cotton mill where he worked the night shift. Mum would give him his packed dinner, while my sister and I waited in the back of the car. I wonder what he had dreamt of when he was the same age as me.

When the mill closed down and was replaced by a supermarket, Dad rescued the old carp from its pond and dug a new pool for it in the garden. The large grey fish, held in his cracked and oil-stained hands, curved its thick body into a sickle-moon shape. Dark, bottomless eyes. Yawning mouth. Glistening scales. It entered the water with a plop, and after a second or two, it swam slowly into the reeds.

Powell, Cartwright and I crammed into the tent. The night was one of the worst I had spent on a mountain. I had drawn the short straw, which meant lying between the others – unable to move or even turn to lie on my side. The morning arrived and I was wrecked. Grey, Gore-Tex-filtered light spread into the tent and I lay awake, much as I had throughout the whole night. I waited for one of the others to start the stove and begin the arduous task of melting snow. An alpine start this was not, but eventually, breakfasted and packed, we were ready to move.

Cartwright approached the ropes fixed the day before intending to climb them alongside Powell and me who were going to lead and second.

'Are you going to take these ice screws, Jules?' I asked, wondering what other gear was going to be left for the last one up the hill to carry. I remembered the time he and Jamie Fisher had left me to retrieve everything when I followed. This was on my first expedition in 1997 when we had attempted the Shark's Fin on Meru Central in India.

'No!'

'Oh, why's that then?' I asked, a little taken aback by his shortness.

'I'll just do everything, shall I? Yesterday I broke trail, carried all the gear, and cooked,' Cartwright continued. 'This morning I even melted the snow while you and Al lay there. How the fuck are we going to climb this thing if there is only one of us doing the work?'

Age had mellowed me a little but I still wore the effects of prison and some of the early-morning rant was unfair.

'Oh, so of the three pitches led yesterday I'm wrong to say I led two of them?' I snapped back.

Powell being Powell said nothing and took Cartwright's rant while sorting gear. Cartwright, in full flow by this time, continued.

'Hey, I know if we continue finishing at three o'clock and starting at eight we're never going to climb this thing.'

Cartwright climbed alongside the fixed rope, kicking hell out of the snow, still angry and obviously replaying the argument with each step. He would thank me later. He didn't notice the early morning strain of climbing – the sting of freezing air sucked into a heaving chest. I also replayed the disagreement in my mind and I vowed to push myself harder.

The runnel twisted and turned. Cartwright apologised for the argument. I accepted the apology and we both accepted that we all needed a kick up the backside. For hours we moved together, pitched, soloed and cajoled, until the final pitch of the day: a beautiful steep ice overhang, which I led and fixed the rope upon, ready for the morning. Our progress was good. Cartwright's words had done the job. Shadows lengthened, colours deepened, breath froze, the darkness beckoned, and a ledge for the tent was excavated.

Returning from fixing our high point I could feel something was not right. As Powell and Cartwright dug, I milled around trying to sort myself out. For two days my stomach had seized and I felt bloated. The cold penetrated my bones and my head felt light. Stamping a ledge into the steep snow I ripped at clothes until my bottom half was naked. Gaining a crouching position was difficult. I really didn't want to tumble down the slope, but the snow was not solid, there was nothing to hold on to and lean back from. Eventually, stance assumed, my bowels decided I had frozen my backside enough and the feeling of release was fantastic. I pulled my clothes back on quickly, causing snow that was blown into my underwear to melt and wet my legs. Finally, half an hour from starting the procedure, I rejoined the others.

Crawling into the pitched tent, I forced myself into a corner. Wrapped in all my clothes, I slid into the normally comforting down sleeping bag, but still I felt cold. Then sick, then light-headed.

'Give me the pan,' I yelled.

Powell passed the cooking pot over quickly.

Throwing up, head stuffed into the pan, I felt proud that I hadn't missed – that would have been a disaster at 5,400 metres in a small tent.

'Hey, bet you were worried I'd miss and throw up all over the tent, weren't you?'

'You mean like you did half an hour ago?' Powell whispered.

'What do you mean, "like I did half an hour ago"?'

Looking at Powell I could see the worry in his face and the obvious relief.

'You've been unconscious; we've been planning how to get you down.'

'Oh, well ... no need to worry now as I feel fine ... just give me that pan again, will you?'

The throwing up continued for the rest of the night.

Retreat and run away was opted for in the morning, which added to my guilt that I had not pulled my weight, and several hours later Cartwright and Powell crashed through the door of the lodge at Thame. I arrived half an hour later, completely drained.

The Everest Summiteer Lodge, owned by Apa Sherpa, holder of the most Everest summits, was dark and quiet. The three of us were sitting on our own on large cushions surrounded by colourful posters of Buddhist deities and Everest, when the door swung open and a slim German woman with red hair and a big smile walked in and took over the conversation. I was immediately intrigued and attracted to this intelligent and confident woman. She introduced herself as Brita – 'like the water filter,' she explained – and instantly our leaving for Namche was delayed by an hour.

After a few days, Cartwright and I prepared to attempt the peak once more. Powell, on a three-week time schedule, had to return to Britain. Saying farewell in Namche, we hugged before heading in opposite directions. The feeling of loss I felt with Powell's departure was huge. Powell and I had become close over the last few years, sharing some very intense times together while climbing in Peru. I enjoyed spending time with him: the mutual understanding and respect; the closeness; the feeling of being able to tackle anything, no matter how difficult; and the deep trust that can only be built with time and shared experiences.

The face had been blasted and a high wind was cause for concern. The summit ridge had extended further and great plumes of spindrift stretched into the sky as snow-powdered fingers grabbed at the speeding clouds. Avalanches poured from above. Rocks whirred and flew off the cliff bouncing down, down, down on to the snow cone. Five days had passed since the previous effort and unseasonably warm weather had stripped the snow, revealing loose rock. As insignificant dots – dots lost amongst powder – we picked a way following the same line as before. We were lost in the maelstrom. A rowing boat fighting a crashing sea of white. As we hid behind a pillar of rock, straws were drawn for who should push out into the open ground ahead.

'I don't want to go out there; it's an artillery range,' Cartwright said.

'I agree, this is madness.'

So we waited. We waited for a lull but eventually we had to force the issue. I led sixty metres and then another sixty as Cartwright followed. Tied to the same ropes, we moved together with an occasional piece of gear between us and no belays – speed was our friend. I was still smarting from my poor show on the first attempt, so I forced the pace; my nerves jangled at the likelihood of being hit by debris, but this forced me harder. Yet, I was actually more nervous of the sensible option of retreating; I was more afraid of what failure would do to my mind. We had already spoken of retreat. The large blocks of freshly hewn rock scattered half buried in the snow indeed lay testament to the direction in which, sensibly, we should head.

We continued to climb with haste … in the wrong direction. Both scared of being killed, both scared of failure. Both just *scared*.

Two nights we endured, cowering in the corner of our tent like proverbial lambs, hoping for the wind to drop, for a chance to continue our climb. Throughout each night repeatedly we tried diving for cover into our soft sleeping bags as boulders whirred, sometimes it seemed just inches from our tent's skin.

Finally, it dawned on us that something from this ricochet-rattle menace would eventually seek us out, and would punch through our tent as fast as a slaughterer's bolt. We could stand it no more, and so taking advantage of the wind's early morning lull, we ran away. We ran all the way back to Thame. Cartwright had seen enough to convince him he wanted to live a little longer, and I wanted to stay to look at an easier, safer line on the north-east face. This line didn't look difficult – it was for the taking. It was a line I had suggested to Cartwright as we retreated from the north-west face. His answer was typical.

'Nick, I would rather sit in Sheffield, smoking and drinking beer, than climb up there!'

I guessed then that if the weather settled, it would be a solo attempt.

Cartwright prepared to leave. Shaking my hand, he stared, intense, stern. Gripping hard, refusing to let go, he spoke in a stern voice and reminded me of our friend Jamie Fisher, and the trauma and pain we had felt several years before upon the news of Jamie's death in Chamonix.

'I don't want to be the one visiting your folks, Bullock – delivering the news. Having to come back up here and search for your body. So come back, OK?'

Turning away from my friend, I promised him I would try my best.

Darkness surrounded. The cold penetrated. Clouds of condensation poured from lungs stinging with raw air. I had begun walking and then climbing at 1.30 a.m. and I had been wading in thigh-deep snow ever since. The day before I had been bored resting. Warmth and safety felt undeserved. At last, level with the dominating feature of Teng Kang Poche's north-east face, the north pillar, my urge was to go up, not across – but height was elusive. A direct line was the objective. But standing beneath the shortest way to the east ridge, the top section looked broken, uncertain. A right-rising traverse to meet the fluted runnels beneath the summit appeared to be the way. As I turned to gaze down to the valley, the dim yellow lights of the monastery above Thame flickered reassuringly. I felt comforted that I could be seen and that I was not alone. I was no believer in any god or even an afterlife, but I hoped the monks would say a prayer for me.

The climbing took a long, rising rightward traverse. The sky turned pewter and on the horizon the Himalayan giants of Everest and Lhotse glowed. Tenuous and steep, I kicked, punched and pawed at unconsolidated snow. I stood, looking over a deep couloir threatened by séracs standing guard over the east ridge. No way would I cross beneath these. Some in the climbing world used to think me a little deranged, a bit crazy, but I knew in myself I wasn't mad enough for that. Not ready to give in, a broken ridgeline of rock and snow led direct to a vertical wall of ice. The ridge was still beneath the sérac band, but I tried to convince myself, should they collapse, the ice would be funnelled either side. I chose to forget the massive avalanche we witnessed sweeping the whole of the face when one of these séracs had calved on our first week of acclimatisation.

My spirits surged once I was climbing the ridge. On my own, in the middle of this unclimbed territory, I felt honoured. I felt alive. I was living and in control. Warm and yellow glowing tendrils of rejuvenating sun flickered and occasionally touched my cold body. Steep ice reared up – a dangerous barrier at the base of the séracs. Quickly, as if a few minutes would make a difference, I kicked and picked around the obstacle and climbed the steel blue-green ice. At last the east ridge was mine and I worshipped the sun's rays. The summit reared not 200 metres away.

Staggering and happy, I moved toward the steep ice cone leading to the final section of the east ridge. Brooding slots snickered across the flat section of ridge, covered in part by fresh snow, whipped to meringue. This was a dangerous place to be alone. A bergschrund appeared – large enough to crawl inside and give protection against the strong north wind gusting across the col. I didn't need an excuse to stop and warm myself; the cold had been causing me to stop and warm fingers and toes since midday. The temptation to bivvy and wait until tomorrow for my summit celebrations was too strong; I dug into the side of the crevasse and burrowed into my sleeping bag with both feet wrapped around a bottle of hot water. A few hours later, I lay in the dark, enveloped and waiting for sleep.

But the summit celebrations would never come; a seriously crevassed summit cone meant that my lonely vigil at 6,350 metres was to be my high point.

Running from the mountains, I met Brita again in Namche Bazaar. She was walking back to Lukla and convinced me to meet up for a beer at Paradise Lodge in two days' time.

When I arrived at the lodge in Lukla, Nick Carter and Dave Hollinger were sitting drinking beer. They had both returned from guiding Ama Dablam. I hadn't known Carter long, but knowing that both Powell and Cartwright were out of the equation for the following year, I was on a mission of recruitment. Two beers later and a hard sell, and I had my partner for a return match.

Later that evening I shared another beer, this time with Brita. At the end of the evening she asked, 'Why don't we go upstairs and you can give me a goodnight kiss?'

It had been a long time since I had been close to someone, and here was an attractive woman hitting on me. What harm could there be in a goodnight kiss?

2
immortal?

Autumn 1985
Dilhorne, England

The Rose and Crown is a dirty, white-painted pebble-dashed pub in the small coal-mining village of Dilhorne, Staffordshire. Soaking motorbike leathers hung above the coal fire. Steam merged with sweat, condensation and cigarette smoke. A jukebox played heavy rock and country and western. I don't remember how I ended up drinking in there as a youth, but that was where we all hung out.

Even now, nearly twenty years later, I can still see them all. Keatsey removing his helmet and shaking his long, blonde mane. Diddy, arrogant and oozing immortality, demanding attention without seeming to care who was taking notice. Stod, delivering dry one-liners, tapping the ash from his cigarette into a brimming tray. Bung, proud as a pearl in his tailored cotton jacket and patterned tie. Deb Chatting, with dark bubbly hair and a voice as warm as the sun on the sea. Gypsy, dangerously thrilling and darkly attractive. Harry, bearded with large geeky glasses. Big Tracy, friendly, charming and understanding. All roads generally led to – and at some point, from – this pub with its quarry-tile floor, sticky with smears of spilt beer.

My white Yamaha with its lawnmower engine couldn't keep up with the others, so occasionally I'd ride with Keatsey. Straddling the blue fuel tank, it was as if the force of life entered his body and made him invincible, despite his short legs. The footrests of Keatsey's Kawasaki Z650 stuck out at right angles. They had no rubber on the underside; it was chewed like a lump of carrion. The rod of metal was also grated, prepared by the gravel of the road and served up by the immortality of youth; this was the dish of the day for most of my mates when growing up. Life was lived at full speed and close to the gravel.

I sat on the back behind Keatsey and watched his black leather gloves as they pushed the small red starter button and wrapped the throttle. The race was on. High-pitched wails of engines. The roads for us led anywhere and everywhere: it didn't really matter so long as the cops didn't catch you, and you were the first to arrive at the destination. Young life was a never-ending kaleidoscope of thrills without repercussions.

Without repercussions? Two friends from my teenage years didn't live to see their futures. Harry's girlfriend and Stod's brother were killed in motorbike accidents. Stod was left disabled. Keatsey, whom I'd always considered the most skilful and reasonably cautious of us all, was riding with his girlfriend when a car sideswiped them, leaving her arm paralysed. Somehow Diddy survived, although he frequently surfed the gravel. At eighteen, I sold my bike and it wasn't until I started rock climbing that I felt that same intoxicating sense of acceleration into unknown space.

December 2003
Hinckley, England

Dad, in my mind, was messing up. He had been diagnosed with emphysema some time in early 2003 and the doctor had said that if he continued smoking, which of course he did, he had four years to live. The smoking, combined with his newly found taste for alcohol, gave the impression that he was on a long-term suicide mission. Although the way he was going about it, death wasn't going to be long at all – Mum was beside herself with concern. I have never met anyone who appears to be so mentally stable, and yet has such a self-destructive streak as my dad, and it made me wonder what makes a person in their later life self-destruct in this manner.

When I found climbing, I suppose, in some ways, I was similarly addicted. I loved the romantic image of going out and maybe not coming back, of being a nihilistic hero pushing selfish personal boundaries that might cost the ultimate price. I would sit on top of the crag and imagine the clichés and platitudes that would be written about my death. It wasn't as if I thought killing myself couldn't happen. I did think of it and I was very conscious of it; I had smashed myself on several occasions and knew the ground was hard. I just don't think I saw death as final. Death to the younger mind is temporary. It's something to experience and come back from.

I grew up in the family home watching cowboy, sci-fi and police films. Sport was Formula One. John Wayne, Alain Prost, Clint Eastwood, Hans Solo, Ayrton Senna, Niki Lauda, Dirty Harry, Steve McQueen – they were lauded as heroes in our house and there's a fine line between real and make-believe to the young mind. John Wayne fought the bad and often didn't return, like so many Formula One drivers of the day. It is easy to see now why I wanted to become a mountaineer. Even today the heroes of modern blockbuster films and the people I relate to, in some form, are nihilistic heroes. I do understand that true nihilism is not something good, but flawed people with a sensitive side, who appear to hate mediocrity and a system which is unfair and corrupt, I respect.

In the spring of 2003, given Dad's terminal diagnosis, my parents retired. They sold their house, settled the mortgage and auctioned most of the contents. They sold the grandmother clock – the only item I expressed an interest in owning. The clock was wall mounted and wooden with a loud tick and a chime that bonged as if it were a much larger clock than it actually was. The timekeeping was poor and it often needed winding. Sometimes it struck an hour too short or an hour too many. But this old, cobbled-together clock was the one object that I really connected with growing up. When I found out my parents had sold the clock to my sister, Lesley, I felt hurt, a little angry, even let down, but I don't know why I was surprised. I still remember Dad telling me a few years earlier that he would make sure there would be nothing left for me or Lesley when he died, not that my parents had a lot to begin with. Mum and Dad commissioned a narrowboat, and moved into a rental property while it was being built. When the boat was launched they called her *Emma*, and they began a nomadic lifestyle, navigating England's large canal network.

I flew back west from Nepal in December, returning from the expedition to Teng Kang Poche and into the darkness of a wet British December. I had loaned my green Citroën Berlingo – stuffed to the back doors with climbing gear, bed, sleeping bags, books, clothes, and all my other belongings – to my parents, who were moored for the winter at a deserted marina near Hinckley in Leicestershire. I thought loaning my van would help them as there was no local shop and they were still finding their feet since selling up and committing to a life on the canals. My parents had been using my van to transport diesel, stored in large plastic containers, which they needed to run and heat their boat. The diesel had spilt over my bed and belongings and had soaked into the ply lining.

I stood in the dark and rain outside my parents' boat wearing several layers of clothing, topped by a Gore-Tex shell. My head torch illuminated the towpath. My jacket hood – ruffled by the wind – repeatedly covered the torch. Attempting to mop diesel and sort belongings without getting everything soaked was impossible. Cold, wet, light, dark ... numb fingers mopped the viscous liquid. The wind cut across open farmland slamming the van doors repeatedly on to my wet legs. Hawthorn shivered like an excited dog and lost the last of its withering berries. *Emma* thumped against the tyres hanging from the thick wooden balustrades. The tyres creaked and groaned. I had made sure the boat was securely tied; being adrift in this weather would be hell.

The next day, alone, I drove the English roads northwards. I was heading to Scotland, to meet up with my old friend Michael Tweedley. The motorway hard shoulder was barren, occasionally glittering with glass fragments – a strip of no man's land silently following the side of my van. Beyond this sliding strip of waste there were empty fields. In one field I glimpsed a horse chestnut tree, caught in the flat light of dusk, standing alone on an expanse of ploughed brown crust. Services, one mile. White lines rolled in and out. Countdown chevrons: three, two, one ... ticking ... chiming. That old grandmother clock was still sounding in my head. I turned off the motorway and into the services – one of those strange islands of people in transit. The wind strafed the tarmac and bit back into my face. People stooped shivering with smoke trickling from cigarettes clamped between cold fingers. Dead cigarette stubs scattered around tubes of polished steel. Marooned on an isolated island with Costa Coffee, slot machines, McDonald's and WHSmith for company; the world could end and life here on this concrete island would continue as if nothing at all had happened. Life here would remain detached. Here, among this neon mass of motorway consumerism signs, we are informed how many inspections the toilets have received that day.

Detached. Yes, that was me. I had survived so far by being on my own for long periods. This solitude kept my life uncomplicated.

3
nothing more

'Ah, distinctly I remember it was in the bleak December;
And each separate dying ember wrought its ghost upon the floor.'

EDGAR ALLAN POE, *THE RAVEN*

December 2003
Scotland

As the door of the van slams, the light inside dims, darkness swells around us. Is there nothing more?

Michael Tweedley and I leave behind the green Berlingo's creaking metal and carefully tiptoe between frozen puddles. Verglas shines in the full moon. We move with stealth past Lagangarbh, the hut owned by the Scottish Mountaineering Club, not wanting to alert the occupants. Caught at the edge of the torch beam, a stag stares back.

A raven opens his wings and allows the wind to lift his body until he passes over the hut. The wind picks at the body of the bird. Soaring high, high above Buachaille Etive Mòr and the bleak Rannoch wasteland, high above the sods of frozen peat and marsh grass. The wind whistles through black feathers. Far below, pinpricks of light pool to form a shimmering way. The raven caws, an old man clearing his throat.

'Come on, Michael, it's a little steep, but it's OK,' I yell toward the flickering light still in the dark gully. Ice slips from the surrounding rock walls. Water drips from the tips of icicles. The cold is unable to penetrate the thick layer of ice covering the stream. The stinging water gurgles beneath the ice, over rock, through constrictions, until eventually it meets the River Coupall.

The fault that Michael and I now follow leads directly to our climb, *Raven's Edge*, a climb I had once driven north to attempt with Cartwright over

New Year. On that occasion we had climbed on The Cobbler and then Beinn Eighe's *Central Buttress*, but after spending New Year's Eve in the Kings House – I had retired to my van, leaving Cartwright laughing and drinking – and eventually both rising on New Year's Day to rain, we said goodbye and bailed south.

This fault has been the grave of many. Seven bodies once quietly waited for spring. The steep walls often funnel fresh snow. Fortunately, the snow this winter has been kind. A compact crust covers the boulder-strewn slopes. There's a dusting on the crags, and névé in the gully above. It won't be an avalanche that ends lives today.

Stringy ice, snow-dusted walls, the wind whips around razor-sharp crystals that find exposed skin. I lean into the wind. A matchstick man. Insignificant. The grey of first light gives clues. Shadows creep from overhanging corners. Tufts of turf, fragile like tissue, poke from the cliff face. The gloom of *Raven's Gully*, directly above, remains mysterious.

Raven's Gully is a deep chimney formed by Slime Wall on the left and Cuneiform Buttress on the right. It was first climbed in the summer of 1937 and remained the hardest climb in Glen Coe for nearly ten years. The first winter ascent was in 1953 by Bonington and MacInnes where they endured the night just metres from the top of the gully.

Knowing Michael will have sussed out the pitches to suit his sensible aversion to falling, I gear up donning not a lot, considering the length and reputation of the climb. Four camming devices, twelve quickdraws – *for heaven's sake, how many quickdraws do we need?*, a few pegs and a double set of wires.

'Loads of gear,' I say, reassuring myself while secretly wondering about the lack of equipment. *Raven's Edge* has only been climbed twice in winter. Of the six pitches, four are given a summer grade of VS 4c, and knowing the second ascensionists, who rated their outing as 'pretty tough', I wonder if this is too much of an undertaking for us.

The first sixty metres are a turf romp. Doubt falls away and arrogance takes hold.

'Are you sure this is the correct line? It isn't very difficult. Maybe I should try to make it more difficult?' I ask, smugly.

'No, no, don't do that. It says here to take the line of least resistance for the first pitch; I'm sure it will get harder.'

'OK, but it really isn't very hard … ' I reply.

Above, the raven circles, before landing on a jutting rock high on Slime Wall overlooking the gully. The wind puckers and spikes feathers … and nothing more.

Sixty metres, hanging on the front of Cuneiform Buttress, I belay Michael who is leading into the bowels of the mountain. White, grey, black, green, blue – colours of a winter ascent. Lichen, moss and rock. Earth to earth. Ice-encrusted and snow-dusted. Moving left, we enter the yawning mouth of *Raven's Gully*.

'Watch me, Nick,' Michael shouts from around the corner, a position in which I have not the slightest chance of watching him.

The noise of his attempt begins to echo from the darkness. Curses mingle with scratching and clearing.

'Ach, this is the pits, man! It's the living end.' Scottish vernacular spat in a broad cockney accent.

'I would really like some gear, maybe even a hold that doesn't slope in the wrong direction. WATCH ME!'

As the rope inches, time ticks by. Eventually, I follow Michael's lead. A left traverse following small sloping holds, not one big enough to grasp, not one in-cut enough to confidently hook. Michael, leaning from a corner beneath a large roof, laughs.

'What's the idea behind this then?' I ask. 'Did you really think this was going to hold you?'

Michael has hammered a piton into some turf. Happy to be at the safe end of the rope he replies, 'Psychological, man, psychological. We don't have any warthogs, that was the next best thing.' Michael's face shines as he laughs his reply.

'Whatever, nutter!' Now it is my turn to lead again.

'My, this roof is big,' I say, stating the obvious, and attempting to keep the intimidation at bay before squeezing beneath the overhang. I clip into a mangy piece of hawser threaded through the eye of a rusty peg, no doubt placed on the first summer ascent. The eye of the peg has to be first chipped clear of ice. Reversing is difficult and stepping right, on to a steep slab beneath the roof, is delicate. Pleased to find a flat hold, an in-cut hold, a peg, a torque, a good wire for protection and frozen turf, I settle.

Next I am pushed into a corner and pulled around the side of the roof, which empties my arms. Slotting the picks, one after the other, laybacking until a large snow-covered ledge appears.

Michael seconds. Cold eases from joints and blood creeps along fingertips. Blood returns to toes. The sickening sting until movement brings relief.

Cold air sucked into lungs is savoured. Every moment.

'Full on, man; good lead! That was the best.' East London echoes, while I stamp into the snow-covered ledge. Crampons worn round from use are fastened on to the base of the boots where they collect snow. Michael pulls the last of the layback moves to stand alongside me.

'Where to now?'

'Up that chimney,' I gesture, 'then traverse left beneath the overhang, around the corner, and belay on a cramped stance. Better get moving, it's two thirty, we only have a couple of hours of daylight. I remember reading somewhere the descent can be tricky.'

The raven dives – a black dart, scything pillars of rock. Somewhere below and deep within the confines of the chimney, Michael struggles, pushing with legs, core and elbows, before gasping and sinking a pick into a large clod of turf. Leaning from the chimney, he seeks an easier line, but to no avail. He spots the raven then, hearing the ripping air emerge from folded wings.

'Hey!' his voice restricted in the confines of the chimney. 'Did you see that bird?'

'No … get on with the climb. You did bring your head torch, didn't you?'

'Of course.' The chirpy cockney reply floats down; 'Did you think I would have forgotten something as important as that?'

As it happens, yes, I did think that. Michael is exceptionally talented when it comes to forgetting. I can recall walking into Lochnagar with him, only to find he had no crampons and had left his head torch on the side of a track in Glen Coe a few days earlier. Clothing and other essentials are often an afterthought for Michael and are frequently left some place they are of no use.

I have known Michael for a long time. I really like his unorthodox and truly individualistic ways. We have been through broken bones and travelled the length and breadth of the country together. Once, on Dinas Cromlech, Michael belayed me unwaveringly while a limp and unconscious body was passed over his head. Blood pumping from the injured climber turned the rock around Michael from grey to red. On another occasion, I winced as I watched him attempt a hard gritstone solo only to surf the steep slab and then crash through trees below, amazingly unhurt. I always enjoy his company and his unassuming nature. I know Michael has his faults, we all have, but I have grown to find them a part of his charm.

'Watch me, Nick, this is really sketchy.' He has traversed a steep slab beneath a long, large roof. Ice smears dribble from beneath the roof covering the slab. He taps delicately with his front points to clear the silver dribbles from the small edges. Silver shards of ice spin into the darkening sky. He hooks chockstones welded in the gap between roof and slab, and uses these for protection by placing long slings around the back and clipping the ends together before disappearing around the corner.

'SAFE.'

The guidebook says one remaining pitch.

'Around the corner a deep crack is climbed to the top. An exposed and sensational top-pitch.'

The day loses its battle against dusk. Shadows lengthen before transforming into dark completely. Cold turns colder. Stars appear. Michael stands and listens to the jangle of the axe and the slow *ssshcripe* of rope feeding against rock. His senses heighten with the coming of the darkness. The flapping of wings breaks his trance and then a cough from the raven who is perched staring straight at us – nothing more.

'WATCH ME.' I ask the impossible.

The raven jumps and glides from the crag. The spell is broken. The black mood is lifted for the time being, but Michael is spooked by the sickle outline circling the confines below.

Pulling the final moves of the offwidth before sitting, cold air swirls beneath. A blurred sheet of white in front. Car headlamps light the distant Rannoch road. The last of the day slinks from the river. Below, the Scottish-cockney grunt and strain mingles with the wisps of condensation that rise from somewhere inside the offwidth. I grin for a second and allow self-congratulation. Michael's head, jittery and sweating, appears from the top of the crack.

Spiky white thistles jut from rocks silhouetted by the rising moon. More rocks run along the crest – uneven bumps in an arthritic finger, like Mum's fingers and her mother's fingers before that. I already have the telltale bumps. Keen to move, keen to find a way out from this exposed place, I rise and begin looking for the way off.

While I am checking the descent, Michael pulls and coils one of the ropes. He does not separate the ropes and because of this, the second rope tangles. The wind wrestles my clothing, invisible fingers grabbing at folds in the fabric.

'Why the hell didn't you separate both ropes before coiling them?' I shout, in part just to be heard above the wind.

'I just did, OK, leave it at that, will you?'

Michael's answer isn't enough.

'I really can't believe you did that. For Christ's sake, you've been climbing long enough to know not to do that. I just don't believe you at times, Michael.'

'Look, I know I made a mistake – just leave it, will you?'

But of course I can't, and I continue to rant until something snaps and he has a go back.

'Get *over* it, will you? I made a mistake: that's all. Just get over it.'

The wind brings tiny shards of ice with it to pinprick eyes and bare skin, and somewhere out there in the dark and the wind is the raven, watching, waiting.

Pulling another knot from the tangled rope, I know I have pushed my friend too far. We shouldn't have had this argument and certainly not on the top of a Scottish mountain in winter.

'OK, Michael, I know I've gone on, but that's me, isn't it; I'm a miserable, moaning bastard, aren't I? Come on, let's get down.'

We traverse the silver walkway. I lead, crunching my crampons, driving them into ice. Michael follows close behind – I'm sure his mind is turning, questioning. A terrible year has made him somewhat short-tempered, moody. He had told me he didn't like what he felt he had become. He would change for the better, he had said. He had promised himself. He keeps on stepping. Not the hard, deliberate stamp needed for penetrating the thick ice. His mind must be in another place; he is stepping without conviction, without thinking, without force. The crampon points – worn smooth – refuse to bite. His front foot slides and his body slews forward. The rear foot twists and skitters across the ice surface. Splinters fly into the dark. Michael's body plunges forward with both arms outstretched, arms as straight as if diving into a swimming pool. He screams.

I spin to see Michael sliding feet first, lying on his front, speeding into the gloom.

'MICHAEL!'

I am about to witness the death of a close friend. In an instant our eyes lock. Michael's bulging eyes burn into my own. And in that split second I think how our last moments together have been angry and arguing.

Michael's body gathers speed. The clifftops are only feet away. A vain attempt to grab a flailing axe attached to his wrist fails. The axe bounces, chiming the hour.

I can only see the torch attached to his helmet now. Michael has seconds to live. I can watch no more … but just before turning away, I see his body convulse … and he stops. He actually stops. The beam of the torch fixed to the helmet is stationary, and then it points into the ice. Michael's forehead bumps into the snow. Crystals diffuses yellow. His chest heaves and he gulps air. A piece of his clothing has snagged on one of the little rocks poking up through the ice … that is all that has stopped him … nothing more.

'For Christ's sake, Michael, what the hell were you playing at?' I say, my concern and relief coming out as anger.

'Don't know … one minute I was following you, then I was falling. I thought I was dead.'

'Don't ever do that again. What the hell would I have told your girlfriend?'

I can see Michael is going into shock – we need to move.

'Come on, let's go. Stamp your feet, keep them flat and keep your axe in a position where it will help you if you fall.' Michael moves forward; it is obvious he wants to crawl. He shakes, but not from the cold. He tells me later that he had thought about those he would have left behind. He thought about those he had been angry with and those he'd fought. Did the raven enter his thoughts also? Did he hear the bird or was it just nothing more than a trick of the wind?

As we step into the upper section of *Great Gully*, I badger and harangue to keep my friend moving. Until at last we reach our rucksacks that we'd left at the base of the climb. We slump down in the snow, relieved.

With yellow and piercing eyes, the raven stares. Looking down the length of his long black beak, he watches with curiosity, anticipation. The dark and the freezing cold of the winter evening penetrate his jet-black primary feathers and no doubt the downy layer beneath. He shakes and puffs up his feathers to circulate trapped warmth.

As the door of the van opens, the yellow, soft light from inside spills out, darkness receding. Yellow filters from the rear of the van – light ruling once again. We step inside, relishing the security it gives.

'Did you hear that bird, Nick?'

I stop and listen to the world outside. I can hear water freezing and the wind blowing but nothing more.

Thick verglas shining in the full moon marks the path we have just walked. The raven lifts one leathery foot. The day is over. Tomorrow will be another day, just that, and nothing more.

4
the cutting lap

December 2003
Leicester, England

It was just before Christmas. I had driven south from Scotland after dropping Michael back in Edinburgh. Having no base, I was discovering every change of location needed planning and packing and organisation. After a few days over Christmas at my sister's house in Hertfordshire and a visit to my parents' boat still moored near Hinckley, I spent a week on my friends Nikki and Mark's narrowboat that is permanently moored near the centre of Leicester. Nikki and Mark were away for the week, and staying on their boat gave me a break, some sort of brief stability until I drove to Chamonix with Rich Lucas in the New Year.

Rich was young, talented, shy and one of the most naturally gifted rock climbers I had ever met. I know this sounds clichéd, but his skinny frame and strong fingers could hang and pull the smallest edges without much in the way of training. Rich always reminded me of a hare caught in the headlights – those big, dark, shocked eyes opening wide and then somehow even wider, while sitting and waiting to be hit by life. I met Rich for the first time at the Tower Climbing Centre in Leicester. We had rock climbed and trained together often since that first meeting. I began calling him 'Boy Wonder', and the name stuck. I wasn't sure what Rich wanted from life, and I don't think he knew either.

January 2004
Chamonix, France

On reaching Chamonix, Boy Wonder and I would share an apartment with Boz Morris, another Leicestershire escapee. The three of us would live in a one-room apartment that Boz had lived in for a few winters while odd-jobbing for a French mountain guide who owned the building.

After settling in, learning to ski and allowing the weather to settle, Rich and I set off to climb.

Mont Blanc du Tacul, to our right, was an ice-cream dollop oozing unconsolidated death. The Aiguille du Midi, to the left, stood tall and slender, fragile but strong, the veritable supermodel of the range. Whereas the Gros Rognon, in our faces, rose dramatically out from the Vallée Blanche, that immense sea of pristine snow, criss-crossed by ski tracks and glowing red with the setting sun.

Small dots hung forlorn, suspended from thin, rusty steel cables running between the Aiguille du Midi and the Gros Rognon. The dormant telecabins swung in the wind. The cold would need to subside and the tourists return before they would move again on freshly greased cables.

Maybe my arms needed greasing? They had locked at the elbows forming perfect right angles. My fingers had turned to gnarled claws and refused to open. My stomach churned, my legs wouldn't work and I was starting to think my dream of climbing full-time was over before it had even begun. All I needed to climb at the moment was one wooden step into a small rickety shed perched at the end of a knife-edge of snow and rock rib below the Cosmiques Hut, but as I sat at the door, taking in the savage scenery, I was sure I couldn't make it.

'This is it then. Game over,' I mumbled to myself.

At worst it was a stroke or a heart attack, maybe cerebral oedema. At best, my body had obviously decided it didn't want to work at altitude any longer – not ideal for an alpinist. Twisted and warped like an old stick, I swung my head to look across at the Vallée Blanche and wondered how to get myself out of this. This being the latest episode in the *Bullock Gets Sick* series. At least this time it wasn't above 5,000 metres on some unclimbed face in the Himalaya.

Boy Wonder was looking worried. With several alpine trips behind him he only had the Frendo Spur and the north face of the Tour Ronde in the bag. He did have several epics to look back on: a life-saving rescue from the Midi Arête and a benightment on an icefall. This was the winter he promised himself he would do it. Unfortunately, it was looking like his string of bad luck was continuing and the curse of the Boy Wonder had now struck me.

I didn't want to let him down, but earlier that morning, as I sat on the toilet wondering how so much could pour out from someone so thin, I warned Rich that all was not as it should be and maybe we should hang on for one day. He agreed. Then, in a sudden rush of 'it'll get better when I'm on the hill', I decided to ignore the pain and go for it anyway.

Pins and needles coursed through my body and I lost the use of several limbs. I was regretting my decision. Boy Wonder busied himself around the small wooden shack, given the grand title of 'winter refuge'. I worked up enough energy to drag myself on to a damp, snow-covered bunk before violently throwing up. Not known for doing things by half, I am pleased to say that also goes for puking. The concern on Boy Wonder's face now intensified, although I suspect it was not due to my condition but rather concern for his own safety. He was now stranded on a deserted mountain-side with someone re-enacting a scene from *The Exorcist*. If my head had begun to spin, I'm sure he would have been out of the door in a flash, eyes wider than ever.

As it was, the projectile vomiting put paid to all of my dysfunction and the climb was back on. The climb in question was the *Supercouloir* with the direct start, a Jean-Marc Boivin and Patrick Gabarrou classic from the mid-1970s. A climb I had long lusted after.

At first light, we took our lives in our hands and skied to the start of the route. I had only started skiing weeks before and Boy Wonder was not far behind in experience. Snow swirled in spiralling clouds, scrubbing the surface of the glacier and taking to the air. In those clouds there were worlds yet to be explored. The Vallée Blanche was deserted. Slithering, unseen, we weaved our way precariously avoiding crevasses – not to mention broken limbs and embarrassment – until stopping near the base of the climb. The wind whipped spindrift all around us, and the weak light refracting from the aurora of fine powder twisted its colourful spectrum around ripples of snow.

I left the skis halfway up the cone beneath the start of the climb and plunged deep steps into unconsolidated powder. The condition of the slope was worrying, but I consoled myself with the fact that on this mini-adventure I had already survived food poisoning (six-month-old mayonnaise likely was to blame ...) and the skiing. So, realistically, nothing untoward could possibly happen to us now, and a relieved Boy Wonder pulled up alongside me beneath the start of the first pitch.

'Right, clip to that, put me on belay. Let's get moving – it's ten o'clock,' I gabbled.

Desperate to get to grips with the climb, the first for the both of us this winter in Chamonix, I could not move quickly enough.

'What the hell is that you're belaying me with?' I shouted, pointing at some form of metal device with limited use that Boy Wonder had pushed the ropes through.

'It's a Magic plate!' the cocky twenty-two-year-old retorted, the statement dripping in *can't-you-see-that-old-man?* arrogance.

'Yes, I know *what* it is,' suddenly reminding myself of many conversations I'd had with my father, 'BUT WHY ARE YOU BELAYING ME ON LEAD WITH IT?'

The need to speak loud with forceful condescension was the way I had learnt to deliver statements such as this.

Not so cocky now, Boy Wonder suspected there might be bad karma heading in his direction for reasons unbeknown to him.

'Is there a problem with belaying you on lead with one of these then?'

Son to father. Enquiring, learning, growing.

'Yes ... so don't do it again.'

Standard, non-committal, non-explanatory answer from father to son. Similar to other well-used parental advice like, 'do as I say and not as I do' and 'children are to be seen and not heard'. And on occasion if I had done something really bad, a cuff around the ear could even follow.

Being adult brings rebellion of its own – who will cuff the ear of a grown man who decides life has become empty and cigarettes and alcohol are the cure? When I was a child, Dad hardly touched alcohol, but in his late fifties he began drinking at least half a bottle of Scotch a day. Pressure of society, advertising, a compulsive disorder, unhappiness, lack of worth, lack of fulfilment, who can say what suddenly makes a person decide it's time to implode and to do it with such conviction? Dad's drinking wasn't a steady creep; it was a conscious decision.

Axe picks sank into the névé glued between grey-pink granite. Ten, twenty, thirty metres. The diminishing form of Boy Wonder was below, looking up with those big innocent eyes. The promised hooks we'd dreamt about didn't materialise, but ice-choked cracks and edges gave security. The first pitch passed in a meandering trance, delicate and decisive. Boy Wonder sampled his first taste of modern mixed climbing, and on reaching the belay he was red-faced, alive, caught in the lights and loving it.

'You need to move faster,' I said in what I hoped was a not-too-bossy voice. We were now into the climbing. I was focused and determined.

At that point in my life I didn't do pleasant days out for fun, I climbed for success and the summit. My fun was retrospective. I really did think like this. This is what climbing was. It was a way to feel value, to feel good about myself. For me, if it could not be gauged, ticked, logged, accredited, worshipped, revered, it was hardly worth doing. I was due for a kicking with this attitude of course, but I didn't see it at the time. How could I see it when climbing gave such validation? Despite all my successes, I still hadn't grasped the full implications of what *being happy* meant. I had not yet begun to understand how to be truly happy. The experience of climbing in good company while in wonderful surroundings should have been enough. It wasn't. I felt like I had to prove myself and I wanted acknowledgement from my peers.

Climbing was everything and relationships were low on my agenda. I was panicking because Brita – whom I had stayed in touch with after hitting it off in Nepal – was sending me gifts through the post and talking about visiting Chamonix or flying me to see her in South Africa where she worked. I was so determined to climb, the thought of hanging out with someone who cared for me instead of going climbing filled me with dread. I worried about missing opportunities in a life I already felt was in fast-forward. Guiltily, I thought about how I had ignored Brita's emails and wondered: why at times is being honest and talking about our fears so difficult?

I realise now that climbing is only important for the personal experience and the ability to grow as a person from that experience. The time shared with a valued partner can be more rewarding, albeit in another form and only if balance can be found, and the validation I once sought through climbing now means very little.

Having run the ropes through and sorted the gear, I led the second pitch. It proved to be less technical than the first as ice flowed over small edges and filled cracks. A broken jumble of large blocks, steep corners, tight chimneys and bulges was cemented and solid with the flow of ice. In no time, I was clipped to the belay, leaning back and swinging from the melange of tat threaded through a collection of old and rusty ironwork. Life was good. I was climbing. I was proving myself to myself. I was proving that I had made the correct decision to leave behind what I deemed was the safety net of a regular income. The sun was shining – unfortunately no longer on us – and if the guidebook description was to be believed, we had already completed the most difficult climbing on the route.

Boy Wonder pulled up alongside and suggested that maybe the next pitch should fall to him. In a controlled environment where skills can be developed and honed, bringing on talent is fine, but bagging a long-lusted-after climb in the Alps, and in winter, is not the friendliest of situations in which to learn. Looking at the third pitch, it certainly didn't resemble easy ground. Diplomacy at this stage in my life was not my greatest trait. In fact, diplomacy was nearly non-existent, especially when there was climbing to be done. But on this occasion, I surprised myself.

'OK, go for it.'

Boy Wonder's face lit up like a child on the verge of seeing Santa.

'Really?!'

'Yes, really. But beware, that overhanging chimney up there is going to be desperate if that bulging ice at its top is rotten, and there is a strong possibility it will be.'

Puppy-dog enthusiasm reduced, Boy Wonder was deep in thought.

'Hmm, maybe you will be a bit quicker leading the next pitch,' he said, deflated.

'OK, let's sort the gear and get going.'

Friendly, thick ice turned to thin, hollow and rotten. I had moved with relative ease leaving the belay, but on entering the tight confines of the chimney, my cocky attitude crumbled, just like the brittle and aerated ice that balanced into the back of the chimney. On occasion, the ice was strong enough to hold bodyweight, but mostly torques and hooks in the rock were sought. Thin axe picks, far too thin for such demanding climbing, twisted and creaked. Hanging from the right arête of the chimney, I swung and struggled to maintain my balance. Delicate foot placements were all I could find on the left wall and inside the chimney.

'WATCH ME!' My repeated call to Boy Wonder, who hung twenty metres below, echoed across the Vallée Blanche.

'Is it difficult?' The naivety of the young sometimes astounds me.

'NO, IT'S REALLY EASY. That's why I'm swinging around up here battling ice and snow and shouting at you to watch me, YOU BLOODY NUMBNUT!'

Yes! A bloody peg. Finally. Thank God for that.

I clipped the peg, which gave courage. To make things more challenging, a constant flow of powder poured from the top of the chimney. The wind caught the powder as it cascaded from the edge of the overhanging tube. A spinning vortex of fine white weaselled down my neck and frosted my face. Eyebrows now clotted with lumps of ice. Breathing became a chore; crystals were sucked into my lungs. For a second, just a second, I was once again a teenager, working in the hayfields of North Staffordshire. For a second, battling that spindrift, I leant against a pitchfork's polished handle.

I see grass croziers pushing from beneath the cold earth. I watch the nurtured grass in the meadow appear to lengthen. It reaches towards the sun, escaping the shade from behind the hawthorn. The grass sways. Wood pigeons set wings before a smack of feathers. Chaffinches nest in the hawthorn, and below, the fox primes his nose, his puffed red firecracker waving behind. Weasels spark from the decreasing square of long grass as the mower completes another cutting lap. The cut grass dries in combed rows until golden hay bales are delivered from the womb of the baling machine. Packed and roped, transported on trailers, the bales wobble. A stacked mosaic of gold trundling along narrow lanes. Hay streamers drift in the hawthorn tops before finally, at the end of the day, we stack the bales into the old corrugated metal barn where they are left to sweat.

For just a second, I clung to this memory of a teenage summer, if only for the warmth, and then in the next second I continued struggling in the cascade of spindrift until eventually I crawled out the top with images of clock hands turning, tractors cutting laps of grass, and the setting sun. The release from the confines of the chimney combined with the unfolding mountain vista lifted my spirits.

'Climb when ready.'

Boy Wonder began to climb and fight. He sucked powder, breathed, gulped. He cranked, pulled, twisted. The learning curve for him was as steep as the climbing, but finally he inched into sight, covered in snow and gasping.

'Mental.'

'Yeah, strenuous … in places, anyway.' I felt it wouldn't do to let on that the climbing was difficult; where would that lead? After all, I had climbed long and hard over the years and this was Boy Wonder's first hard alpine climb. No, it would not do to let on that he had just climbed really well and had impressed me. Why inflate his ego and belittle my experience?

Belaying and watching Boy Wonder climb towards me, wrapped in sheer granite cliffs, I didn't realise at the time how similar some of my attitudes and actions had become to those of my father.

'Get on with it then.'

I pointed him into the wide couloir above. A dark, steep, ice-covered back wall hemmed in by even steeper sidewalls led the way to an easing of the angle and an end of our difficulties. We climbed the swathes of ice running the length of the deep couloir until the light faded and the sun sank. The chill was instant. Rich climbed to my side. Standing huddled close, we dug out our torches and attached them to our helmets. Ropes were tied, threaded and allowed to slither their way back down the route.

'Ready then?' I asked.

'Yes, I'm ready.'

5
the rain

April 2004
Siurana, Spain

I never imagined rain …

The Berlingo's windscreen ran with rain. It was like looking through melting glass. Heavy drops bounced off the steel exterior, the clatter relentless. A lightning flash gave Boy Wonder and me a visual treat. The van's stuffed and festering interior lit for just a second and just as quickly returned to gloom. A car passed, its tyres sucked, headlights glowing yellow and illuminating the drops that sprang off hot tarmac.

I had fallen from *Omega* on the Petites Jorasses a month previously. I never imagined breaking an ankle, a helicopter rescue and a return to Leicestershire for recuperation. This was not part of my dream plan. I never imagined driving to and from Chamonix. I never imagined any of this when I packed up. The rain wasn't in the dream. The picture I'd conjured, during those dark days of imprisonment, was one of health and sunny freedom. Freedom with fresh-smelling pine trees and raptors sailing in the powder blue. Tanned skin, long hair, freshly baked bread; no rules, timings or constrictions. No fear. I'd left my home and allowed strangers to move in. I didn't imagine rain when I gave up £25,000 per annum.

I hadn't imagined driving once again to Chamonix to collect Boy Wonder and setting out for the south. Driving for nine hours, we had passed through tollbooth after tollbooth, handing over euros neither of us wanted to hand over. We drove past the turning for the Écrins, Briançon and La Grave, and had ignored the road for Gap and its miles of Céüse sun-bleached limestone. En route to Spain, the land of promise. The land of sun, hot rock, sizzling skin and San Miguel. Land of olives and cheap red wine.

Southwards. Costa del this and Costa del that. South. Nine hours' driving without a break. The Berlingo had gasped in the increasing temperature, second only to our increasing anticipation. We had run from the brown patches in the middles of white ski runs, and the white patches in the middles of brown faces belonging to ski bums. Always south. Towards twenty-four hours of sun-drenched rock. Time to get strong, time to get thin, time to get tanned.

Time to get wet.

As we drove into the depths of the Spanish countryside, it began. And it got stronger. The olive groves dripped with fresh rainwater. The terracotta pantile roofs gushed waterfalls with large wooden barrels catching the spate and overflowing. The Berlingo struggled. Hairpin after hairpin after hairpin. Finally, we arrived at the focal point of my prison-time fantasy: Siurana, land of golden tiger-striped rock. Golden tiger-striped *wet* rock, as it turned out.

Boy Wonder and I sat in the van for most of our first day, venturing out between downpours to check the crags and watch water weep from limestone pockets. Later we called into the campsite and drank espresso. We bought a copy of the climbing guide and talked to fellow climbers. We found a place to park and call home, sorted food, kit, clothes and climbing gear. Read a little. Dreamt a little more.

On the second day, the rain stopped by midday. The mist, swirling from the deep ravines surrounding the plateau, thinned to reveal the ancient village with narrow streets and a church, with warped and rickety wooden doors that creaked when the wind opened them. On the edge of the village, perched on a precipice above the steep orange, were walled-in patches of dark soil – rich, dark soil lined with rows of broken onion candles, filling the air with an earthy metallic tang. Acres of spruce, larch and shrub with finches hanging like Christmas decorations stuffed the bottom of the ravines. The woods shifted. The undergrowth dried. The scent of wild rosemary and thyme lifted from the valley base. Small birds chittered and large birds soared. We avoided the water caught in rock scallops as we walked to the crag. We climbed. Not well, but we climbed.

Day three dawned rainless and we climbed.

Day four dawned clear; we donned shorts and flip-flops and climbed in sunshine. Days five and six, hot and clear and we climbed more. Day seven, hotter still. But thin skin, aching muscles and stinking armpits signalled a rest day, so we moved the van to the side of a large lake and washed away the grime in the cold water.

Returning to our spot beneath the old pine tree, we cooked a meal with fresh vegetables and added handfuls of herbs that were growing nearby the van. We ate fresh olive-oil bread and drank red wine straight from the carton. We walked to the campsite for an evening coffee and checked out the hand-scribbled topo describing the newly developed crag where we had been climbing. Returning to the van in the dark we laughed and scoffed at the supposed grades of the climbs we had thought a lot more difficult.

Fed and recharged, we retired ready for a return to the golden walls in the morning. Only by then the clouds had returned, and in the distance, thunder rumbled. An hour later, a flash of lightning etched silver into the pines.

I hadn't imagined the rain; it didn't enter into my dream. But what I couldn't possibly have imagined was enjoying it. I realised then that I had started to pack away the past. And I let the rain wash over me.

6

the emotional tightrope

June 2004
Luton, England

Waiting patiently by the National Express drop-off at Luton Airport, surrounded by large duffel bags, was a stooped six-foot-four, gaunt and rangy frame, almost like a wolfhound. Unmistakably Al Powell.

I like Powell's attitude. I like his no-bullshit, quiet and humble demeanour. I like his no-need-to-give-it-the-big-one-and-advertise-his-ware, his no-hashtag. Scrape away the lichen from his green, unclimbed surface and you will find passion, drive and determination, a deep knowledge of climbing history, and a purveyor of style.

'Ey up Mr P, how's it going?' I called from the window of my van. I drove the wrong way around the car park system to park on double yellows, as close to the pile of bags as possible.

We headed toward my sister's house, deep in conversation, to exchange ski gear for expedition gear – Boy Wonder and I had returned home from Spain via Chamonix – and to sort climbing gear ready for the next chapter with Powell. The van rattled. Powell mumbled, another one of his traits. I nodded, frowned, shook my head. Added an 'oh' and an 'ahh', hoping they were in the right places. Not that it would matter, as he was so engrossed in stories of fatherhood, business strategy and work he probably wouldn't have noticed.

'So when exactly do you need to fly home?' I asked nervously.

'Oh, it's err, hang on, let's check.'

My god, he doesn't even know when he returns.

He pulled a small notebook from his pocket and flicked through its pages. Intense eyes slid from side to side and lips moved as words were read but no sound came from his taut mouth.

'Yes, here it is,' a note of triumph at having found something in this topsy-turvy filing system.

'The 23rd.'

I narrowly avoided driving the van off the dual carriageway. Composing myself, I attempted to answer in a neutral fashion.

'Oh. That doesn't give us long to nail Chac, does it? What was wrong with the flight on the 31st I secured for you?' I knew the answer before it was spoken, but had to let my disgruntlement be known, if only quietly.

'Under a little pressure from home.'

Not surprising really; he was never at home, and with a young family it would strain the most settled of relationships. Al's partner Sima was very forgiving of his obsession.

Huaraz, Peru

The familiar journey had gone well. Hours of flight and dossing on the floor of Lima airport. Taxis. A whole day of crushed and sweltering bus transportation and then finally meeting friends as we stepped from the bus in the middle of the bustling town of Huaraz.

We rushed the acclimatisation. I secretly cursed Powell and his limited time for affecting my chances of climbing a new route on the stunningly pointed Chacraraju east face.

A visit into the dark interior of Mount Climb in Huaraz, the local gear shop and collator of all new routes and topos, delivered us a hammer blow. Two Slovenian climbers had climbed our line in 2000, then both had subsequently been killed later that year in Nepal, thus, news of their Chacraraju ascent was left unreported. Left to be buried …

We decided to go anyway. They had used aid to climb the line. Maybe we could free it. Could we? Maybe another unclimbed line would present itself. Maybe?

We walked with heads full of dreams and aspirations, following the donkeys that carried ten days' worth of food and a full rack of climbing equipment. We walked into the steep-sided valley covered with Quenal trees – vivid green leaves, flaking bark like burnt skin, stunted. We marched into loneliness and solitude, into the unknown. I lived for this feeling. This was my life, my chosen route, my preferred way. But also I longed for some form of female closeness: a friend whom I could trust with my inner thoughts. Someone to share with.

Above us were broad open slopes covered in pampas, glaciated slabs, rivers and underdeveloped trees; the ground promised a lung-stretching time ahead. I hoped I could fully acclimatise with the stocking of a high bivvy beneath the icefall and the massive and intricate east face. Time would tell, but we didn't have much of it.

Two days of bad, snowy-rainy weather made our route decision for us. We no longer considered the direct and steep line that followed a shallow runnel, following the route of the Slovenians – men who had dreamt dreams similar to our own. Snow dusting the face made the technical rock climbing impossible. And since finding out that 'our' line had already been climbed it had lost its new-route aura.

We sat together close to the campfire. Silent, immersed in our own personal thoughts, watching the shimmering of embers that sparked as the wind caught the growing mound of red-hot charcoal. The wild and windy west coast of Scotland came to mind. Handline fishing. Dad, my sister and me. Mum had remained inside the car listening to a Radio 4 play. Feathers of bright blue, red and green disguised the brutal sharp points of the fish-hooks. Mirrored shoals of sun-reflecting mackerel. Hit the shoal and drag them in. All blue and silver and shimmering.

Tomorrow we would go.

We sat quietly, contemplating the mile-long ridge.

The following night we begin our climb. Freezing temperatures make the snow and ice we methodically kick sparkle by the lights of the head torches. We easily reach the lowest point in the ridge and turn right. A mile of Peruvian, mush-roomy, overhanging uncertainty awaits us. But first a red-grey, moving and crumbling granite step bars the way to the scary white stuff above.

I lead. It's difficult climbing; I'm out of balance, unprotected. I remove my gloves to feel the rock, but it doesn't help. I remove my rucksack, and immediately I feel a let down. Still the impasse, still the nagging feeling of being a waste. Have I lost it since breaking my ankle on *Omega* a few months back?

'This is desperate, I'm coming back down, I've broken one ankle this year and that's enough.'

I feel justified in my decision, as Powell won't even contemplate leading the pitch. He scuttles off following a gangplank to the right. He secures himself at the foot of another difficult-looking rock pitch and informs me it will be easy; 'look at all the holds,' he says. *So why don't you lead it?* I think.

Fortunately, with gear and a little technique, it goes. Powell follows on a top-rope.

'How did you move right?' he shouts, quite loudly for once.

'I did it by using all those holds you helpfully pointed out ... '

Powell completes the pitch and moves past to lead the very loose but easy way until we are standing on the knife-edge. Moving together is the only option. The snow feels solid. Overhanging at times, and corniced, but solid. The sun shines now. It shines worryingly on us and on the unstable platform in which we have to trust. We continue moving together, close but apart, balancing, tiptoeing. It's a circus performance, a live performance. Large gargoyles push out at an angle, barriers to easy progression, barriers working against time – time we just don't have.

The day continues. All of the tightrope walking is tenuous, thought-provoking, attention-grabbing. Large snow formations continue to grow at right angles to the ridge.

Over. Under. Around to the left. Then right. Tunnel. Cut. Move together.

The ropes hang in a great arc across a knife-edge of mushy white. Powell confidently stands. I crawl. We sit and talk.

'This is a fine spot for a bivvy, isn't it?' I say, having coped with the tension for long enough on this first day.

Powell enlarges a tent spot; he's keen to try his new toy. Purposeful and precise, super-light, he plays and studies, adjusts. I sit on a perfect crescent-moon-shaped scoop beneath an overhanging roof of condensed rotten snow, and watch. He is constantly on the move, constantly planning, working, competing. All day we are on the edge, walking this tightrope. Defying the inevitable.

The previous year on Jirishanca, Powell and I were involved in a search for two Austrian climbers who were buried and killed in an avalanche. I witnessed the heartache and trauma felt by friends left behind. It was then I started to understand. I had no wife or partner or children, but my parents were still living and I had a sister and many close friends. I'd lived away from Britain for long periods already since taking up climbing full-time. Mum was growing old without her son nearby, and every time I returned to Britain she was older still – more grey hair, thinner. She worried. At times I feel guilt about this life I have chosen. Is it fair to inflict this on my parents?

Especially my mum? But equally can we live a life of less for others? If we do, will this type of life, a life where we never attempt to follow our dreams, wither the heart, dull the light?

Powell talks of his son Adam. His hair, his smile, the way he moves, plays, cries. I cannot begin to comprehend the feelings of a doting father. I watch Powell's face light up when he talks to me about him.

The night passes and the sun hits the ridge. Immediately the temperature increases from deathly cold to just cold, even warm on the north side. I grow concerned. The ridge ahead is becoming more serrated. A dinosaur spine of unconsolidated snow lumps. Gothic formations that will have been weakening. The rock ribs we climb to bypass the increasingly wafer-thin snow overhangs are loose and moving. I pull on blocks of granite as large as the base of a mature tree trunk and watch, horrified, as they rip from the face and fly past the ropes. The ropes hang in arcs across gullies, over fins of ice, around arêtes of snow and back to Powell who is out of sight, unable to fathom what is happening.

Continuing, more blocks pull, crumble, spin and tumble into the void. They become lost to the deep snow and the glacier hundreds of metres below. The ropes tighten at my waist. Without shouting I wait for the telltale release. When it comes I know Powell has stripped the belay and is moving. He moves over the same unstable, uncertain ground as I had. I try to remember what gear I placed. Was it good? Would it hold both of us should one of us fall?

All the climbing now is pitched. Ninety-metre pitches are the norm, moving together is the norm. The only time I feel safe is when Powell is on one side of the ridge and I am on the other. I plan what I could do if he falls when belayed forty metres away on the opposite side of the ridge, beneath an overhang of snow. How long would I wait before it became apparent he had fallen and hurt himself?

He has been over an hour now leading this pitch. The ropes have remained stationary for ages. I hear tumbling, rock blocks crashing down rubble-strewn gullies, then slowly the ropes inch.

'Al, are you OK?' I shout as loudly as my dry throat allows.

No reply. Sitting under an overhang of ice, the wind whips spindrift into my face and I long for the sun. Fingers are numb. Feet and toes cold. I want to move and see that this is just a bad dream. I want to wake up to my old life, back in my house in England, making coffee in my kitchen, sitting in front of my fire, eating toast and reading a book. I don't want to be scared any more.

The ropes pull. Following Powell's trench through the overhanging ice funnel, it becomes apparent why he took so long. Balancing on the crest, the ropes run away, down the opposite side of the ridge, across loose crumbling blocks held in place by rotten, sun-bleached ice and aerated snow. He had placed a wire lower down, but the ropes had pulled it up, later an ice screw driven into crud, and a wire thrust into crumbling rock. His best piece was one of his tools smashed into ice. I don't fancy my chances should I fall. I traverse down, following a four-inch ledge of gravel, on to a flake system of loose granite ears, on to rotten aerated ice, then the *pièce de résistance,* a vertical downclimb of a loose corner. Powell cheers me up by calling to me from his hanging position.

'I call this the Paul Daniels pitch.'

'Why's that then?' I call back, glad to delay.

Powell grins and shouts the well-known Daniels catchphrase, 'You're going to like this ... But not a lot!'

I can delay no longer and begin the traverse. It reminds me of entering the headmaster's office years ago at school, but fifteen minutes later I am down-climbing the corner and actually enjoying the looseness of the pitch.

'Jesus, you wouldn't want to be climbing this at the top of your grade, would you?'

'No, this would really freak some folk out; you definitely need grades in hand for this stuff.'

Yes, about ten of them, I think, scrabbling to Powell's position.

Exchanging gear, I wonder about the worth of what we are doing. Are we ever going to reach the steep stuff at the end of this horror show? The next pitch is just as tenuous as everything before. I don't want to lead it. I want to descend the rotten rubble-strewn gully to escape. I want an end to the insecurity.

'We're never going to reach that headwall, you know,' I moan. 'Let's just bail now while we can. Did you see the ridge further on? It looks more dangerous than anything we've done yet. Two days of climbing I reckon.'

'Yes, I think you're right ... but lead this pitch and then we'll have a better idea back on top of the ridge.'

'OK, I'll give it a go.'

An hour later I feel pleased that I had had the conviction to lead the pitch. Vertical, air-pocketed, a warped and twisted wall of layered ice. It was wood grain without wood strength, and only three pieces of protection within sixty metres: one crumbling ice bollard, one loose ice screw and one good ice screw.

Tucked beneath another overhang of rotting ice waiting for Powell, I look at what is to come. The way is dark and twisted. The two days of climbing to this point have been the warm-up. Buoyed up by the success of the last pitch I feel inspired to continue, but feel it might be pointless.

A feeling of worthlessness threatens to overpower me. I battle with these emotions. I crave safety, security, solidity, yet still I crave to continue. Why would it be pointless to continue even if we only reached the end of the ridge, then have to escape? Would it be because it would be *another* failed attempt? Not newsworthy? Not worth printing, not worth the space for a picture? A Facebook post? Here I am pushing myself. I am doing what I set out to do eleven years previously. It shouldn't matter if we don't reach the headwall, it shouldn't matter if we run away and escape … but it does. What matters is that we don't attempt to complete this climb for the wrong reasons. Reasons that no one should climb for: money and perceived fame. That really *would* be a poor reason to die.

Powell climbs over the point of the crest, and downclimbs to my shivering form beneath the ice roof.

'Have you seen the ridge?' he exclaims. 'Jesus. It looks impossible, two days of climbing at least, and that's only if we live that long.'

I am glad he has come to a similar assessment of the situation. It helps when one so driven decides the situation is getting out of hand. I still feel like a fraud though. What of the alpinists of the past? Lionel Terray, Maurice Herzog? Would they have retreated now? I don't think so. They were the real heroes. They were hard and driven. They were pioneers, enforcers of style and tradition. The alpinists of the past didn't have all of this new technology, light gear, synthetic, breathable, quick-drying, as-warm-as-you-like clothing. But look at all they achieved and the style in which they'd done it. They were the *real* pioneers.

Enough is enough. Although ironically for once we still have plenty of food and gas to continue. We still have energy to carry on the climb. The weather is settled and stable, and we have all the equipment we need to continue. But it is time to descend. Time to lick wounds and learn to live with 'failure'. There will always be failure with this style of climbing. Summits missed by metres. Disappointment. Self-analysis, self-deprecation. And this is OK.

7
bad shit

July 2004
Huaraz, Peru

Bad shit

The subject of the email screamed from the computer screen. I sat in the gloom of the Peruvian internet cafe, tucked away above a vegetarian restaurant in the centre of Huaraz. Powell had left Peru, and as planned I had stayed on. I was scared to hit the button to open the email Powell had sent from back home in Otley, Yorkshire. I was scared. Hands trembling. Eventually I opened it. In green words that blurred as I read, he told me that Jules Cartwright and his client, Julie Colverd, had fallen from the Piz Badile in the European Alps. Both had been killed.

I walked the busy streets of Huaraz in a daze, surrounded by the vibrancy of chattering people, the smell of roasting meat over open fires, the grind of an engine, the peep of a car horn. It was all just noise. I felt so incredibly alone. Numb. In my mind I was a thousand miles away, a thousand miles away and running from the summit of Mont Blanc in crisp early morning air. The crunch of firm snow beneath my feet, racing Cartwright. We were laughing: day four, two routes in the bag on the Italian side of the Blanc with the promise of beer and pizza.

The bustling South American street swayed and jostled around me. Colourful, a kaleidoscope of stimuli. But all I could see was Jules. I felt angry. Really angry. I was desperate for someone to start a fight, desperate to lash out, desperate to get drunk; I needed someone.

Owen Samuel, Mike Pescod and my partner for the Nepal expedition in the autumn, Nick Carter, were sharing a room with me at Edward's Inn. All three of them were somewhere in town. I bumped and jostled around the streets until I at last found Mike. He could see how upset I was and took me to a small cinema where Owen and Nick were watching a film. Mike went inside and spoke to them. When he returned he told me that they would meet me later in a bar after the end of the film. I knew Nick Carter did not really know me and had not known Jules, but I could not understand why Owen, who'd been on an expedition with Jules, preferred to watch a film instead of consoling me.

I walked away on my own and bought a small glass, narrow at the base, broadening to a wider rim. The glass was thick and green with 'Cusqueña' in painted red lettering, and cost the equivalent of twenty pence. Cartwright deserved more than the plastic measuring jug that I had been using as a mug, though he would have taken the piss now about my cheapness with this glass. When I returned to Edward's Inn, I filled the glass with Chilean red wine and toasted him.

I filled the glass for a second time and toasted his drive. I toasted his strength and commitment, his skill, and his bloody annoying habit of always being right … even when he wasn't.

I sat on my own, thousands of miles from where I wanted to be. Thousands of miles from people suffering the same pain as me.

Thoughts and fond memories filled my head, threatening to overflow and burst like the tears that were now pouring down my face.

How could you leave us, you bastard?

Drinking deep, I toasted the climbs we'd done together: *Point Five, Central Buttress, Eagle Ridge.*

Cartwright, you were the benchmark I struggled to attain. You were much, much more than the benchmark.

I toasted the close times in faraway countries – India, Pakistan – and I toasted running from the summit of Mont Blanc. I toasted our five-day round trip from Britain to the Grandes Jorasses. We'd been stormed off the *Colton-MacIntyre,* were frostbitten and had had hardly any food for three days. We'd struggled to the Montenvers train station in deep snow – me following while cursing Cartwright and his long legs. Sitting outside the cafe in the centre of Chamonix, we drank beer and ogled the college girls like a pair of dirty old men … although he wasn't that old. We had been so pleased to still be alive. We felt full of life and happy to have shared such an adventure.

At times I hated him. I hated his confidence, his commitment, his ability to carry a bloody big bag without complaint. He made me feel inadequate. But I loved him like a brother. I loved being with him and the way he tolerated my quirky personality, my moods and my inability to drink a lot of alcohol. He never tried to push. He never cajoled. He knew who I was and respected me for it. He always encouraged me.

Most of all, I remembered that summer when he was between expeditions. I was struggling to find someone to hold my ropes at North Stack Wall and without a moment of hesitation he agreed. 'Of course I'll climb with you, just don't expect me to follow.' He did though, with style and laughter, and afterwards I had held his ropes at Wen Zawn. The waves had crashed against the cliff and our fingers were frozen. I remembered the grey seal that popped his head up from the deep, and the forlorn cry of swooping seagulls. Later, sitting at the Trearddur Bay campsite, a sea breeze blew our way. The long grass moved in swathes and the smell of salt filled our heads. We recalled tales of daring. We bullshitted. Cracking a second bottle, we toasted each other.

How could you leave us, Cartwright?

8

deception

December 2004–January 2005
Chamonix, France

Rising and falling. Reflective. I was sitting by myself on the cross-Channel ferry, which always feels like a transition. The before and after. Driving to and driving from. Leaving behind. There is something about the break in the road and the passage over the surface of the sea. The smell of diesel and oil, of salt and rusting metal. The rattle of chains. The tides. Ferries remind me of crossings from childhood. Bright painted steel, floral carpets, plush upholstery, vomit-splattered toilets, anticipation of hours on the road. Spray flecks against the ferry windows. Ferry crossings in adulthood are most often by myself.

> Mussels for bait. Dad, Lesley, me and Tami – the golden Lab. That rainy holiday at Toscaig pier. The small wooden structure near Applecross off the west coast of Scotland. Mum in the car. The islands of Skye, Scalpay and Raasay somewhere across the Inner Sound's white-capped waves. The pier is attached to land on one side, while on the sea side it stands on telegraph-pole legs – legs that are tide stained, growing green, covered with constellations of barnacles. Sea otters poke their heads from the sea and large birds dive for fish. Tami, with a spiky golden coat, smells of salt and wet dog; she hunts between the rocks and eats mussels.

I drove through the night toward Chamonix, staring for hours through a rain-splattered windscreen thinking about Toscaig and the sea and the purple mussel shells. I thought about the *Omega* accident with Bracey on the Petites Jorasses last March – less than a year ago …

> The thudding and whine of the red helicopter was heard before we could see it. Bracey and I hung side by side and said nothing. For two days we had not seen another soul. We had relied and depended fully upon each other. For two days we had climbed as hard as we were able. I had dreaded the arrival of the red dot and what it signified and where it might take my life.

Driving, covering the dark kilometres with the smell of unseen farmland all around, this would be my second, full winter season in Chamonix. I hoped this winter would not be cut short like the previous one. I wanted more than anything to engage with all a winter in Chamonix could provide. But this time it felt different. This time, I was leaving someone behind. On my early return to Britain after the death of Jules, I had gained a connection amid the loss, and now there was someone in Wales ...

> White salt crusted together the brown shingle underfoot. I stood alongside Helen looking up into the maze and confusion of the rock in Mousetrap Zawn, Gogarth. Helen and I had known each other for several years; she had always been friendly and interested in what I was doing. I had always enjoyed the occasions we met, and for me there had always been an attraction. After our brief meetings I would occasionally wonder what it would be like to be close. A cacophony of sounds: bird calls, the sea filtering through shingle, scurrying insects, the wind through grass. I breathed deep and smelt the salt and the damp rock. We stood close, and the approaching storm combined with complicated emotions.

Recently – well, since discovering climbing – there have been few close relationships in my life, and this single, simplified life is something I have fiercely guarded. I find it difficult to give to someone with whom I do not feel fully connected. I would rather be alone than spend time in a relationship with someone to whom I am not completely committed. At times I feel I stand on the outside of society and look in and watch people forming relationships because of the expectations placed on them by society and the fear of being alone. I cannot imagine how terrible it would be to go through life waking next to someone who was there to make me feel better about myself or to fill a supposed gap. I've never understood how people can go from one relationship to another without time for reflection and recovery. Are relationships another of life's commodities? Am I a commodity?

I was not sure what I was leaving behind in Wales, or what was to come of our relationship. Helen had young children and had not long separated from their father. My climbing ambition and sacrifice combined with her drive to be a good parent and to live a fulfilling and rewarding life for herself and her children made for a delicate and complicated mix. My emotions and feelings could be nothing compared to hers. Through the summer together, in times of doubt, she had told me to move on, to continue living the way I had envisaged. But I convinced her that we had a future. I convinced her that we could make what we had work. But I was being selfish, I should have listened. We continued to muddle along, never knowing quite what it was we had. It's easy to be attracted to someone, but it's something else to actually turn that attraction into a lasting relationship. Timing is everything, and there has to be sacrifice. I'm not sure I was ready for sacrifice.

Omega translates as 'the end of everything'. My fall and resultant broken ankle from the attempt to free-climb Patrick Gabarrou and Ferran Latorre's masterpiece on the Petites Jorasses was literally the end of everything for my winter of climbing in the Mont Blanc range in March 2004. I vowed to return to the climb and a pact was made with Bracey that if either of us was in the area and we heard the climb was in condition, we would get in contact and try again. *Omega* was a prize for any driven alpinist, but a line like this felt more important; for some reason it went deeper than other climbs. Until this point, *Omega* was a climb overlooked – or at least, left alone – because of its reputation, but my heart ached to experience it. The climb had not had a second ascent in the ten years since it was first climbed. I had to get back to the climb. I had talked and thought about successfully climbing *Omega* for ten months; the climb was unfinished business. Hot and cold. My emotions, like those of my parents, had little in the way of middle ground. But it was also something like a trophy, something to own, something to feel proud of and satisfy the ego, a status symbol. I should have been content with the experience I'd already had, but I wasn't. Last time it ended short of the prize and the admiration from my peers that a successful ascent would merit. I really needed to own this climb and I didn't want to share it with anyone apart from Bracey.

Bishop Rawle, the primary school I attended, had a tarmacked area between the walls of the Victorian school building and the schoolhouse. Blue cornices, blue mullions, white-latticed lead windows and, at the head of the playground, a red brick wall with blue wrought-iron gates. I remember playing there one day and my sister coming to me to say that there was a lady at the gate who wanted to give me some sweets. I went to the gates where a woman whom I had never seen before said hello and smiled. She wore a long brown coat. She passed a white paper bag of sugar-coated sweets to me. And after a few minutes of chatting she walked away without another word. Over the weeks, this lady visited the playground a few more times and each time we chatted. Each time she passed me a paper bag of sweets. My parents eventually heard about this, and told me that if the lady visited the school again, I had to ignore her. It turned out the lady was my gran. My dad's mum, who I didn't know existed because of some kind of family dispute. All she wanted was to meet and get to know her grandson. But I was told not to see her. So, when a school friend came to me and told me a lady was at the gates, I refused to see her. And I still remember watching as she walked away from the gates with a paper bag in her hand.

When I was a teenager, probably seven years after I was instructed to ignore Gran, there was some kind of truce. I think it was Grandad, my dad's dad, who took the plunge and in a way forced himself upon the family. Very quickly I became close to Grandad; he was such a loving and gentle man. This was something I had never really experienced from Dad. Dad's ability to ignore his family confused me then, and it still does now. Was I angry about being robbed of time with Grandad? No, not at the time, but maybe a little now. I suppose we just have to deal with what is dished up and do the best we can without allowing it to affect our lives in a destructive way.

Climbing in whatever form can teach humility. Climbing can be life-enhancing, even life-saving in some cases. But it can also be torturous and damaging. I should have been concerned about my obsession about completing this climb, because it was possibly for the wrong reasons. In a world where so much is wrong, my being obsessed about a climb was not a particularly worthy cause to spend energy on. But in some way it gave me direction and helped me come to terms with all that was going on in the world. Besides, I had history with *Omega,* I had spilt blood and broken bones and it was my gear that hung three quarters of the way up it; it was my gear caked in rime, swinging in the breeze. I could still see the cams that Bracey and I had abseiled from. Frozen solid, they waited. Our attempt had been the only serious effort to repeat *Omega* and certainly it had been the only attempt to free-climb it. I arrogantly viewed *Omega* as our climb; Bracey and I had earned the right for another go.

'Hey, Nick, have you heard? Bracey and Sue Nott have been on *Omega*.'

A mischievous spark glinted in Jonny Baird's eyes – my housemate for the coming winter season.

No I hadn't.

Bracey has been back on Omega.

It was quietly spoken and it burrowed into my subconscious.

' … Did they do it?'

'No, they bailed from low down.'

That was all I needed, and I quietly vowed that all pacts and promises made were now off. Open season on *Omega*, and with the imminent arrival of Stu McAleese, I knew, given favourable weather, where we would be heading.

The heavy snow over the Christmas period had subsided and things were now looking possible for a ski to the Leschaux, and the weather continued to settle when Stu arrived. We discussed possibilities. Before I had left Llanberis, the plan had never been for the two of us to jump on *Omega* – that was for Bracey and me. We had planned to go to the Grandes Jorasses. But I must admit, I was excited by the opportunity that now presented itself.

After fifteen years working and living inside a prison, I had escaped without the closed mind and cynicism often associated with the work, but it made turning the other cheek difficult. It had been a little over a year since I had resigned and it was going to take a lot longer to shake its impact on me. Inside the walls of a male-only prison, acceptance and forgiveness are viewed as weaknesses. I still had a competitive and vindictive streak as wide as a French motorway. I didn't blame Bracey for wanting to jump back on *Omega*, but I did take it to heart that he hadn't told me. Integrity and loyalty were things I felt to be important and, if these were betrayed, there could be some fallout. On several occasions while growing up I experienced Mum cutting someone out of her life who she considered had betrayed her friendship. This intensity had come from her mum, who had refused to share her grandchildren and had been the cause of Dad falling out with his family.

Finger-numbing cold hung in the night. McAleese and I breathed deep with our skinning efforts. The mountain cirque surrounding was invisible, but still the atmosphere was daunting. Walls hemmed us in. They imprisoned our ambitions while the devious reefs of white hid slots large enough to swallow us up. On the steep slopes, the snow waited for a trigger. McAleese was in front cutting a trail. He stopped frequently and attempted to use his experience to gauge the danger.

'I don't like this, there's a lot of snow here.'

'Of course there is, Stu, it's winter in the Alps. Come out of the way, I'll go in front, I'm not worried by this.'

Stu's reply was succinct and to the point.

'Well, you should be.'

Breaking trail, immediately I felt the threat, but the prize, or at least the dream at the head of the glacier, was too great. Was I focusing too much on the endgame and not enough on the overall experience? Now we were on the way it would take a lot to turn me around. Jirishanca in Peru had been similar, but also very close to a suicide mission. But pushing myself physically and mentally makes my life what it is. At times, when all of the factors appear to fall into place, I feel you just have to push. I sensed similar in McAleese, but he appeared to have more demons and complications than me. We had only climbed together since the summer and already we had a string of rewarding climbs under our belts; we made a good team. Stu had climbed several new routes in Alaska and always appeared to be looking for that extra bit of time and that extra week of unpaid leave in preparation for the next big climb. But a McAleese trait that had surprised me was his ability to fret. Concerns were regularly voiced, not only working himself into a nervous wreck, but also bringing doubts to me. I wished he would keep his knowledge of everything that could go wrong to himself. I was happy in my ignorance.

We were on our own with only the early morning breeze for company. Plunging and kicking, spindrift caught and blew up the dark rock looming above.

The bergschrund was easily crossed and the memories from the effort and the fall from ten months before flooded back. A white ice streak poured down the vertical wall to the right of the line Bracey and I had climbed.

'That wasn't there last time … guess we should climb that instead of that loose overhanging corner,' I speculated.

'Do you think I'm up to this?'

'Stu, you're one of the best climbers I know. Let's just nail the bastard then eat pizza in the valley and get pissed.'

'OK, I'll try my best.'

Stu had good looks, he was blonde and popular, but he was unsure of himself. Was I *too* confident, too proud, in contrast? Was my ego too big? Many friends were more skilled than me, but in my mind they under-achieved and suffered doubt. At times I find it difficult to accept that people are different and their differences should be respected.

I climbed a corner that had perfect ice. I hammered in two hooks for protection. McAleese joined me and took the gear. I marvelled at his change in character. Fretting and cautious one second, then, with the exchange of gear, he became sure.

The next pitch was a steep wall, ice-streaked and blobbed with lumps of névé. Vertical. Direct. McAleese barged until overhanging mush blocked the way to the snow slope above.

'Watch me.'

Hunting for placements, the Cumbrian cleaned and hammered.

'WATCH OUT!'

Front points kicked into a skin. Picks flicked and quivered. And it was at this time – this most insecure time – that the mountain chose to shake itself of snow. Spindrift poured. I ducked while taking in rope. The snow bellowed, before slowing as it hit the glacier. Snatching a glance, I revelled in the fight happening above before McAleese crawled from sight.

Two pitches and not even midday. We were already in the snow gully, but the bolt Stu had belayed from and the brand new abseil anchors I had just clipped were concerning. It was obvious another party had recently been on the climb.

I stamped into the soft snow and counted the anchors I passed at sixty-metre intervals. A snow step and pee stains were evidence of a bivvy, a mere sixty metres beneath where Bracey and I had bivvied on the previous attempt. I tried to figure out who and when it could have been. I couldn't make sense of the clues. The weather had only just settled enough for an attempt on such a technical climb, hadn't it? If the party had found the same conditions as us, why would they bivvy so low? The explanation I arrived at was they had walked in and started to climb full of confidence knowing they could bivvy in the gully. The competitive element in me hoped they had woken on the second day and bad weather had forced them down. I prayed the new tat stopped below one of the difficult pitches. But I had a feeling it would be keeping us company to the top.

McAleese climbed quick and sure. Wedged tight, immersed in ice, he battled with the first of the hard pitches above the snowfield. A sheen ran the length of the pitch. Ice was moulded on to the right wall of the overhanging V-chimney, the same chimney that had taken me two hours to climb ten months earlier. Scabs of blue helped. Picks tapped and, on occasion, smashed. The ice tore, leaving the flesh of the mountain exposed. After only thirty minutes, he eased from the clutches of the dark and rotten and clipped into another newly constructed anchor.

I stood only fifteen metres above McAleese and eyed a snow-topped buttress for bivvy possibilities. I had been airlifted from the gully above after the accident – the déjà vu was strong. I pictured the mountain guide and the helicopter. I pictured Bracey's face and I could feel the torment slipping away. McAleese joined me and side by side we dug.

An inky sky filled with stars. Silhouetted and serrated, the mountain ridges lit by the moon. I pulled the bivvy bag over my head and leant against ice.

At the end of a camping holiday on Anglesey in North Wales, Mum and Dad packed the orange house tent and its contents. Metal poles, thick canvas, a large blue gas bottle, pump-up mattresses and a Tilley lamp that burned so bright it attracted moths with large dusty bodies and eyes as big as moon craters. Dad was proud of that lamp; he would sit and watch and rescue moths. He would cup them carefully in his hands, ease out of his camping stool and release them into the dark before sitting back down and wiping away silver from his skin.

With the purple Austin Maxi packed, the trailer connected, kids packed in the back, and after saying goodbye to friends, we drove away from the campsite heading home to Staffordshire. Sycamore and oak bordered the August Anglesey road. Dappled sunlight and a uniform motion of white lines. After about half an hour, I watched as Dad glanced into his rear-view mirror and said something about a car approaching fast from behind with flashing headlights. Dad pulled into a lay-by where an overflowing bin cascaded chip wrappers and plastic bags and empty cigarette boxes. The car belonging to the friends we had left at the campsite pulled in after us, and the whining of a deserted golden Labrador could clearly be heard. Tami burst from the car whimpering, excited, tail wagging. Dad was happy to be reunited with Tami

> and fussed her, while mystified and musing as to how he had forgotten her. Dad loved that dog and her unquestioning loyalty.

Following steps kicked by McAleese, I shook the early morning fog from my head. At last my time had arrived to climb something more challenging. On the previous attempt I had climbed my share of the hard pitches but this time the hardest climbing had fallen to McAleese and I was beginning to feel like a passenger. Setting up the belay, McAleese stood at the foot of the mirror image of the overhanging V-groove from below. I had been scheming through the long cold hours. If I could get to lead this first pitch, I would be back in sequence for the hard climbing above, including the broken-ankle pitch.

'You don't mind leading, do you? It does mean you will be leading the pitch you broke your ankle on though.'

I admitted that I would have asked to have led the broken-ankle pitch; I wasn't yet content enough in my life to allow McAleese to climb that one.

'Thank God we left our sacks at the bivvy!' I yelled, while trying to escape the grip of the chimney. Knees were rammed beneath my chin and thighs burned.

A confident McAleese climbed, passed and cruised the pitch I had been selling from the start of the climb, the pleasant and safe pitch. I savoured seconding the pitch while praying the rock above would be covered in thick ice.

My eyes darted and I wondered why the bulging chockstone I had fallen from previously looked so different from the way I remembered it. There was more ice, certainly. The streak in the narrow chimney was thicker, and the corner below the overhang was also covered in ice. But it still looked different from the pitch I remembered. Maybe it would turn out to be disappointingly easy ... ?

A cam, two wires, an ice hook hammered into an expanding flake and an ice screw in crud. Five pieces of gear and each piece was poor. Five pieces of gear, four more than last time and still I was sure I would break bones if I fell.

I floundered while searching for a foothold on the right. There was nothing but smooth rock. The confines of the chimney constricted arm movements. My shoulders wouldn't fit. I couldn't see my feet and once I committed, there would be no return and no gear. I planned which pick needed to be placed first, because once I started, there would be no stopping and no room for placements alongside each other. Everything depended on the picks holding, as my feet would be hanging.

Three pick-teeth placed into ice, a mono-point smeared on to rock. I committed and pulled into the confines of the overhanging chimney. I began to breathe heavily. Locking one arm, I wedged in hips, elbows, knees – any body part I could push against rock. Tapping, tapping, tapping. The pick eventually stuck, but only to a skin. I wriggled hips, and braced again.

I swung an axe and caught a placement first time. Swing. Pull. Feet in sight. A final pull and I was above the bulge; I was above my previous high point. Inside a weight had lifted; I felt light.

I climbed a few more metres before belaying off two new in-situ pegs.

'You thought that was the last hard pitch, didn't you?' I said. McAleese had seconded and stood by my side looking up. The corner we had been following for the whole climb appeared to get even steeper with less ice.

'I reckon we still have two more difficult pitches with one easy pitch to the ridge,' I said, feeling disappointed.

'You're right, and that above is definitely going to be harder than anything we've done so far. Do you think we have time?'

I realised McAleese had reverted to his cautious mode once again.

'You've got your head torch, haven't you?'

'Yes.'

'Then we have time,' I reasoned, bluntly.

McAleese set off.

'Watch it; the whole of this corner is loose,' he called.

A rock pulled and flew past me. I ducked as another came close. McAleese had reached a large square boulder blocking the corner and chose the vertical wall to its right. Vertical, technical, unprotected – he teased his way around the boulder trusting to a frozen ripple and climbed to the belay.

I looked above at the smooth vertical walls, dusted in swirling powder. The walls were towering ramparts either side of the overhanging split. There was no ice. A large flake of rock looked ready to pull.

'Do you think it'll go?' Cautious McAleese again.

'Aye, looks OK?'

McAleese looked up again. 'Are you looking at the same thing as me?'

Passing over the gear, McAleese looked at me, watching for any sign of hesitation. I sensed his doubt in my ability. I understood his doubt because I felt it also, but I had convinced myself that the pitch would succumb.

I fooled myself into believing I could avoid the smooth vertical wall to the right and climb the loose corner, but the gear placements ran out. Out right, in the middle of a blank wall, the first bolt now made sense. This was the start of the A2/3. I surprise myself at times with my naivety. The obvious can stare me in the face and I will still not see it. This was one of those occasions. I delicately edged right on small sloping edges and clipped the first bolt. Stood beneath the large flake, I looked at my options.

I gripped the side of the flake. Verglas stuck to its edge. My gloved hand started to slip, but a slap for the top found a handhold. Swinging my right foot high, and with one quick heave, I manteled the flake.

Just visible to the right were tiny edges. The sharp mono-points of my crampons struggled and my eyesight without glasses blurred. My helmet brushed against pink rock. Emptiness. At full stretch, my axe pick fished behind a flake for something positive. The pick slotted in an inch, but not the safe and sure placement I longed for.

My only hope was to aim for a decent fang of rock in a shallow depression. I stopped and opened up my mind. The possibility of serious injury was once again nigh on certain should this sanctuary of holds turn to mirage. Every small move up would result in a bigger fall. Another move. The pick twisted behind an expanding flake. Higher, the fang was in reach. I placed hope in the hands of the fang. It was all-consuming. I gambled. Ambition and desire had raised the stakes. Comparing and competing against others was part of what had driven me into this possible cul-de-sac.

Dirt poured from behind the fang as I grasped it. High on this deserted mountain, I teetered in the clear winter air and all I could taste was salt and disillusionment.

Shouting to McAleese, thirty metres below, I used every trick in the book to relieve tension. Hanging in balance with an axe pick hooked over the flake, I placed a thin Knifeblade and carefully tapped. The blade began to sing.

'Keep an eye, Stu.'

'OK; give it everything.'

I didn't know how to tell McAleese that I already had given everything. A wobbly layback led to another, and another. A rockover on a rounded foothold, a foot change, and then thin ice before the picks securely thunked. I clipped a third bolt to belay from. McAleese joined me and asked if I minded leading the final pitch. Forty metres later, we sat on the crest looking into Italy.

Sitting on that crest, McAleese and I smiled. We felt together, a team, and the surrounding mountains smothered in white looked innocent. Alongside us, draped around a spike and with a karabiner hanging from it, was that new red tat that had been with us all of the way.

9
the web

January 2005
Chamonix, France

Jonny Baird, my roommate in our overpriced rabbit hutch in the centre of Les Houches, lay festering on his deathbed, moaning and whining. He coughed and hacked all through the night, much to my annoyance. For three days I had waited. This spell of high pressure bringing cold and settled weather with styrofoam ice wasn't going to last forever. I was twitchy. I don't wait well.

'Jonny, we need to be out there. I need to climb. Get well or die because if you die, I will be able to plan something with a living partner, or at least go soloing.'

Jonny Baird was a good friend. We met in 2002 when Al Powell, Owen Samuel, Jonny and I had travelled to Peru. Immediately I had warmed to Jonny and his Scottish down-to-earthness. On the surface he appeared stoic and dour, but beneath the surface he had a dry and dark sense of humour. He could appear tough, but actually, chisel away that pale Highland exterior and you uncover a caring and sensitive man with a penchant for mischief. He was also humble, and at times self-deprecating. Jonny, like me, appeared to work hard for results. But, unlike me, he appeared to lack ego.

The *Colton-MacIntyre* on the north face of the Grandes Jorasses is the route Jules Cartwright and I had attempted on our first winter alpine climb in January 1998. This was the climb Jonny had suggested before being hit by the Chamonix lurgy. Bags were packed and stood in the corner of the room. Axe picks were sharp. Freshly filed crampons sat sparkling. Bivvy food, gas and new bundles of tat had been bought. The stove had been serviced and clothes patched; I was being wound into a frenzy of frustration.

Another clear and cold day dawned along with reports of routes climbed in perfect conditions. Baird watched me like a fly injected with venom. Paralysed and prone, he was wound in a web of sickness and self-pity. His bed, which doubled as the sofa bed, had a Baird impression in it from days of inactivity. Turning, escaping the threads, he hacked and coughed and I'm sure I saw lung hit the bottom of the bucket. Red-rimmed and sunken, his eyes peered from a waxy-white cadaverous face and he watched me pace.

'Are we going today or what, Jonny? I can't take any more of this inactivity.'

'NO!'

'Right, OK, well I'm going to the Droites.'

'Please go, you're driving me crazy! Bloody super-alpinists are all the same: fine when you're in the hills, but like caged animals in the valley. Go! Please!'

The summit crests of the Chardonnet and the Argentière were beginning to glow in the late afternoon sun. The slope beneath my skis was rutted, and the skiing style adopted was 'survival mode'.

Chunks of ice, so blue they could have been from the Mediterranean Sea, guarded the end of the Argentière Glacier. The ice chimed frequently, shattering the late afternoon serenity. The glacier was broad and bright, a stretch of frozen water inching slowly between monoliths. I stopped at the junction between slope and flat to fit skins to skis.

The Aiguille Verte, a glistening fortress bathed in vermilion hues, was the first mountain in the horseshoe surrounding the Argentière Glacier. The second in the chain of mountains, leading towards the head of the glacier, was the Droites. The north face cast a 1,000-metre shadow and somewhere in the dark folds of ice was the memory of my friend Jamie Fisher who had died in January 1999.

Jamie had been pinned by high winter winds while in the brèche on the summit ridge. I first met Jamie as he and Jules Cartwright rolled up at the Camping du Glacier d'Argentière one evening after spending three rainy days beneath the Eiger North Face. On that first meeting, life and energy almost exploded from the two of them; it was impossible not to be mesmerised and fall in love with their vibrancy, impossible not to be a little intimidated. And here I was, years after having met Jamie and Jules and many climbs down the line, on my own skinning into the shadows of the Droites.

And the guilt of outliving both of my friends simmered somewhere deep.

I lived in Cheadle with Mum and Dad from the age of eighteen to twenty-one after my job as a gamekeeper in North Wales had not worked out. I was working at the time in the warehouse at the theme park Alton Towers. Mum and Dad were away on holiday and had left behind the keys for Mum's car, a black and Martini-striped BMW 323i that was bought by the computer stationery company that employed Mum as a sales rep. The car was far from new and was included as part of the job package, but I think I'm right in saying both Mum and Dad were very proud to have such a status symbol parked in the drive. The engine was race tuned, although I'm not sure what this means apart from it growled and was temperamental, but when on form the car was fast and difficult to handle.

Dappled shadows from the oak tree canopy painted a pewter stencil across the road's surface. The soon-to-set sun peeped over the top of the hawthorn. Staffordshire farmland. Fields of grass swaying in the westerly. The shadows on the surface of the road blurred. I sat behind the wheel of the BMW. Keatsey, his girlfriend and Bung sat in the car with me. Nobody spoke; it would have been nearly impossible to hear with the growl of the car. The lane was narrow, barely wide enough if a car appeared from the opposite direction. Grass and hedgerow and mature trees lined either side. The needle on the car's speedo flickered at 100 miles per hour. The stiffened suspension made the car bounce with each dip and rise. Grass, flowers, trees, shadows, fence. I concentrated hard while gripping the steering wheel and holding the car steady; Diddy Turner, riding his Kawasaki Z550 with his girlfriend riding pillion, was attempting to overtake us. I stared to the front, at the road. Elbows were pinned to my side. The roar of the motorbike was just inches to my right. Through the tinted glass I saw a rubber grip, a black leather glove, dials, keys and instruments. The straight was running out and a sweeping right-hand bend was looming. The bike inched past my window. No one said a word. One hundred and five. The BMW juddered. I fought the steering wheel. The bend. The hedge. The verge. In the corner of my eye a black-helmeted head turned and looked into the car. Inches. Seconds. The car, the bike and six people were racing along a narrow lane at over 100 miles per hour. We could have been motionless.

Skinning deep into the heart of the mountains, the evening chill began to bite. I lost myself to dreams. I was still undecided on the route I would take to climb over the Droites. I really wanted to climb the north face but I suspected it was lacking ice. If this turned out to be the case, I would go for the 'really easy option' of the Lagarde Couloir. *The Lagarde was climbed in 1930, how difficult can it be?*

There was no doubt in my mind; whichever climb I chose there wouldn't be a problem. The following day would find me abseiling from the brèche and heading toward the Montenvers train station, ready for something more testing with Baird – that was if he ever managed to drag himself out of bed. The only problem I could envisage was arriving on the summit too early. *Rock gear? Why bother, I'm climbing snow and ice.* To save weight I had no guidebook, no extra clothing, no food, no stove or a sleeping mat. But I did have two ropes for the descent and an ice screw.

Merging into the rocks and moraine, the Argentière winter refuge stood on the opposite side of the glacier. The hut was cold and dark – it felt like entering a walk-in freezer – so I decided the most sensible option would be not to go there at all. I skinned beneath the Droites, and the clouds that had swirled, covering the complexities of snow, ice and rock, lifted. The 1,000-metre north face came into view. The higher section of the face looked doable, but not guaranteed. Streaks of ice followed runnels but there were also sections of blank rock where the wind had stripped the face. This, I decided, was not the domain for a solo climber. The Lagarde Couloir it would be.

I continued until I was beneath the initial snow cone that poured from the Lagarde. I couldn't see into the couloir, but I had passed it several times this winter and I knew it looked in condition. Stamping a ledge into the snow, I swapped skis for crampons and poles for axes. Hopefully, as arranged, Baird would be feeling better and crawl from the sofa and collect my skis tomorrow.

I started to climb the snow cone but after a short time I pulled up, stopping to stick my nose over the lip of a crevasse. The edge of the slot had blended with the slope above; it was not until I had nearly fallen that it had become visible. Overhanging like the eaves of a house, I reversed from the edge. I laughed nervously at my stupidity before continuing on my quest to rub Bairdy's weak nose right into his bucket of self-pity, although how soloing this climb would do that I was not entirely sure!

Deep in thought, my legs broke through a snow bridge while crossing the bergschrund. I plunged both of my axes above my head and out of sight. I must have looked like a small child fighting to grasp the top of a steering wheel. My legs pedalled and eventually crampons caught something and I pulled myself free.

Thick, squeaky ice. Thin, rotten ice. Soft snow and hard névé. My nose bumped into a buttress of rock. The dark shrouded an ephemeral sheet of ice that continued direct, almost mystifying, as it swathed away disappearing into the dark. I had been climbing for an hour or so and had reached the foot of a rock buttress splitting the couloir. Direct couldn't be the way. The clue was in the name of the climb. The climb was not called the Lagarde Couloir for nothing. A deep, deep dark – darker than the dark outside the couloir, and leading into the heart of the mountain – this had to be the correct line. Into the couloir: walls enclosed. And in the confines of this place, my stomach sank. I could sense a turning of the tide.

Living on a narrowboat and navigating the canal systems, my parents travelled up and down the large system of canals over the summer months. I lost track of them and where they were staying for the night. Looking it up on the map and visiting them was quite exciting. In the spring, they planned which system of canals and rivers they would explore before setting off.

Walking a section of the Grand Union Canal towpath in the centre of South Wigston, Leicestershire, the sun warmed the brick houses with their fenced gardens that butt against the towpath. Drops of rain glistened on nettles. While training to become a PE instructor, I regularly travelled through South Wigston heading to Glen Parva Young Offenders Institute. I hated Glen Parva: red brick and razor wire; volatile, confused, abused, disassociated, ill and sometimes dangerous eighteen to twenty-one-year-olds with whom I had a really tough time connecting. All of my experience within the penal system had been with adults. Generally I could connect with adults, or at least reason with them. I didn't *get* juveniles, and with my lack of understanding came intolerance and stress.

A lawnmower buzzed in a garden and swallows skimmed the surface of the still canal water. If they danced, they would pirouette, and so would I. I was returning to an area that now held no torment but which once did. I could enjoy the day and the day after and the day after that.

Emma came into view. Eighteen metres of blue and green steel, and with her, walking the towpath, windlass in hand, was Mum. Mum had lost weight, if that was possible; she couldn't really get much slimmer. Her dark hair was greyer, and tied into a ponytail. 'Hi my love,' she called as she spotted me. Her skin was as dark as ever. We hugged. She smiled, a tired but content smile, a smile created by navigating the canals, jumping on and off and opening the locks all summer long. I helped push the heavy wooden balance beam that opened the gate, allowing Dad to steer *Emma* into the lock.

Since the onset of my climbing obsession, the weight of time and the lack of time had played on my mind. The lack of time and even the act of climbing did not feel much like fun on occasion. This weight and drive had always been selfish. The weight of never having enough time to do the things in climbing I wanted to achieve was at times heavy; but what exactly was it I wanted to achieve? I suppose the thought of being a known climber appealed to my ego, but this really wasn't what drove me. I just wanted to push myself and extend personal boundaries that at one time in my life were not entertained, not on my radar. I wanted to surprise myself with how far I could take the climbing. Walking the towpath that day and seeing Mum, I realised that for my parents, time was running out, and the thought of being without Mum somewhere in my life was daunting. Dad was still smoking and he had almost used half of his four years the doctors had given him to live, but he appeared to be no worse. Out of breath and coughing, but no worse.

On occasion in the past I had felt angry when I had lost valuable climbing time in order to visit Mum. It was a distraction and I begrudged anything that took me away from training and climbing. I used to think: *If I come and see you and miss a day's training, I may die when I fall from one of my dream routes on North Stack Wall.* But seeing her now, frail and old, made me feel guilty for ever having thought that way.

Dad steered the boat into the chamber. I leant against the smooth wood of the balance beam, pushing my feet against the edge of raised bricks set amongst damp cobbles. The gate shut with a judder and I jumped on board alongside Dad. He held the tiller, his strong freckled fingers clasped like he was holding the grip of a motorbike. Mum fitted the iron windlass and started winding. The metal bar with its teeth engaging lifted the paddle – a shutter covering a hole in the bottom of the gate – and water was released from the chamber.

The sun disappeared. Gushing water with creamy brown bubbles surrounded. Dripping and dank. Green algae between black bricks. Gloom.

Imposing walls. Surging water. The heavy oak gate at the head of the lock trapped us inside this man-made tomb. Eventually the water equalised and the slime-coated lock gate gave up its battle with the weight. Escape was successfully navigated at four miles per hour, and once again we were into the sun and the vibrant banks of the canal surprised with a punch.

A vertical corner with loose granite blocks stacked one on top of the other obstructed the couloir that was no longer a couloir, but a chamber. The feeling of uncertainty wrestled at last into my thick skull. The Lagarde is a popular climb. I began to look for in-situ gear above the frequent steep sections. There was the odd piece of rotten tat or an old peg, but the normal melange of fixed gear that usually festoons the walls of popular alpine climbs was nowhere to be found. I stopped and removed an old rusty peg. Arrogantly, I had dismissed the Lagarde as an easy outing. But this mountain, the Droites, had killed my friend.

I imagined Baird, prone and coughing but at last escaping the threads that had entwined him over the days. The threads were now threatening to entangle me. I continued and refused to accept the obvious.

Fifty-four degrees and two sections of Scottish grade IV. It'll be OK, it'll open out soon.

The overhanging chockstone blocking the chimney that prevented my passage was not fifty-four degrees. A slither of thin and fragile ice dribbled down the left side. Above, the ice disappeared. I climbed beneath the overhang and stretched up. Scrabbling, I attempted to find some ice thick enough to plant a pick in, but there was none. I reversed and begrudgingly kicked my way to the right of the chockstone. Dread. A clot of compressed powdery snow that had formed between the chock and the smooth vertical wall on the right of the couloir blocked the narrow overhanging chimney. The clot was a big marshmallow. I burrowed beneath it and began to dig upward. Lumps of dense snow broke free and punched me in the face. The wall to the right was smooth. There were no holds, nothing to aim for or grab. Digging, digging. An inch was made, and then another. I plunged the shafts of both axes up to the hilt into a soft snow step. I was running on faith and hope. I heaved and wedged my shoulder against the wall on the right. Both legs cut loose and dangled into the dark. I lifted my knee and rammed it repeatedly into the snow. I began to scream at myself and doubt my ability. Cutting and digging, my body wedged against smooth rock. Hyperventilating.

Questioning. Manteling. Kicking … Praying.

An inch higher. *Come on. You're not going to die here, you stupid bastard.*

Every inch was relief. I forgot about the cold. No placement felt secure. At any moment, I expected both axes to rip and my feet to cut through the powder. Nearing the top of the chockstone, squirming and bracing into the snowy confines, I kicked a high boot hole and just hoped it would hold. Rocking over, putting all of my trust into the boot hole and reaching over the top, I hunted for something secure but all I found was powder. My heart sank.

Fuck! Fuck! Fuck!

My foot slipped with a jolt and my head almost blew apart. Pushing a shoulder against the rock, I hoped the added friction would hold me just long enough to find something solid. I fought and started digging … then caught a sliver of water ice at the back of the corner. It was enough. I nearly threw up as I pulled above the chock and established myself into a narrow snow gully above.

An hour later things were more serious. My euphoria at surviving the chockstone had worn off and controlled panic had taken its place. Move after move after move of technical mixed climbing had me stood on a knife-edge arête with unseen gaping exposure to my right and steep walls above and to my left. I was in control but I also knew my control was close to crumbling. Several hours after a rational person would have arrived at the conclusion, I conceded that I had taken a wrong turn. I blamed Baird for being ill and not having moral fibre. *You just wait, Baird; it'll be on your head when I die up here, you bastard.*

Beeeeep.

I had forgotten to turn my phone off – I couldn't believe it, usually there was no signal in the Argentière basin. Now, at least if I couldn't find a way up, I thought, I could let someone know where I was and share the concern. I left the arête, dropping down on the right side overlooking the north face. It was obvious: I had followed a minor couloir to the right and was balanced precariously somewhere near the top of the north-east spur, approximately 200 metres from the summit.

A hidden chimney cut back to the top of the arête. Climbing the arête, I willed it to lead to the summit, but almost at once the walls reared up. Trying not to panic, I followed a ledge that led left beneath more vertical walls. The yellow beam of my torch followed the ledge until it ended at a sheer cliff. The corner was my only hope for continuing but it was very steep. Once committed, there would be no turning back. I wasn't prepared to blindly start climbing and hope that everything would turn out rosy.

A little late to begin using some sense don't you think, Bullock?

I needed daylight. I would have to wait, and if I couldn't climb the corner I would return to the arête and look around the top of the north-east spur in hope of finding another way. If all else failed I could call a helicopter, but I was sure I would rather attempt to downclimb before I took the little-red-dot option.

An hour passed while I chopped a small ledge. Feet, still booted, were pushed inside my empty rucksack. Wrapping and folding my arms under my knees, I pulled my chest to my thighs and began the wait. Stars flickered, satellites followed arcs. The moon was a perfect crescent. Bouts of shivering startled me awake as I drifted in and out of consciousness. Foetal, cramped and twisted, I stared at the silhouetted crest of the Pré de Bar for telltale signs of dawn. There were none. Teeth tapped like castanets and my heart thumped.

Pinpricks of light, thousands of metres below, emerged from the Argentière Hut and floated across the glacier. Two, four, six lights left the hut. Time passed. At last, after about seven hours of sitting and shivering, the grey hinted that the end of the torture was close. Light filtered through the black. At the first opportunity I started to move again. The light revealed what I had suspected all night: there was no way up, not for a solo climber – or at least, not for *this* solo climber. I consigned myself to going down and all the effort that may involve.

An attempt at downclimbing failed almost before it had begun. I hooked and weighted large blocks with the axe picks trying to lower myself, but the blocks moved. Pulling back on to the arête, level with the ledge where I had spent the night, I fished out my phone and called the overpriced rabbit hutch. Baird would definitely be in and he knew I was here high on the Droites, so he would definitely answer the phone. *Click*, the phone was picked up …

'Hello.'

… my heart lifted with the sound of his dour Scottish voice.

'Jonny, thank God you picked up—'

In my delight at having contact with the outside world it took a second to register that Baird was still talking.

'Please leave a message after the tone.' *Beeeeep* …

Resigned to the disappointment of the answer machine, I left my message.

'Jonny, I'm high on the Droites, I've taken a wrong turn somewhere. I'm about to start down. I may be a while. Don't pick my skis up, there's a chance I might need them. Hope to see you later?'

Pushing the phone back into my pocket, I attempted the downclimb once more, thinking I probably wouldn't ever need my skis again.

Smashing over and over and over, the picks were unable to penetrate, so bounced. Rock and gravel splintered. I begged for something solid, trying to commit. I tried to be strong, but I just couldn't make the move to lower my body. Fear consumed me. I knew I would eventually try the move, and in doing so I knew I would probably fall when a pick failed. Pulling back on to the arête, I suddenly remembered the old peg I had cleaned on my way up. The peg hung from the one quickdraw on my harness. Relief flooded me. Hammering the old rusty peg into a crack and clipping myself to it I immediately felt safer than I had for a long time. *Maybe things will be OK.* The peg moved and the rock it was hammered into was loose. But in that moment, it felt as solid as a bolt. I pulled the ropes from my rucksack, and tied them together after threading them through a loop of cord tied around the head of the peg, and began, very gently, to abseil.

Five and a half hours later I crossed the bergschrund. I had dug, delved, searched, scraped. I had Abalakoved and bollarded. I had found the odd piece of tat and an old peg or two that I repositioned. With every metre, every inch of ice, snow and rock, my paranoia increased. Each abseil, every down-step, every colourful inch of rope passing through my abseil device, was a test. I had abseiled over the bergschrund and avoided the large slot that I nearly fell into the night before, and then front-pointed steep snow and ice until finally collapsing next to my skis, still driven upright into the snow.

Skiing off the glacier and on to the top slopes of the Grands Montets was surreal. People, happy, laughing and so full of life, skied all around and past me. I sat down and looked at my phone – I had a message. It was from Baird. It was a reply to my poorly disguised cry for help, my this-is-where-to-search-for-my-body plea. The message in full was just two words:

'OK, Bullock.'

10

cravings

April 2005
Llanberis, Wales

Fighting gusts of wind, the van slewed toward the centre of the North Wales Expressway. Chester, Queensferry, Mold, Colwyn Bay, Conwy, Penmaenbach, Pen-y-Clip tunnels – I was desperate to finish the arduous journey. I was desperate to see friends and make last orders in the Gallt y Glyn. I was desperate to spend time with Helen. Rain ran in rivulets. A capillary system, streaked and branched, a living, growing organism etched across the windscreen. My eyes cast a gritty glance out to the dark Irish Sea. White frothing waves, a curling frenzy of cornices. Imagination took me to the washed base of North Stack Wall, to *Mousetrap*'s shingle cave. Imagination took me beneath the mayhem happening on the surface. I pictured long strings of swaying kelp. I was happy to be returning to North Wales, close to the sea. I was happy to have escaped Chamonix.

The previous day I had sent a begging text message to my sister in the south of England:

> Please can you transfer £100 into my bank account ASAP,
> I don't have money to get home.

Half an hour later, my out-of-credit mobile had beeped; the text message from Lesley informed me the money had been deposited, and my 950-mile journey began.

I craved escape and normality. At least for a while. Shopping for food with labels I could understand. The bustle of the High Street with dry feet. The money in my account for new music, my books and CDs close at hand.

Radio in the morning with a stiff-upper-lip-public-school accent, and toast in front of an open fire. I craved solid stone cottages sunken into green rolling hills. Grazing sheep and frisky, gambolling lambs, bumping their mother's underbelly. I craved dark streaks of wet on the cleaved slate of a Llanberis stone mine.

Sailing the Berlingo into Llanberis, a crossword of terraced housing and parked cars, the High Street's brightly painted shopfronts were almost overwhelming. The town grew up in another time – in the late 1700s – when flat-capped men burrowed into the hillsides like moles, risking their lives to mine the green-grey slate. Today, the detritus is piled high in great, grey mounds surrounding the town, a tribute to and reminder of harder times; this town feels like home.

I vowed to invest more time in my rock climbing, and also in my relationship. But somewhere beneath it all, somewhere beneath my good intentions and longing, was a tremor of uncertainty; I was actually hungry for climbing to the point it caused an ache and I'm sure this was easy for Helen to see.

The summer with its warm days, wet days, warm nights and a hundred rock climbs began, and once again my North Stack Wall romance – or was it obsession? – blossomed.

Waves crashed into the base of North Stack and from them the old and whiskered grey seals popped up. They took a look and checked us out. Spume filled the air with sticky, skin-clinging salt deposits. Fine white smoking mist swirled above the sea. Caught on an updraught, the mist lifted and stroked the green five o'clock shadow of lichen growing on the cliff. The mist stroked my drive and my ego. Tides rose and fell. Haze had filled my head for the previous three days, for the previous weeks. Getting into the North Stack zone once again had been good, life was good, life was exciting and free. *Blue Peter* for the sixth time, *The Cad* for the third, *The Long Run Direct*, *Art Groupie*, *Not Fade Away*.

The chime of steel on steel was sweet. The clear tone excited me more than the scream of the circling seagulls. The cackle of the nesting guillemots vying for the space to bring up their young on the shit-smeared ledge opposite once again became my soundtrack. The raucous mayhem, the turmoil, the madness of life on the ledge resembled an overcrowded tube station in rush hour. Thoughts raced through my head. Thoughts that threatened to tangle the twisted trains of obsession and confusion.

This wall was calling me. This wall had called for six years and once again

I had succumbed. I was an addict; I was prepared to give everything for my addiction. My life again stood still until this climb, *The Bells! The Bells!* was complete. The tides pealed a tentative chime. Obsession. I had gone cold turkey, done recovery. This climb had been with me almost from the start. And here I was again. Here I was again.

The chime of steel on steel electrified me. Like the clapper hitting, the pitch increased with each blow: baritone – tenor – alto and finally soprano. The thin, rounded blade, an inch in length, entered into the tight crack with each insistent thrust of the hammer's head. I laughed. It's a mad, on-the-edge sound. The nervous excitement tickled my intestines. Each swing of the hammer, each sweet ring in every millimetre of depth. The black head of the peg flattened with the pounding. Black turned to silver with each repeated hammer blow.

The hammer was borrowed from the woman who lives in the fog warning station above North Stack. The previous day we had brought all of the paraphernalia to place a new peg and dispense with the old, but we had bottled it. What if the old peg was removed and we couldn't place a new one? The climb would be ruined and so would we. The peg had saved my life once. The peg had been nineteen years old then. Cracked and flaking. That was six years ago. But the previous day, when we had come prepared to replace it, it had appeared solid as we brushed and practised moves. The previous day it had appeared strong when I knew I wouldn't be starting out on the lead, when I had cheated with the rope running up.

This time, Dougal Tavener was on for his climb, *Stroke of the Fiend* – the route that traverses the wall from left to right. I had climbed *Stroke of the Fiend*, a Redhead E7 like *The Bells!*, in 1999 with Tim Neill at a time when I was indestructible and immortal. It was a time when I was as arrogant and as sure of my abilities as Tavener was now. At twenty-four years old and with only four years of climbing experience, it scared me to think how good Dougal might become, how full and successful his climbing life might be. But at what point does a person realise their mortality? At what point does life outside the climb take precedence? Would he burn out or just flicker into existence? Would he take a less obsessive path? Would meeting someone special mean more to him than a climb? At what point does life move forward from having to push and test one's strength of mind and one's drive? 'But it's only climbing,' Helen said, but for me, at that moment, it felt more nourishing than food. Was this wrong? Climbing was life. Climbing was as real as anything else in this life. Climbing at that moment was more real than TV, more real than computer games. More real than material goods, more real than families, relationships, more real than comfort. Helen had refused to belay me or be anywhere near when I decided to step from the boulders, but Tavener had stepped into the loop.

Stroke of the Fiend utilises the peg used for *The Bells!*, but as Tavener had started to remove the tat clove-hitched around the neck of the peg, the steel had crumbled like a rotten rag. Dougal quickly retightened the faded tat and gave me the bad news. That was it: game over. Obsession over, move on.

Life waits for no one. Fuck that.

Dougal knocked on the door of the house standing on top of the cliff to beg for a hammer. I ran the steep hill back to the car park to collect the pegs from my van. All my doubt ran down that steep hill with me. Would I be brave enough to attempt to remove the peg placed by Redhead in 1980? What if I couldn't replace it? The thought of not finishing the climb that had become a part of my history more than any other rock climb drove me on. The thought of actually starting on the long lonely lead was less frightening to me than the thought of not starting on it at all.

Desire.

Swinging from the abseil rope I failed to place a thick and strong Lost Arrow immediately above the frail peg. No way would I even attempt to remove the old peg. Trying again, the Lost Arrow blanked out for a second time. I was gutted and relieved.

Move on, what does it matter? Move on. The voice of castigation flooded my mind.

You don't want to do this climb. It scares you. People know you've had the confidence to try it once before, that's enough then is it, run away? Was my life turning? Once I pushed hard, I gave it everything. I was brave enough to try this climb before without practice. Is this what getting older has done? As the clock ticks do we grasp at the ever-decreasing years or has my ego calmed?

Four inches above the peg a small thin crack gave hope. The smallest peg I had was removed from the karabiner. The peg was a blade of thin steel, as thick as a coin and two inches in length. The first hammer blow failed, but then, as if some evil spirit looked down and wished me on my way, the thin steel bit. The heavy hammer pounded and with each resounding blow the peg entered the wall a little further. Eventually, it could go no deeper. I smiled to myself knowing there was no going back. Looking up, Dougal's head was silhouetted against the blue sky. I gave him the thumbs up.

We danced a cautious sideways dance for the rest of that day. Dougal led the crux pitch of *Stroke*, testing the new peg. I was grateful for that, although it would be different taking a lob on it from above which is where the line of *The Bells!* would take me.

I went running the next day, and often when running, thinking takes away the pain. I had cheated. Seven times in fact. Once from the start, practising the traverse beneath *The Cad* flake, five times through the crux section, and once on the final traverse and the exit groove. I was not proud. I pushed my body, pounding the slate of the miners' track – lungs burnt, sweat ran, grey crunched underfoot. I wanted pain. I wanted to punish myself for cheating. I wanted to take the full hit, because I had given so much to climbing, and other aspects of my life, such as relationships, friendships and family, had taken second, third, even fourth place. I needed the perceived success, otherwise what was the use?

I had watched Dad cope with the death of his twenty-eight-year-old brother and Gran and Grandad and not once did I see him shed a tear.

A few years after the death of Grandad, I visited my parents at their house in Cheadle. It was winter and snow lay on the frozen ground. I decided to go for a walk through the graveyard behind St Giles church and visit Grandad's grave. Walking above the town, my footsteps left a trail behind me threading gravestones. Mounds of rotting flowers were covered in snow; the snow hid their withering. Looking around, I knew where the grave should be because Gran was buried there also, but there was no headstone – Mum and Dad had not bought one. I crouched beside the mound of earth and wept.

Dad had a sister, Aunty Jude, that he had not talked to in years and didn't even know where she lived. She obviously shared the same blood because she had made no move to see that her parents had a headstone either. Dad had very few friends: he didn't spend any time away from home, not in the pub, nor walking nor socialising. Dad had walls; he appeared to need no one apart from Mum.

Time would tell if *The Bells!* would mean as much to me now that I had top-roped it. I reasoned to myself that having cheated death once, when I attempted the climb in good style with only the middle spike on *The Cad* for protection, I would now climb it using whatever style it took. I wanted the climb. I wanted the intensity. I couldn't let it go. I would use the climb as a stepping stone to gain the confidence to attempt other routes on the wall in better style.

I slept alone in the Climbers' Club hut Ynys Ettws. The wind caught against the rough-hewn stone of the building that stood beneath the road of the Llanberis Pass. The room was dark. Sheep shuffled outside trying to escape the wind, trying to eke out an existence before the farmer collected them. The gurgle from the stream nearby made me think of six years ago, lying awake all night in Tim Neill's house, down the pass from where I lay, and my near-fatal attempt to climb *The Bells!* the next day.

Driving toward the wall, I was in the passenger seat of Dougal's van. Cars driving in the opposite direction came toward me as if filmed using time-lapse photography. I saw the cars as large snowflakes caught in the headlights while driving through a blizzard. Fixated fascination. I was consumed. I was on a countdown.

> Dad was on a countdown. I had heard from Mum a few days ago; Dad was drinking half a bottle of Scotch a day – obviously his smoking was not ending it quickly enough for him. His liver had hit overload and he had collapsed. Mum was beside herself with worry and concern. After four days he was released from hospital; there was nothing the doctors could or wanted to do. He was drinking himself to death and that was his choice. He could do it at home and not at the taxpayer's expense.

Stepping from the tidal platform I made the familiar moves: edge, flake, spike, touching with tenderness the grey-scalloped rock, rock smoothed by the monotonous caress of the sea. *I will take the gear on The Cad this time.* In my warped way this disturbed me more than top-rope practice. Since the first ascent in 1980 *The Bells!* had seen between fifteen and twenty ascents; many had placed gear in *The Cad*. Maybe I should have been content with living beyond my previous unsuccessful attempt? Maybe I should have left the climb feeling generous, having ejected me still alive? Maybe this time, even with practice, a hold would break and I would die?

It's a stepping stone. Repeatedly, I told myself this. But still the feeling of letting myself down was threatening to overwhelm me. I should be honest with the climb and with myself.

I completed the traverse beneath the flake without emotion or fear

– unlike the last time – thanks to the gear in *The Cad* flake. Self-loathing was consuming. What's driving me? Placing the gear after the traverse, before starting on the upward dance, I wondered about its worth. I placed a sideways number-one wire in snappy rock, sideways numbers four and five in the same snappy rock. I placed an RP in a millimetre in rock as thick as a potato crisp.

Move on. Life will not wait. Risk enhances.

Entering into the intense upward maze of crozzle and crimp, I treated wafer-flakes with respect. I cleaned cobwebs. Focus and belief maintained my momentum. Step up, push down. Weighting, not waiting, life moves forward. Fingers clipped the karabiner that hung from a thin tape joining the old and the new pegs. Trapping the rope inside its oval of shiny metal, the gate snapped loudly. The smell of the sea was strong.

I completed the crux without hesitation, a series of technical and blind moves that had been made easy with practice. The waves jeered.

Standing level with the shield of rock on the final traverse before the dirty loose exit groove, I confronted the move that scared me more than any other move on the climb. Minutes passed. Knowledge helped and hindered because I knew what I had to do. Sharp out-of-sight edges cut into fingertips and, inching sideways, I eventually reached the arête.

A new view, a new outlook. The sea and the breeze and the smell of salt. Random and scattered, boulders balanced on the ledge below like snooker balls. They waited to ease my way should a hold break. Lumps of rusty iron, floats and ripped fishing nets filled the spaces between the boulders. Dirt filled the back of the exit groove and provided nutrients for plant life. Roots clung to the rock and tried to prise flakes from the wall.

Technically, the easiest section of the climb proved to be the most taxing. The thought of falling was traumatising. The rope ran for what appeared to be miles, disturbed only by make-believe protection. I had cheated once with the rope running up on this section. I wished I had pulled on holds and practised more, if only to test the strength of the rock. Had the rot set in? Was I beginning to cling to the decreasing years?

Grovelling in the dirt, I pulled the final moves on to the ledge and then on to the flat grey rock of the top. The pink and green were as before. Unchanged. The white of the fog station wall was still white. Unchanged. The climb was beneath me. Unchanged. But I felt I had let myself down.

I stand above, but really am I beneath?

11
death or glory

June 2006
Peru

White corrugated walls surround us. The metal tunnel will lead Matt Helliker and me to the plane and the plane will land in Peru. I feel relieved. Matt is a great friend, he makes me laugh. I enjoy hanging out and climbing with him, but arranging a trip with Matt is close to being the most frustrating exercise in the world. As great as it is to be with the six-foot-two blonde Helliker, he is, without doubt, the most unreliable person on the planet. Going on a trip with him is a complete uncertainty until the moment you walk on to the plane – only then do you know the trip is happening.

I press the off button on my mobile, ending the call with Helen. Our relationship has been through rough times, more off than on, but once again we decided to resurrect our failing relationship, to try harder to make the relationship work, although going to Peru, I'm sure, was not going to help. But what could I do? I suppose I could change? I wanted the relationship and the closeness, I wanted to be a part of something other than climbing. But this is who and what I am, this selfish climbing life makes me better. Maybe having both isn't possible for me?

After a day of travel Helliker and I arrived in Lima where we caught the overnight bus for Huaraz, that bustling and dusty town in the Ancash region tucked beneath the Cordillera Blanca of the Andes. A few days later we jumped on to another bus taking us to the remote eastern side of the range and a small town called Chavin. The bus might as well have been a spaceship for it appeared to transport us to another planet.

Huantsán? Never heard of it. Once in, no way out. Miles from anywhere.

Miles from anyone. Miles from relationships and responsibility, miles from ageing parents and alcoholism. No rescue, no helicopters, no one. The splitter couloir on the east face of Huantsán was mine and Helliker's line, our life, our chosen route to fame or at least a Facebook spray. Or maybe it was our route to something more permanent?

I stuttered some rubbish from a translation book. The hotel owner welcomed us and after some form of dialogue, that neither he nor I really understood, he ran around the corner to look for an *arriero* and three *burros*, but came back with no one, no donkey, nothing. *Nada.*

The following day he ran away again. Helliker and I sunbathed in the hotel garden. A large and thick, freshly painted white wall separated us from the deprivation outside. The scent of roses and red-hot pokers filled the air that hung above the damp grass on which we lay. The wings of the hummingbirds buzzing around the flowers purred like my old two-stroke.

Suitors started to arrive as the rumours spread of mad gringos with wads of cash. One by one, men from the high meadows passed through the large arch of the hotel. String held their trousers. Cracked and beaten skin hid in the shade beneath their brown felt hats. The first didn't think we had come from Mars, but maybe a Christmas cracker. Eighty dollars one way? We told him thanks, but no thanks.

Waiting ...

Eventually a man appeared. He accepted the stipulated rate without hesitation. Dark eyes beneath the brim of his Stetson. He wore a gentle smile with white teeth across his tanned face. He appeared content and trustworthy. Twenty minutes later and the deal was done. Horses breezed beneath the arch of the hotel, hooves clattering on cobbles. We held their heads while bags were loaded and we were on our way. Another problem solved, one thing less to make life interesting. The hostel owner shook our hands, wished us luck, then with his arms stretched high above his head, like he was about to dive into a swimming pool, he imitated shooting head first down the couloir. He laughed and waved. Turning away he shook his head.

'Gringos, poco loco!'

We walked, and walked. The afternoon sun baked the earth. Up and up. Passing through villages, passing thatched roofs, mud bricks and children playing in the dirt. Corn on the cob hung from wooden lintels, the sun draining the yellow cobs. Dogs yapped and snapped, pigs grunted and scuffled with one leg tied by twine. Dust filled the air. Children ran and hid when Helliker strode past; I had told him his blonde mane and tall frame would scare. Up and up and on and up … Six hours later, day was changing to night, hot to cold, and finally we stumbled across a flat piece of scrub we chose to be our base. Some things remain constant no matter what; there is something primeval about finding and setting up a camp.

We arranged for a pickup in twelve days' time.

'*Hoy* is the 18th.'

The arriero looked confused. I counted eighteen on my fingers.

'*Dia*, 18th. *Sĭ?*'

He nodded his head. The brim of his Stetson fell slightly. At last we understood each other, if only the basics. I then wrote eighteen to thirty on the back of the crumpled boarding pass I still had in my pocket and counted twelve days with him counting also, except he counted in Spanish.

'*Uno*-one, *dos*-two … *treinta*-thirty, *Viernes*-Friday, *aqui*-here. *Sĭ?*'

He nodded his head for a second time, and clutching a wad of dollars and the boarding pass, he moseyed into the distance.

'Do you reckon he understood?' I asked, it being too late now anyway.

For two days Helliker and I walked the walk. Up the hill and down, up and down. Life was simple in the middle of nowhere among the long grass and the lakes. The complications for us both were closer to home. I ran and skipped, like a child in the wake of an angry parent. Helliker's legs were long, his years few, and he attempted to keep his ambitions under check, but he didn't do a very good job. It was easy to see that he craved attention, which was fine; his level of climbing skill deserved some form of recognition, I suppose.

Andean geese broke the tension of the surface of the lake, ripples circling beneath their white plumage. The surface wavered with the growing rings, and the reflection of the mountains surrounding the lake distorted. The cows, left to graze, lifted their heads and looked puzzled as we passed. Left to fatten, their death when it came would be in a stream, the quick steel of the knife severing tissue and tendon. The collective of farmers would share everything and waste nothing.

The gear was stashed beneath a rock at 4,800 metres: a few cams, screws and wires. The couloir waited and we were set. I was nervous. I wanted the couloir and recognised in myself the familiar deadly combination of ambition and fear of failure. The previous year I had failed to summit on both of my big trips. I often thought of Alex Fidi, the Austrian who had been killed on Jirishanca Chico the year Al Powell and I had climbed *Fear and Loathing* on Jirishanca. Friends of his had said in the year previous he had sat in frustration waiting out bad weather on too many occasions. The need to succeed is strong, and driven people do not wait well. In the past I had made mistakes when longing and ambition had taken over. I had made many mistakes. I prayed now that we were ready and the weather would not turn my mind to turmoil.

Huantsán Sur towered to the left of the couloir we had come to climb and had one recorded climb from this side. The 1,000-metre face we were both staring at didn't have a single climb. Dreamy. Helliker stood and stared. This was his first trip to the greater ranges and he was hungry. Like me he had sponsors to please and no doubt felt pressure, though pressure placed by himself as much as by anyone. But with a head beyond his years, his drive was not a substitute for sense. I marvelled at his steady approach and laid-back personality, while I felt the strain being the old hand. Expeditioning had become second nature. Helliker knew this, and was prepared to let me make the decisions. I accepted the role, but I also knew that once on the hill, my ambition and drive could kill us.

Huantsán Sur was a Matterhorn. Ridges of brown rock supported the snow and ice above. It had a wide base, but upon closer inspection the support was rotten. Snow couloirs ran down from the pointed summit, blocked by massive windblown umbrellas of ice. Sharks' teeth, as thick as telegraph poles, hung from the edge of the umbrellas. The middle of the face looked technical and scary, disappointingly so. Séracs teetered at angles that defied gravity. We sat quietly, looking, contemplating. Realisation hit: nothing is as straightforward as it looks from the outside. The question is, I suppose, *how much are we prepared to risk?*

Huantsán Sur is 5,919 metres. It is 300 metres lower than the main Huantsán summit, but we surmised that, being a buttress, it would be safe to climb, no matter what the weather. The objective dangers were not considered. This would be our downfall.

Later in the night, a cloud-filled sky masked the Milky Way. The snow arrived an hour later. Four days of storm followed. The snow covered the grass and built beneath the flysheet of the tent. Both Helliker and I felt impotent. We spoke of sensible options, of having plenty of time. But our vacant looks and wide eyes showed that we didn't even really believe the words coming from our own mouths.

Day five dawned, cloudy but dry. We packed and left Base Camp. Two hours later, the kit was recovered from the snow cone at the base of the couloir and our attention turned left. A curtain of scree spewed from between brown cliffs at the base of Huantsán Sur. Overhead, geese flew in an arrow pointing away from the mountain. Entering into the theatre of loose rock, I felt insignificant. Rocks scattered and balanced, something similar to Craig Dorys on the Llŷn Peninsula in North Wales.

Boulders were pushed, gravel crunched, tiles flew. Big boots smeared. The rucksacks on our backs pulled like an undertow. Soloing, staying close so the tumbling rocks could not gain momentum, we moved with a jagged ridge on the left and a headwall on the right. Helliker and I were hemmed in. A gigantic umbrella blocked our way like a fishing net. Overhanging, creaking séracs leant on either side of our ice gully. The sun beat down. We roped up; fear of falling down a slot or being hit by a collapsing sérac was ever present. Speed would be our friend.

As the evening took hold we forced on to the top of a couloir. Dollops of snow layered like tiramisu formed a delicate and spiked ridge on the right. An ice umbrella big enough to fit a school bus blocked the head of the couloir. On the left, a sheer and unclimbable rock face. I climbed an overhang, breaching the rock wall, and discovered a step big enough for both of us to sleep upon. Helliker joined me and together we excavated.

Wrapped for the night, snow poured through a small hole left in the bivvy bag zipper. The entrance of my sleeping bag froze. Turning from the one side, the side overlooking the void, I turned again, to face the rock. The shelf was about fifteen inches wide and my legs jittered with fatigue. My head thumped. I cursed our abortive attempt at acclimatisation earlier in the trip. Sleep eventually came, however, and when it did I welcomed it like an old friend; it made me feel secure.

The first lump of ice hit and woke me with a start. Several more hit. I screamed. Helliker on a shelf above also screamed. A sérac high on the face had calved. Lumps of ice exploded, breaking into smaller lumps that were hitting us. Large lumps flew over our heads, into space.

'You alright?' I asked, attempting to control the quiver in my voice.

'I think so … '

Helliker and I watched the sun rise in a stippled sea of clouds, and among the serenity we looked up. The danger had forced us from our sleeping bags, placing us in a strong position for reaching the summit that day, if we could find a way from beneath this behemoth – the biggest ice overhang on the face. I belayed from beneath icicles that were too thin to climb but plenty large enough to maim.

Reversing, Helliker informed me that there was no way out on the right. So, up, up beneath the centre of the overhang. He disappeared, reappeared, disappeared. Forty metres to the left, silhouetted against the blue sky, he pulled from beneath the fringe. The Amazon basin was a blurred weld of green in the far distance. Up and around, out of sight, a way had been found.

I sucked oxygen-thin air. Blood pumped. Traversing from edge to edge of a runnel I thought of looking up, but it wouldn't help. Embedded deep into the snow, large lumps of freshly calved ice littered the way. The cause of a sleepless night had been discovered; we had to cross beneath the shedding sérac. Reaching the far side, I placed a wire into a wall of rotten rock and ran out the remaining rope.

Helliker climbed an ice runnel leading to a small version of the massive umbrella below. This time escape was found through a keyhole on the right that led to a steep slope of snow. Looking at an image on the screen of the camera, Helliker pointed me left, assuring me it would lead to easy ground and the summit. I was doubtful. Helliker displayed all of the signs I had once shown on my first forays to the big hills, an underestimation of the sheer scale of 1,000 vertical metres being one of them.

The easy ground didn't materialise. After reversing, I climbed a mixed line until I reached a small snowfield. A large, open expanse of flutings, runnels, icicle-draped overhangs and rock spread to my right. There would be a way amongst this maze if I chose, but the effort needed and the time was more than I was prepared to give. I sensed the summit snow slopes and down-climbed to a runnel of ice hidden on the left.

Helliker led out from the runnel and on to a vast ploughed field. Some time later the snow began to melt, wetting my legs as I took in the ropes while sitting on the summit. Clouds swirled about Huantsán's 1,200-metre face to my left and in the distance I could see the Huayhuash. I tried to spot Jirishanca, but couldn't. This was my first success on a big hill in a year, and it felt good to have succeeded, but in some way it was an anticlimax. The experiences along the way are often more fulfilling than the arriving.

Five days after sitting on the summit of Huantsán Sur, Helliker and I wallowed in the comfort of Edward's Inn, the place I had always stayed in Huaraz. Pink flowers adorned white walls. Beyond the walls were dogs, bars and drunks. We had returned from our climb the day before with a week remaining before the flight home. It would have been easy to go climbing again but neither Helliker nor I could muster the mental energy.

The route on Huantsán Sur was new, of course. Who in their right mind would go up there in the first place? The name I came up with for the line was *Death or Glory*.[1] At the time it appeared apt; I associated it with prison tattoos, machismo and the punk band The Clash. It reflected my personal feelings at the time about climbers that appeared willing to risk almost anything for perceived fame.

1 I regret calling the route *Death or Glory* because when we were on Huantsán Sur – and at the time we were out of touch with our base camp – Sue Nott and Karen McNeill, both accomplished climbers and much loved, were missing, presumed dead, on Mount Foraker in Alaska.

12
slave to the rhythm?

Winter 2006–2007
Chamonix, France

The M6 leads to the M1, a blurred passing of white lines and lights. Full to overflowing, cumulus hang in the night sky, and behind the clouds I know there are stars. Cones, balustrades, chevrons. Cars, fields, rivers, electricity pylons. One day Kathmandu, the next Ynys Ettws in the Llanberis Pass, and the day after, the road south. I call in to my sister's house to collect ski and mountaineering gear before setting off again and visiting Mum and Dad. My parents are moored for the winter at a modern marina near the centre of the large town Hemel Hempstead.

The marina is clean and functional and convenient. There are shops close by, and life for them on the narrowboat – a new boat to Mum and Dad called *Jasper*, but a second-hand, more traditional and longer boat than their previous boat *Emma* – appears OK. Mum is thin and grey but radiant in a tired and happy way, and she is pleased to have the convenience of shops close at hand. Dad smokes and drinks tea and reads novels. Mum hands me a bag of Christmas and birthday gifts including a Christmas cake bought in Marks and Spencer.

A swan glides toward the boat and taps the hull for attention. Mum opens a small side door before breaking up bread and dropping it on to the surface of the brown water.

They will be moored at the marina for the winter. I can tell that being stationary for a while is welcome. But no doubt, once again, in March they will be ready to begin exploration of the canal system. It's strange seeing my parents, people who were fixed for so long, appear to be so free and transient. I wonder why they waited so long, why did it take a doctor's death sentence of emphysema for Dad to wake up? Although that diagnosis was obviously incorrect as he's still smoking and still going. After the scare of Dad collapsing with the effects of drink he now appears to have dried out and looks healthier. Humans are strange; many of us appear to need a scare to appreciate life.

This will be my third full winter season in the Alps. I'm sharing an apartment in the middle of Chamonix with my friend Kenton Cool. Kenton has asked me if Andy Houseman, a young Brit I last met in Peru, can also live in the house. I've told Kenton I'm not sure, that the jury is still out on Andy … but the prospect of the rent going down by a third, and the fact that I have a room so I can get away and hide, has swayed the decision.

'OK, Kenton, whatever.'

Surrounded by new red brick, white concrete, glass and bright lights, I park close to Mum and Dad's boat and sleep in my van. Climbing gear is stacked all around. In the morning, after saying goodbye, I begin to drive south once more, heading to Dover.

By early evening I reach the outskirts of Chamonix. Up above, in the moonlight, the slender spire of the Aiguille du Midi is visible. Lights shine through windows cut into the slender rock spire and pierce the dark. The weather is settled, and as I drive I text Jon Bracey and arrange to climb with him the next day.

Scotch on the Rocks was first climbed by Stevie Haston and Laurence Gouault; the name supposedly came about because Haston said climbing in Scotland was in decline and, literally, on the rocks. I didn't know Haston, I had never met him, but the folk tales in Llanberis abounded; he appeared to be a forceful character with strong opinions, some of which I liked, some of which I wasn't so sure about. Climbing seemed to be becoming more mainstream, more conformist, so I thought it was OK to have someone who was unafraid to vent, someone who stirred it up, and the stories about the aggression and the fights were surely exaggerated, right?

Bracey and I skied from the first Midi telecabin the following morning and climbed *Scotch on the Rocks*, but we bailed from above the crux pitch with two pitches remaining. Bracey said it would cause bother at home if he missed the last lift to the valley. I hated not finishing climbs; convenience and comfort always seemed a poor excuse to bail. And it made me wonder how a person went from being so free to becoming concerned about getting home on time? Though, maybe this was my problem, maybe this was why I was single once again, Helen and I having written off the relationship for good this time.

After climbing *Scotch*, unacclimatised, I skinned back to the Midi alone. Bracey, acclimatised, fit and in fear of the fallout should he not make it home, shot ahead. I skinned and accepted that I was in for a cold bivvy in the back corridor of the Midi station. Strapped to the side of my rucksack, top-heavy skis weighed me down. Leaning against poles, I plodded the middle section of the steep Midi Arête gasping for breath. I stopped and looked up; a member of staff stood on the bridge crossing from the summit of the Midi to the subsidiary summit. He shouted and beckoned – the staff were waiting for me, but I had to keep going. Reaching the tunnel, my lungs felt like they were about to rip apart, but I caught the bin and made it down to the valley.

Later that evening, Bracey called.

'Don't be a slacker, Bullock!' he said when I suggested a rest day and going up again the day after tomorrow.

So there we were, once again stamping into ski bindings on the wind-scoured col beneath the Midi Arête. The Grandes Jorasses, the Dru, the Verte, snow-dusted monoliths so familiar to me now. So solid and ancient, but so young in comparison to the stars in the night sky, and so much more attainable.

Bracey and I were hoping to attempt a new line we had spotted the day before on Pointe Lachenal, a small subsidiary rock face near the Tacul's east face. After stashing the skis, I followed Bracey's steps until we stood beneath the intended line – a clean welt cutting through pink granite. A sliver of ice thinning to a dribble at the back of the welt reminded me of the well-documented pitch of the Twight and Parkin route, *Beyond Good and Evil*. Above is a slab, and the slab is topped by a turret of large and overhanging blocks that lead to the final spire and summit of Pointe Lachenal. At 260 metres the climb is short, but it was 19 December and daylight was even shorter.

Several hours later, engulfed by dark, torquing, laybacking, I almost fell when I was hit by a cascade of spindrift lifted from the snowfields above. I forced into an offwidth and at the top, stopped, cleared myself of snow, and regathered my composure. I couldn't see a bloody thing; my head torch was at the bottom of our one, almost empty, rucksack that Bracey was carrying. Bracey joined me and set off, shivering his way into the night, until at last he pulled the top of Pointe Lachenal. I heard a shout of success, and our new route, which we later called *Tentation*, was climbed.

Climbing slowed for Christmas, but in the space between Christmas and New Year, *Omega* had a line of devotees as long as the streaks of ice that shone from its blank walls. On the countdown to New Year celebrations, the crowds left and Tim Neill and I were left alone to clean up in a bitterly cold auditorium. On New Year's Eve, a moonlit ski descent from *L'Oeil au Beurre Noir* on the Petites Jorasses – a wave of water-ice leading to a steep silver pencil compressed by overhanging granite – led us through heavy, thigh-deep crud beneath the Grandes Jorasses north face. Burning thighs. Lungs on fire. Two friends skiing into and out of the shadows made by the moonlight and the mountains.

Wind and snow battered the Leschaux's aluminium skin. Fully clothed, I wrapped thick woollen blankets around myself and dreamt with eyes open. A shaky forecast and New Year celebrations had no doubt kept other climbers away, and as 2006 slipped into 2007, I thought it fitting that my most prolific and successful year of climbing had finished with such an interesting and unusual route alongside a great friend.

The rock and ice up high had been generous in 2006, and the crumbling, vegetated cliffs at the edge of the Irish Sea, forgiving. Experiences were packed away, stored like yellowing newspapers – people, places, climbs, countries – experiences that would steal into and out of my mind that infrequently slows. Pulling the blankets around me, flushed with success and warm for a while, the thought of what I had lost in 2006 tempered my contentment. Maybe there are a finite amount of relationships out there that work – that *really* work – and the rest of us just take whatever comes along to ease the passage?

New Year's Day and the return to the valley was a wet one. Driving sleet and rain thrashed the glacier. Tumultuous rivers cut gorges through the ice, the wind almost gale force, carrying the hail and rain. Climbing the ladders that lead to the Montenvers train station, my fingers felt almost frostbitten they were so cold gripping the metal. But after an hour, Tim and I sat side by side, steaming and warm inside the train carriage. Celebrations that night had been earned and the stars in the sky shone brightly.

Again, nervous, competitive glances flickered across cold faces in the hewn and cavernous gloom of the Midi tunnel. Numb fingers fumbled crampons. Skis strapped to the sides of sacks caught on the sculpted ceiling of blue ice. Stepping from the tunnel, the brightness was blinding, but once eyes are adjusted the mountain vista always thrills. Glaciers ripple and rough wrap around the base of the mountains, squeezing. In this settled winter, a winter more suited to climbers than skiers, Jonny Baird and I set sail towards *Pinocchio,* another Haston route also on the east face of the Tacul. And many hours later, and once again in the dark, Jonny and I bowed our heads, the torch beam picking out old ski tracks etched by the wind. Ice mounds erupted out of the night, now shockingly familiar on this winter sea. Skinning. The wind burned our faces. Skinning, spindrift scrubbed like pumice. Skinning. Names of the routes successfully climbed kept time with the edges of the skis cutting the crust: *Pinocchio, Scotch on the Rocks, Tentation, M6 Solar, Vol de Nuit, L'Oeil au Beurre Noir, Slave to the Rhythm.*

Later in January, once again in the dark and beneath the stars, Houseman and I left the Fourche bivouac hut bowed like two aged men, wrapped in layers and wearing balaclavas. We headed to the base of Mont Maudit fighting deep snow flutings. And in the snow, ghostly nine-year-old steps took form …

Nine winters since the wind blew spindrift and the clouds swirled, and Cartwright, with long legs stretched out in front of him, sat on the summit of Maudit wearing a goofy grin and giving a double thumbs up. We had both sat on that summit burning with life, glittering with emotion. There had been no ulterior motive behind our climbing; it was climbing for climbing's sake and the experience of being together in a wild and empty place. But five years down the line I stood at his wake, tear-stained and angry. Cartwright's love and passion for climbing was a force to be reckoned with, but near the end even he was a little affected; I suspect he felt the pressure of securing a future. Are any of us free?

Houseman kicked a weaving trail for us to follow. *Overcouloir,* into *Country Couloir,* a slender icefall flickering at a height of 4,000 metres and almost hidden in a deep gully. Later that day, we were joined together by the rope, moving together, living together, trusting together. Downclimbing the Tacul in flat light, I reversed an ice overhang and the edge collapsed. Screaming, tumbling, crashing … *waves hit Gogarth's green cliffs. Cackling guillemots bobbing in a line on white shit-covered ledges, the old whiskered seal with big eyes* … screaming, sliding … the swing of an axe, a tight rope and a firm stance from The Youth (Houseman was still only twenty-eight and so young for his age that I called him The Youth), stopped my fall.

1 Jamie Fisher acts as expedition doctor patching up Jules Cartwright after he fell from the path on the walk to Tapovan base camp. This expedition was to the Shark's Fin on Meru Central, India – my first expedition in 1997, alongside Jamie, Jules and Owain Jones. **Photo**: Owain Jones.

2 North Stack Wall, a dangerous obsession that stayed with me for many years. *In the small hours, the wall calls!* **Photo**: Ray Wood.

3 The crux section of *The Bells! The Bells!* – I fantasised for a long time about standing in the grass atop North Stack having successfully climbed this route. Style is everything. **Photo**: Jude Spancken.

4

4 North Stack again, and the crux of *A Wreath of Deadly Nightshade*. I was actually attempting to climb *The Angle Man*. In my endeavour to climb *The Angle Man*, I racked up five ascents of *Wreath* – a dangerous route to start running laps on. **Photo**: Ray Wood.

5 Matt Helliker and me on the summit of Huantsán Sur after the first ascent of *Death or Glory*. I regret the name of the route but it is quite apt. As climbing becomes more mainstream and seen by many as a sport, I wonder which other sports have such a long list of casualties?

6 Kenton Cool on Kalanka.

7 The Hippy and his poorly finger! **Photo**: Ray Wood.

8

9

8 *Lord of the Flies*. I'm not sure what number ascent this was, but I've now climbed *Lord* ten times; a great route that always brings joy with its movement. **Photo:** Graham Desroy.

9 *Mister Softy* in Wen Zawn being given the Nico Favresse treatment. Completely pumped, I fell miles while leading the third pitch: Nico was having a laugh with Sean Villanueva O'Driscoll and James McHaffie who were climbing *Conan the Librarian* at the time. **Photo:** Ray Wood.

10 With new-found skills – footwork and sport fitness – I thought it time to finally try *Strawberries* at Tremadog. I took the philosophy that every piece of gear had to be placed on lead because this makes such a difference to the difficulty and grade of the climb. **Photo:** Ray Wood.

10

11

12

11 I always wanted to go back to *Mister Softy* after falling from the third pitch. I eventually climbed it with Tim Neill. After a rainstorm the third pitch was a waterfall, but I was adamant we were going to climb the whole route, and we did. **Photo**: Tim Neill.

12 *All the Pretty Horses*, a great Cormac McCarthy book and a great climb. I'm most happy when I become fully embroiled in places: the situation, the wildlife, the climbing, the ambience, the partners. **Photo**: Ray Wood.

13

13 Tim Neill was drawn into my Equestrian Wall relationship. This is the E5, *Captain Mark Phillips*. I had to lower in more gear from the top so he could finish it. Afterwards I counted the runners; he had placed over forty.

14 Andy Houseman on the summit slopes of Chang Himal. One of the best trips ever with a great friend.
15 Andy Houseman at our highest bivvy (6,550 metres) on Chang Himal. We sat wondering if it would go; I was certain we had made a route-finding error.
16 The north face of Chang Himal. **Photo**: Andy Houseman.
17 I always wanted to climb what for me was one the most striking lines at Gogarth: *Rubble*. Having James McHaffie on my rack was an astute move. It's one of the few summer rock climbs on which I felt wearing a helmet would have been sensible. **Photo**: Ray Wood.

I dropped my forehead into the snow and saw a single cormorant standing with wings wide. So many climbs, so much sacrifice, so many close calls.

The sun set once again on yet another climb as The Youth and I burrowed into the side of the Nant Blanc face of the Aiguille Verte. Headlight beams illuminated the road between Chamonix and Argentière and I could see that road, its signs, the tennis courts, the river, the bars, the ski shops ... familiar. The blood pumped inside my arteries, my head bursting. Across the valley the piste bashers were flashing yellow, smoothing the snow for skiers who appeared to be able to find peace without discomfort. I couldn't. Not yet. I climbed here with Cartwright on a five-day hit from Britain. Five new pitches joining the ridge of the *Brown-Patey*, but still only halfway up the face, our crampons blunt from two days' mixed climbing, kicking and kicking and kicking. Kicking, Cartwright and I exited the iron-hard runnel of the *Marsigny-Mohr*.

'I hate fucking ice climbing!' Cartwright screamed on the abseil descent. I remember him leaving cams as backup, and that was when he said it, that was when he said the words that haunt me.

'When you do as much of this shit as I do, Nick, it's a matter of percentages. You need to cut down the chance of being killed.'

A second night sleeping on snow. Street lights in Argentière quivered and scintillated as I lay shivering. The helicopter beam swept the north face of the Dru searching for the Slovenian with a fractured skull.

I lost myself in the swirling facets and intricacies of the past months. I was changing. I had changed. All of the approaches in the early hours, sleeping in damp clothes, hunger, humility, success, togetherness, these things were honest, they had integrity, they formed me.

Standing on that summit alongside The Youth – that summit with so much history – I knew the descent would be numb fingers and feet, the hot aches and the fear, and it would lead me back to warm rock, swaying grass, bleating sheep, birdsong and appreciation. My third winter in the Alps was at an end; it was time to return to Llanberis.

13

bittersweet desire

May 2007
Llanberis, Wales

The now-familiar carriageway from Chamonix to Calais was driven in my ageing Berlingo. The ferry took me to Dover and the roads led, via a detour to visit Mum and Dad on the canals, to Llanberis.

Dad's collapse two summers ago had shocked him into sobriety, and it had shocked Mum into hard love; she now refused to buy him whisky. And for the first time in a long time, when I had visited, I had found myself chatting with the old man and enjoying the experience. He was becoming something like the intelligent conversationalist I knew he could be and had once been, and his selfishness was diminishing.

I shouted in Mum's direction – her hearing was terrible but she refused to even entertain the idea of a hearing aid. 'Hearing aids are for old folk.' She had also nearly completely lost her vision in one eye because of a cataract.

Dad sat in his chair drinking tea and smoking a roll-up.

'She's deaf as a doorpost – I can have a better conversation with the parrot now,' he said, laughing.

'What did you say?' Mum piped up.

'You see what I mean?'

Arriving in Llanberis the hills and the sea relaxed me. I had five months before I would leave for India and I intended to fill these months with as much adventure rock climbing as I could.

Waking inside my van, parked outside Ynys Ettws, the morning light filtered through the blue-striped Peruvian blanket I used for a curtain. I could feel the warmth of the sun as I lay listening to the sheep. The water in the stream gurgled and small birds tapped with long toes along the van roof.

Occasionally when lying there, I would worry about money, or the lack of it. I had left the prison service with some savings – about £12,000 – and my house was fully paid off and rented. But if car insurance came along, or I was staying a winter in Chamonix, renting a room and paying for a lift pass, I was drawing on savings. The rent of my house paid for food, and my writing was growing in popularity, which gave me a small income, and the pay from an occasional lecture was welcome, but it was still a worry and I would lie in the back of my van at times wondering how much longer I could go on before I had to look for some form of employment. DMM, the climbing hardware company who sponsored me, occasionally gave me work – which was welcomed. In fact, everyone at DMM based in Llanberis were now good friends and I could walk into their offices whenever I chose, which gave me a bolthole for rainy days. In Britain, mountaineers are very fortunate; there are many expedition grants to apply for and with some added money from savings, this was generally how I funded my big trips.

September 2007
Kalanka, India

Bursting from a billowing dust cloud, the lorry has a battered, pugilistic face. Its split windscreen, a pair of dark, evil eyes and the white-painted grill wears a fixed sneer. Thundering by our taxi with inches to spare, the horn screams, 'Get out of my way.' I slide along the sweaty plastic seat to the side furthest away from this menacing spirit of the road. The humidity is stifling, the noise deafening. Cars, bumper to bumper, screaming horns, revving engines, the jostle of so many people. Bumper to bumper. Returning from the solitude of the mountains, the interior of India is too much. And my mind has not stopped ruminating since Kenton Cool and I left Base Camp.

We should have tried harder.

We saw, we climbed. Then we turned and ran. I felt a fraud. The year previous had brought new routes in Peru, the Himalaya and the Alps. I had tasted arrogant brilliance, or so my ego thought, and now failure burned. I remembered a line from a conversation I'd had with Sam Chinnery at a party in Llanberis before travelling to India:

'In the mountains, if you successfully climb everything you attempt, the climbs are obviously too easy.'

Well, returning to India for the third time had brought failure for the third time. The failure hurt, but not as much as the end of a relationship. Sometimes I feel death is almost easier to cope with. The loss of a relationship is different, especially in a small community, because you see each other, hear snippets, catch a brief glance here and there. Friends talk, not realising your pain. You leave parties, scared that the person you least want to see will turn up, or you don't even go in the first place. Failing on a mountain hurts, but it is nothing like the end of a relationship.

'Set off in the night, climb through the next day and we'll be on the shoulder. We'll have a big bivvy site, sun, warmth and recovery before climbing the pillar to the summit. Three days up, two down. We'll take four days' food.'

Kenton and I stood beneath Kalanka's massive north face trying to decide on tactics. Snow shrouds swept around the face. Two rock bands cut the face horizontally. Ice glistened. Nobody had attempted the left side of the face. Hardly anyone had attempted the north face at all. And nobody had walked to its foot with just two ropes, their rucksacks packed, and begun to climb.

Plugging through the night, the nervous anticipation was left behind when we crossed the bergschrund. This was my first big climb with Kenton and his brooding beforehand had affected me. I wasn't sure how to deal with brooding and concern. I now only climb with a group of very experienced friends who are mainly mountain guides. I nearly always bow to their training, but the climbing partners I most relate to are those who realise I am not a client. Tim Neill, Matt Helliker, Bracey, Jonny Baird and Neil Brodie – they are all mountain guides and all treat me as an equal. Kenton falls into this category, but I did get a feeling his 'new' path, one of Everest expert, someone who had made guiding the highest mountain in the world a career, had taken away his edge. Climbing Everest is obviously very risky, but using oxygen actually reduces the height by the equivalent of 2,000 metres and there is a whole support infrastructure at hand. Climbing a large technical face in the greater ranges in alpine style is something very different indeed.

Moving together, with the occasional ice screw placed between us, was the way this climb would end in success. However, as dawn arrived the first steep rock band had to be pitched. Near-vertical snow-ice that would not take protection or even secure pick placements gave sickening hot aches and deep concern, but once through we carried on moving together. The afternoon brought cloud and the summit hid behind a white mist. The snowfall began soon after. Earlier than expected, and a long way from the top of the shoulder, we cut a small ledge into hard ice to sit out the night.

'You should be climbing this with someone else.'

I was surprised at Kenton's comment. He had climbed so many hard routes in the past and suffered. The bivvy was uncomfortable and the constant spindrift was tiresome but it could have been worse, it could have been much worse. I wasn't going to allow Kenton's negative attitude to affect me. I knew deep down he would not give up. He had climbed Everest five times, although the style in which he had summited didn't impress me. Annapurna III and the climbs he had done in Alaska were much more impressive, but on a climb and a face like this, it takes both of you to be driven and supportive. I prefer to try and suffer in silence, and for my partners to lie rather than be honest. Honesty is for the valley.

The second day passed in a fight for the ridge.

'We'll be there tonight, sitting on a big flat ledge out of the spindrift … no problem,' I said optimistically.

'You're fucking mad if you really think that … it's miles.'

I knew my optimism was distorted, but optimism on a big face is sometimes all you have and Kenton's angry negativity annoyed me.

We moved together all day but the ridge didn't appear to get any closer. Scratching and inching, we grew tired and deflated by the lack of progress. The afternoon snow started and we continued to climb until the hunt for a bivvy began. I climbed a steep corner and looked down on to a rock covered with a triangle of snow.

'If we dig that out, it may be flat enough.'

Slings tightly bound Kenton while my harness cut me in two. Once again, spindrift poured. We attempted to drape the tent over the two of us but it wasn't big enough.

'This is shit. I'm not doing another of these trips,' Kenton barked.

It was miserable and frustrating, so we decided to forgo the direct line toward the summit spur and head left to the ridge in the sun and what we hoped would be a good bivvy site. But the nagging voice of failure whispered.

Once on the shoulder you'll never get across to the spur, it will be game over …

We had seen the corniced ridge running along the top of the shoulder from the acclimatisation slopes opposite. It reminded me of unclimbable things I had come across in Peru. But what could we do, we needed a good night, didn't we? I knew a good night with a good bivvy would not go amiss, but I was certain we were doomed heading to the shoulder. But then I was also certain we were doomed if we didn't, because no way would Kenton continue without a good night.

Plunging arms to the shoulder and manteling on buried axes, the cold singed our lungs as chests heaved. We had reached the snow arête leading to the left-hand side of the shoulder. Over to our left, Kalanka's neighbour, Saf Minal, appeared to have its own perfect weather pattern and easy access along its summit ridge. I imagined John Varco and Sue Nott attempting Kalanka's central buttress to our right and I also imagined John looking – like we were now – with longing, at Saf Minal. It was obvious why Varco had returned in the company of Ian Parnell to successfully climb this striking peak.

Kenton and I had chosen Kalanka and I didn't regret it. I needed a climb that would challenge me completely. I just didn't know if I wanted to face the disappointment of failure once again. Stopping early, we dug a large cave and for the first time in three days we could sit without the fear of falling. Some ten kilometres away the tiny specs of our tents could be seen at Base Camp. I didn't long to be there just yet. I was content, wrapped in damp down and eating a mere fraction of the food my body required, but the thought of what tomorrow would bring used more calories. Tomorrow would decide the outcome of the climb. Would we make it across the shoulder to the summit buttress or would we be abseiling? What else in life was this simple? I realised I had not chosen this mountain, it had chosen me. Climbing had chosen me much the same as climbing had chosen my friends.

I slept fully clothed in the snow cave without a harness. Stars filled the night sky. Spindrift poured over the roof of our ledge, missing us. The wind rocked our perch, reminding me of sleeping in my van through the summer in North Wales. Tomorrow would be day four on Kalanka, our imagined summit day. Kenton's altimeter put us at a height of 6,300 metres. The estimated 800 metres to where we now were had actually been 1,300. Seven hundred metres to the summit. We surmised that if it were possible to reach the bottom of the summit pillar, it would then take another two days to climb to the summit and a further two days to abseil the line. We reduced our food intake.

'I don't know how to climb this,' I said to Kenton.

Standing in knee-deep snow on the crest of the shoulder I was confronted with a snow-covered rock tower. I expected the ground beneath my feet to collapse. The ridge was overhanging on the left. Brown rubble welded together with grey ice fell straight to the glacier. There was no walkway, no ramp or secret hidden path; I felt cheated. Ahead, I could see the twin summits of Nanda Devi beyond Kalanka's south ridge, behind were Kenton and Saf Minal. Kenton was sitting in a hole with the rope running around his body. Gravity was the belay.

I don't know how to climb this.

'How about dropping down on the right?' Kenton shouted.

The 'right' was nearly vertical snow flutings, unpredictable and uninviting, but if we were to get anywhere I would have to give it a go. About an hour later I had passed beneath the rock tower and climbed a deep fluting to hang beneath the crest of the ridge and belay. It had been nothing but unprotected roulette, but seeing what was to come, I realised it had only been an hors d'oeuvre. Kenton's lead!

'That was sketchy,' Kenton said while sorting gear, having seconded the pitch.

I leant out from the fluting.

'If you think that was bad, take a look right.'

He leant out and stared at what was to come.

'I'm not going out there, it'll be suicide.'

I was disappointed and relieved; Kenton had made the decision I was too proud to voice. That was that then.

After another night on the face and another night at the base, we escaped the hill and made it back to Base Camp. A few days later, with a forecast threatening a big storm, we left.

The taxi weaved among cyclists and tractors pulling trailers stacked with sugar cane. Another lorry burst from the cloud of dust that hangs permanently over Indian thoroughfares. I gulped hot, humid air and fought off travel sickness, my mind ever racing. Replaying our climb. My first thought when I had seen the ridge ahead with its twisted snow mushrooms had been to carry on, but was this irresponsible and pointless given our dwindling food supply? Had it been someone other than Kenton with his wealth of experience, would I have pushed to continue? Should I have been more forceful? Or would it merely have delayed the same outcome? Was Kenton waiting for my insistence, needing that impetus to continue?

Questions, too many questions. But that was the problem, and the problem was I felt like a fraud, and in the end, I always came to the same conclusion. We should have tried harder.

14
strange eden

January 2008
Chamonix, France

A cold wind funnelling through the jagged V-notch in the summit ridge of the Droites stripped the warmth from my face. This was the first time I had stood in the Brèche des Droites, but looking around I recognised a ledge above me. Fixed, staring at the ledge for a minute – although it felt a lot longer – I eventually dragged my eyes away and turned once again to face into the bright sun. The dark and brooding Grandes Jorasses north face, the Géant icefall, tumbling and erratic, and the Vallée Blanche were all visible. I closed my eyes … immediately I returned to that winter evening, nine years before.

I remembered leaving the warmth of the climbing wall and the yellow sulphurous glow while driving through Leicester's cold city centre. I remembered passing abandoned, graffiti-daubed hosiery factories, kebab houses with papers blowing in the gutter, and the high walls of the prison. I remembered the dark deserted park …

> Driving out of the city, leaves illuminated by the van's headlights blew across the country lane. Trees stooped either side of the road, twisted and skeletal. Sleet hit the windscreen. A news report between songs on the car radio: *'British climbers are trapped on a mountain in the French Alps.'* I arrived home, switched on the TV, closed the curtains and waited …

Taking in, pulling the ropes through the belay device, my swollen wrist hurt. Ross Hewitt was still on the dark side of the mountain beneath my position, plugging away on the last few metres of the *Ginat*, the classic ice climb of the 1,000-metre north face. I had met Ross several years before while walking in to Creag Meagaidh in Scotland. I liked him, he was a Scot with an unusual accent, or at least I took it as an unusual, posh accent. I was more used to hearing Glaswegian or Highland which sounded more abrasive than east coast. Or maybe Ross was just posh? Whatever, I liked Ross, mainly because at least in his climbing he appeared to lack ego.

> I stared at the TV, watching the two climbers stranded on the ledge that was now above me. One wore a yellow jacket, the same make, style and colour as the one I had removed after I had walked into my house that evening, nine years earlier. Four days before I had spoken over the phone with Jamie Fisher, who had been with me on my first and second expeditions to the Himalaya. He was heading to the Alps with his flatmate Jamie Andrews to meet Jules. Jamie Fisher, Jules and I all had the same distinctive jackets that had been given to us for our Shark's Fin expedition in 1997. Watching the news, recognising the jacket, I knew it was either Jamie or Jules pinned by atrocious weather on the summit ridge of the Droites. The rest of that Sunday evening was spent sitting with the rain hitting the window and the dark and the memories …

Ross was nearly to me now. The spell would be broken with his arrival. Rock walls hemmed him into his snowy runnel. The Matterhorn and Monte Rosa were behind, standing head and shoulders above a million other mountains. The Argentière Glacier flowed, a rucked sheet butting its head against the rock barrier of the Pré de Bar. I had skied along that rucked sheet so many times now.

We had climbed 1,000 metres of ice, rock and history, and as I stood belaying, I could hear the BBC reporter say my friend's name, Jamie Fisher, and the other Jamie, Jamie Andrews. Taking in more rope I could see Jamie Fisher's cheeky smile and his shock of unruly red hair.

This would be my final climb in the Alps that winter because of my wrist. I was disappointed it was all coming to an end but thrilled to have at last climbed the Droites, not once, but twice in a matter of weeks. It had been long overdue. I had a connection with this mountain, and as I pulled the ropes, my mind replayed the climb.

Thunk. The pick penetrated ice, shining in the light of my head torch. Reverberations travelled through the shaft of the axe and into my arm. The deep, nagging ache from my wrist took the baton and sprinted to my brain. I had broken my left wrist eight days before; I fell while bouldering with ice axes at Le Fayet and only a metre from the ground. Four days after the fall, after being wrapped with bags of frozen peas and taking a whole load of anti-inflammatory tablets, some of the swelling had reduced and I had regained partial movement. I convinced myself it wasn't broken. The fifth day after the fall, I skied the Vallée Blanche, and on the sixth, I skinned beneath the Droites to check out the conditions on the north face. Ross and I walked in to the Argentière Hut on day seven and at 1.30 a.m. on day eight, we broke trail to the base of the climb.

I had been nervous. Would the pain be too much? I didn't want to let Ross down and I desperately needed to climb, but more than that I needed the mountains. The thought of catching a ferry and returning to Britain was more painful than actually climbing with the injury. I had been nervous about what memories the climb would stir up. I heard Cartwright's voice telling me of the relief and catharsis he received from climbing the *Ginat* some years after Jamie's death … and now he was also dead.

Thunk. Again I threw the axe toward the ice. The teeth penetrated just enough to stabilise me before I forcefully swung the right axe and planted the pick deep. I couldn't remove the left axe as I normally would by holding the handle and twisting, the leverage from the full length of the shaft caused too much pain. So, I slid my left hand halfway up the shaft and twisted. Shooting pains ripped up my arm; grimacing, shutting the pain away, I lifted the axe, hooking the pick into the ice at shoulder height, before I grabbed the handle and threw it again and again and again.

We had soloed from the bergschrund, but at the beginning of the Messner variation – a steep icy gully leading to the large central ice field – Ross had asked to tie on so we could move together. I grumbled, having soloed to the top of the ice field five weeks before when Houseman and I had climbed the line to the right.

The *Colton-Brooks* had been my first successful climb on the Droites. Houseman and I had climbed it without any problems in nine hours. It had felt great to be climbing with The Youth again after our previous winter together. We were beginning to know each other well, which meant understanding and respect, and at times forgiveness. Spending hours, days, weeks and sometimes months together with a climbing partner is similar to being in a relationship; I didn't want to spend time with people out of convenience – being in the hills with someone is as important to me as the climbing itself.

After the years of wondering, skiing beneath the dry, grey, out-of-condition face and imagining the hell the two Jamies had been through, the *Colton-Brooks* was almost too good to be true. I had stood alongside Houseman on the summit ridge, basking in the sun, looking across at the brèche wondering, *why them? Why not me?*

At the time of the tragedy Jules had been in the Chamonix valley. I had asked him afterward if Jamie Fisher had had a sleeping bag with him on the Droites. I was trying to bring some sense to what happened and knew Jamie was an advocate of moving fast and light. As it turned out he did have a sleeping bag and bivvy kit. People, including myself, are always trying to find explanations and somewhere to place the blame for accidents in the mountains, especially people in the press looking for a story or some way to hype it up a bit. But sometimes there is no blame, no underlying story, no hyped newsprint. The mountains may have been tamed with time but on occasion they still present a worthy challenge.

Ross had been climbing cautiously and admitted to feeling exposed without leashes. Soloing without leashes meant if he was hit by a rock, or a large lump of ice, he would fall and be killed. He said he would move quicker if we climbed simultaneously, tied together and placing protection. This was the first time we had climbed together but I had skied with him and watched him throw himself down steep slopes, slopes so steep as to have a climbing grade. It came as a surprise to find that someone so bold on skis was thinking of what might go wrong on a relatively easy climb. My mind didn't work like that, not yet anyway.

Belaying, stood in the brèche, I started thinking that moving together attached to the rope did make sense. If I came across grey, steely hard ice, I wasn't sure I would be able to swing the axe with enough force to make the pick penetrate, but time was our main concern. We carried no sleeping bags or bivvy gear and the thought of the two Jamies' fate had been with me every step. Three years had passed since I had spent that very cold night on the Droites by myself and I wasn't eager to repeat that experience.

Ross moved a lot quicker once tied to the rope. I followed, while imagining him sixty metres ahead pushing himself, and thinking, *come on you bastard, complain about the speed now.* We took turns in front. The ice was thin but chewy and didn't need a forceful swing – I was glad about that. Gently placing the left axe for support and pulling with the right arm had us weaving around the constrictions following thicker streaks. On one occasion, in the lead, I leant back to look at a bulge of ice blocking the way. I knew I would have to swing the axe with force to enable me to pull over. Nervous of the pain, I swung the axe from behind my head. The shockwave hit, turning my stomach – but looking over my shoulder, the red glow of the sun creeping over the horizon helped. Being in this wild, empty place always helped. I was almost free, almost content.

Ross climbed into the brèche alongside me and we shook hands. Five weeks before when Houseman and I had easily climbed the *Colton-Brooks* the winter had only just begun, and my head had been spinning with the possibilities. Now I was savouring the last of my time in the mountains for the season. Melting ice glistened all around me like mirrors and in these mirrors I imagined the face they reflected was one of contentment. Almost. Jagged snow icicles, warmed by the sun, wept. Braced, buffeted by the wind, I took it all in knowing this felt right, but still I felt sad. The mountains around me were friends I would be leaving behind for an indefinite period and already I missed them.

Ross sorted out the ropes and rigged the abseil ready for our descent. I threaded the rope through my abseil device and clipped it to my harness. Stamping my feet clear of snow, zipping zippers, changing gloves – I did anything to delay leaving, but eventually I could delay no more. Leaning back from the ropes I turned to look at the ledge above and quietly whispered my goodbye.

February 2008
Luton, England

Driving back to Britain, I stopped at my sister's house so I could visit Luton A & E to have my wrist X-rayed. I walked into the sterile hospital and approached the reception. Trollies clattered and rattled, people sat in chairs looking morose and bored. The white, almost sci-fi, decor felt otherworldly having just come from the mountains; it felt grey.

'Hi, I've broken my wrist.'

The two women behind the reception looked at each other before finally tilting their heads, looking over their glasses.

'You *think* you have broken your wrist.'

'Yes, I suppose, but I'm pretty sure it's broken.'

'How did you do it?'

I explained how I had fallen and hit the ground and when I had done it.

'It's been two weeks since you injured your wrist? What have you been doing until now?'

'I climbed the *Ginat* route on the north face of the Droites.'

After explaining what the *Ginat* and the Droites were, I watched as one receptionist looked at the other, rolled her eyes and on a piece of paper I saw she wrote 'timewaster'. I was pointed to a chair and the wait began. I didn't mind the wait, I was receiving free health care and communicating in a language I could understand; I didn't have any complaints at all.

After a few hours my wrist had been X-rayed and I had returned to the chair expecting more of a wait, but almost immediately a doctor came out from behind a curtain holding my X-ray in the air.

'You did this,' he lifted the X-ray even higher and pointed ' … two weeks ago, and you've been alpine climbing?'

'Yes, doc.'

'Follow me.'

We went into an office and he slid the X-ray on to a light box on the wall.

'Can you see that?'

He pointed at the X-ray of my wrist. I trained in anatomy and physiology, and later extended my studies to pass a diploma in the treatment of sports injury, and having had many injuries, I said yes, I could see *that.*

'You have broken the distal head of the radius; I can't believe what you have been doing and the length of time it's taken for you to seek treatment. Usually, people are in so much pain they come to hospital immediately.'

I left the hospital with my wrist in plaster. Guess I wasn't a timewaster after all.

15
how soon is now?

February 2008
Llanberis, Wales

The edge had returned to the Welsh hills in February. There was no snow, only frost thistling the yellowy slabs of rhyolite. Each morning the grass was white and the black slate wore frozen cling film. I stayed on my own in Tim and Lou Neill's house next to the chapel in the centre of Nant Peris. The sun filled the sky, melted the frost and cast shadowy crosses on the white walls inside the house. After breaking my ankle on *Omega,* when my first winter season in Chamonix was cut short, I returned to Britain feeling sullen having been ripped from the mountains. On that occasion I stayed with my friend Janet in her house in Quorn, Leicestershire. I counted the hours and days and weeks before I could remove the plaster and return to Europe. I sat inside Janet's terrace house in stasis, inert, stuck – the waves washed over me and I almost drowned. Time, that most valuable commodity, was spilling. This time my winter had been cut even shorter, but returning to Llanberis felt like coming home. The town had taken the place of my home in Burton Overy; it was somewhere I was starting to become very attached to. Friends that were still in town and not in Scotland or the Alps welcomed me and I didn't begrudge being back or even the injury.

Every day I ran with the frozen bog beneath my feet. Sometimes my foot would break the crust leaving a dark footprint with a white outline. The hills directly accessed from the house were my favourite: Elidir Fawr, Foel-goch, Y Garn – sheep-shorn mounds, all frozen and crisp. I ran across the worn track at the top of the Devil's Kitchen. Open space. A buzzard cried. The open Glyderau plateau with spikes of rock, like hewn standing stones. On the lee of these jagged monoliths was soft moss, but the rock was as rough as a terrier's coat on the windward side.

One day I ran and scrambled Tryfan's North Ridge. Where it was possible I jogged, and where it was not, I scrambled. Passing people, they looked aghast when they saw my arm in plaster. I waved and said hello and continued. I climbed direct, the cold friction felt clingy and safe. I remembered climbing the same ground, the same rock and the same features in April seventeen years before when I trained to be a PE instructor. I jogged a wide ledge where I could still picture Mark Bentley, my roomy and friend from Bolton, as he crawled on all fours with the wind snickering at him like a magpie, and afterwards I remember him brushing away the sleet that had left dark damp patches on his knees. The air around me now was frigid and empty; it caught images and dreams and carried them over the heather.

Crossing Bwlch Tryfan, I looked once again to my past. I saw a group of trainee PE instructors trying to remember how a compass worked. My toes crunched on the surface of rock covered with moss and grains. I smiled thinking that some things hadn't changed. On and on and on – panting, chest heaving, deep, desperate breaths, the streak of dried sweat. Scrambling Bristly Ridge, swinging legs and pulling. Empty air with blank, open space. My broken wrist ached, but not enough to stop me. Then, once again, I was out of the dark and on to the glaring Glyderau tops. The rocks and the hills looked like an over-sharpened photograph, and in the shimmering distance the sea was a dark green. Jet aircraft screamed across the blue leaving white scars for the buzzard to thread. But eventually the scars faded and the buzzard disappeared.

I ran from the summit of Glyder Fach, dodging and balancing, my feet catching edges, stubbing toes, *nnnrrrrgh* ... The pain, like a broken heart, was only temporary, although the pain from a broken heart would hurt more.

I stood on the edge of Cwm Cneifion. Skidding feet turned sideways. Rocks bounced and whirred and hummocks of grass broke off, revealing the red earth beneath. I stopped and stared at Clogwyn Du, the little black crag at the top of the Glyderau. The raven coughed. I could see ghosts of winters past and the climbs that were a part of my history, *Travesty* and *Cracking Up*.

Running the edge of Llyn Idwal, around the well-worn path, the water sucked and filtered through rocks rubbed smooth. I watched Sam Sperry, my ex-girlfriend from Leicestershire, with Blue, the brindle Staffordshire bull terrier, pulling on the end of his fully stretched lead. I saw Sam's long blonde hair blowing wild in the breeze and her torn jeans with flickering frays and I watched her 'take me or leave me' twenty-eight-year-old attitude catch in the wind and carry across the ancient water.

I jogged on to the Ogwen Cottage car park and saw a group, including myself, huddled tightly together on the tarmac, cooking in the cold having navigated the Carneddau all the way from Drum to Pen yr Ole Wen on our summer Mountain Leader award. I ran the roadside by Llyn Ogwen, the water unruffled. Gulls skimmed the water's clear surface, looking down at a version of themselves. Cars sped past. The people inside with heavy right feet and heavy heads, rushing to somewhere from somewhere, going nowhere or anywhere. I could smell fumes and warm, worn oily engines. A silver wheel trim lay in the gutter, a plastic starfish, washed up and winking.

Whatever happened to Alison Parker?

Alison Parker and I went out for a while when we were both twenty. She had a small upturned nose, short to medium-length blonde hair, white teeth, taut suntanned skin and an amazing smile, which she wore most of the time. She laughed and she made me laugh, and I think for the very short time we were together I loved her very nearly as much as I have loved anyone. She introduced me to Neil Young and Crosby, Stills and Nash and Leonard Cohen and The Smiths.

The night before this run I had watched Morrissey on iPlayer – he looked similar to how Tom Briggs looked the time we first met and climbed together in Australia. And later in the evening, I watched a YouTube clip of The Smiths on *Top of the Pops* from 1984. 'What Difference Does it Make?' – the song I ribbed Alison Parker about when we first met, standing next to the cooker in the kitchen. I refused to admit I liked it.

The night before, watching The Smiths from so long ago plunged me into renaissance, swinging my plastered arm and wishing I had a bunch of flowers.

Where the hell did it all go?

It had been twenty-three years since Alison Parker had bullied and cajoled until at last I admitted to enjoying the music of The Smiths, and then we moved close and kissed for the first time while leaning against the cooker.

Morrissey gently shuffled around the stage with his shirt buttons tested to the limit by a paunch. Then, with a bit of a shuffle and the occasional arm swing, he attempted to be dangerous. But he wasn't, he was just old and a little overweight. His voice and presence were still electrifying even after all of this time, but *how* time stops for no one. Not you, not me. Not Morrissey nor Alison Parker nor Tom Briggs nor Mark Bentley nor Sam Sperry. It stops for none of us.

The music of The Smiths takes me back, back to an attitude of 'What Difference Does it Make?' and 'Panic'. And while I always left the club on my own, I never did think: *what difference does it make?* Or at least, not until now, not until I could run no further and wring every bit out of this short life. The Smiths remind me so much of Alison Parker with her vitality and energy and intelligence; she was carefree and dangerous and so much fun. I wonder where Alison Parker is now and if she has children and if so how many? Does she still have that spark or has life beaten her to grey?

I ran the last few metres until I stood at the side of my Berlingo, parked at the side of the road near Little Tryfan.

Watching Morrissey the night before made me think that for just the short time you are there – in your prime, a handsome devil with hollow cheeks and bendy limbs and strong muscle – just for a short time, you may not care about the world, or at least the world outside your world, and you think the light will never go out.

But while there is a light, one day it *will* go out.

16
you only live twice

May 2008
Llanberis, Wales

Creaking, tearing, ripping, sawing ... the bread knife made it at last through the plaster and my wrist was free. I was becoming quite the expert at removing plaster casts with a bread knife. A few weeks later, still in the grip of dry winter warmth, I met two friends who were heading to Llandudno to climb at the Great Orme.

Turning off the A55, we travelled through the small coastal town of Deganwy near Conwy. The marina was full of white yachts and speedboats, and the shopfronts had an upmarket air about them. Turning a corner in the old Volvo 940 saloon, the three of us were suddenly faced with a police roadblock. Sitting in the front, my usually laughing and joking and boisterous friends became subdued, almost wake-like. I was in the back, foam poking from threadbare upholstery, and a strong smell of mould, but stronger still was the smell of fear. My friend who was driving, who I will call Jim, is short in stature and bouncy and vocal. Although it sounds like a cliché, he nearly always has a big smile, and the only time he isn't smiling is when his mouth is moving because he's savaging and taking the piss out of something, or someone. Sometimes he has a long, unkempt, 1960s Beatle-esque bouffant, and sometimes he is as coiffured as David Beckham. Originally he was from somewhere near the Wirral and he can certainly do a good Liverpudlian accent when pressed. His nickname relates to his hairy feet, but any more will give the game away. I had climbed rock many times with Jim and no matter how much he had abused himself with 'substance', he could always climb much better than me.

The passenger seat was filled with the large frame of Robert. Robert is more serious than Jim. Sometimes he appears to carry the weight of the world, and a lot of the time he is stoned. He works at being professional and fixing injured people, so he is very much a man of two lives and should one life collide into the other, it might have serious repercussions. His dark curls on this occasion were bubbling, but on seeing the roadblock they stood straight, almost touching the yellow smoke-stained plastic peeling from the Volvo's ceiling.

Slowing in a line of traffic, the Volvo chugged and belched. Jim had bought the car from a mutual friend called Lee and paid a tenner, and to be honest, Lee saw him coming.

Crawling forward the tension in the car was as thick as the smoke coming from its exhaust. Putting each hand on the top of the fading black plastic of the front seats, I leant forward to hear the whispered conversation.

Robert to Jim: 'What's the documentation like on the car?'

Jim to Robert: 'No MOT, no insurance.'

The pair straightened and looked ahead. The car coughed and staggered forward a few more inches.

Jim leant over to Robert. 'Please tell me you haven't got any weed on you?'

Robert leant closer. 'Big bag of superskunk ... I've pushed it under the seat.'

Jim to Robert: 'That's OK, that's OK ... they won't find it ... this isn't about that, they're not looking for drugs ... it's OK.'

In unison, all three of us looked forward. A police van had pulled up and a dog jumped from the back wearing a yellow coat, and on the dog's coat in big black lettering was a word, and unless the dog's name was SNIFFER, I had the feeling we were fucked.

'Hi boys, now where are you all going today?'

Robert gave the policewoman his most alluring smile combined with big dark eyes. He spoke in his deepest and most eloquent tones.

'We're going to the Great Orme, rock climbing.'

'Oh you rock climbers, my hubby is one, you're all mad!' she laughed, but the laugh didn't ease the tension.

Jim chose this moment to give his best John Bishop impression – the comedian from Liverpool – which actually appeared to hit home and cause another laugh.

I sat in the back wondering how my life had gone from being a PE instructor in the prison service, to almost certainly being arrested for drug possession in an uninsured car with no MOT. But then I thought, *hang on a minute; I'm not in possession and the car isn't mine, so no problem – home free.* I eased back in the seat and the mould suddenly smelled of roses.

The dog bounded and barked while wagging his tail and jumping around the inside of a car that had been pulled up in front of us.

'Well,' the policewoman said, 'you do know you're in trouble, don't you?'

Jim didn't appear to be John Bishop any longer, and Robert watched his hard-earned medical qualification burn like a big fat bifter. I sat smug and righteous.

Fuck em, fuck em both, silly sods, brought it on themselves!

The policewoman stuck her head in the car and looked directly at me and said, 'Who's a naughty boy then?'

And the righteousness dropped right out of my arse.

'You aren't wearing your seatbelt!'

I couldn't believe it. There was a big bag of superskunk under the passenger seat of a car that had no MOT or insurance, and I was the one getting the dressing down! Just for a second I thought of grassing to prove I was the good guy, but I didn't think it would be appreciated. So I grinned sheepishly and apologised profusely.

'Ha ha, you climbers! Go on, on your way – but wear your seatbelt in the future.'

And with that Jim hit the pedal and the Volvo lurched free to gas the local community for another uninsured day.

The Welsh sunshine continued and after a month of wrist strengthening and climbing I teamed up this time with Nic Sellers. Nic's psyche took us climbing for eight sun-baked days; we climbed on mountain crags and glittering sea cliffs and my arms were kicked into shape for the fast-approaching British Mountaineering Council International Meet, but my head was kicked into shape even more so.

The BMC International Meet has become one of my favourite times of every other year (it is a biennial event). The meet is held in May and more often than not, it takes place in North Wales. Being an exponent of the cold stuff, May is not the best time for my rock climbing. The winter cobwebs are still, usually, clinging.

This was the second BMC meet I had attended, and a few weeks before, I gave Becky McGovern – organiser and friend – strict instructions not to sign me up with a Slovenian superstar who wanted gnarl (as she had on the first meet). 'I'm unfit, it's only just summer, a nice E3 or E4 leader will be great. Under no circumstances do I want a Slovenian wad again!'

So in the Plas y Brenin bar, the evening before the start of the meet, the throng milled. The weather was set fair, and I was reasonably content to spend the week ticking classics with my international E3 leader.

Becky approached. She wore an alluring smile and in that Lancashire twang, she warbled, 'Don't worry, Nick, I've found you a nice Belgian to play with.' I couldn't believe my luck, a Belgian, how cool was that? Belgium, land of chocolate and beer. Flat Belgium, rockless Belgium. I was happy.

I followed Becky until she stood before a small and scruffy, unshaven, non-threatening individual. He wore a massive smile. 'Nick, meet Nico Favresse, your climbing partner.'

Nico Favresse, the name sounded vaguely familiar but I couldn't for the life of me remember how I recognised it. We shook hands and chatted. I asked Nico what routes he wanted to climb, and crucially I asked him what grades he wanted to climb.

'Grades do not matterrr, just the line eez important,' he said in that really annoying Euro accent – kind of like Poirot – the sort of accent that makes British women turn to jelly and British men hate men from across the Channel. Brilliant; game on.

I was still staying at Tim and Lou's and later that evening, when I returned from Plas y Brenin, I flicked through the pages of a magazine. The magazine was *UP* and it listed most of the new routes or significant repeats of climbs in Europe throughout the previous year. Something was niggling. *Nico Favresse, Nico Favresse.* I knew I had seen his name among the pages of this magazine. I turned another glossy page and there he was, a picture of my little inoffensive Belgian strapped to some desperate-looking climb. The picture description read: 'Nico Favresse makes the first free ascent of … ' I turned the page, feeling a little nauseous, ' … *Inshallah*, 8c+.'

Oh shit. *That* Nico Favresse?

I turned the computer on and tapped the name Nico Favresse into Google.

'The first Belgian to climb 9a, the second ascent of *Greenspit*, an 8b+ roof crack led on gear, new big wall climbs in Pakistan,' and on and on and on … I dived for the cupboard and opened a bottle of wine. I wept. Damn that Becky.

Dinas Cromlech, home to *Cenotaph Corner* and *Right Wall,* is very much home to British trad climbing. Brown, Fawcett, Redhead, Crew, Livesey, Whillans. The Cromlech is one of my favourite crags, and so it was on the first day of the meet a bunch of folk, including Pat Littlejohn, were ensconced beneath its towering walls.

Nico was suffering. A debilitating migraine had knocked him for six, and as others were strapping it on, I sat and sunbathed, and felt reasonably relaxed with my get-out-of-jail card.

'I'm sooo sorry, Neeeck, you moost think me one of those type of climbares whooom talks more than he does?'

Which of course I didn't as I had seen the numbers on the internet the night before!

'No worries, Nico, you take it easy.'

Which he did by falling asleep in the sun. On waking, Nico thought he might try *Cenotaph Corner*. Brilliant. And after climbing the corner we both abseiled back to the sunny ledge where Nico, virtually blind from migraine, almost threw up. Another hour passed and once again Nico thought he would test his headache, this time by climbing *Left Wall.*

'Ah, I am feeling zee luuuv a bit more now. I shall go right.'

I started to grow concerned, as going right was the sustained and strenuous finish to *Resurrection*.

'You don't need to, that's another route.'

'Ah, but it eez ze line, no?'

No, no it was not the line, not in my mind, but it was looking like it would have to be the line today. Nico skipped up the crack and breezed the long reach at the top. He was obviously starting to feel better, and with each fluent move my concern grew.

'Now we shall try zis, yes?'

Bollocks.

Zis was a route called *JR,* a sustained and technical E5 6b.

And feeling better, he ran up it. I knew I was in trouble then. As soon as we returned to the ledge he was off on a vertical sprint up *Lord of the Flies*.

As I slapped for the top of the crag seconding *Lord,* I knew I had to do something to get myself out of this upward-spiralling frenzy of Bullock destruction. Already I had mentioned the route that goes up the nearly blank wall to the left of *Lord,* a climb called *Nightmayer*. I had mentioned that it had only received two ascents and that both of these were after quite a lot of practice. I may have mentioned that it was only meant to be a sport grade of 8a. I may not have mentioned that on several top-rope attempts, I had failed to reach the top of the crag. I did mention it was run-out and I certainly mentioned there was a crucial number-one wire placement that Steve Mayers, the first ascensionist, had told me about.

I stood on the ledge alongside Pat Littlejohn as Nico abseiled the line, closely inspecting the holds and checking for gear placements.

'What's he doing?' Pat was looking up puzzled.

'He's going to top-rope *Nightmayer*.'

Pat looked at me.

'But isn't he meant to be good? The route has gear, doesn't it? It is safe.'

I looked at Pat to see if he was serious … And he was.

'Well, yes, it does have some gear, Pat, but not a lot!'

'Poor effort then, don't you think?'

I nearly choked before spluttering to Nico, who was virtually down: 'Pat reckons you should go for the ground-up, Nico; he thinks it's a poor effort if you top-rope it first … '

I looked at Pat; Pat looked at me … and Nico said, 'OK, Neeeck, but I will first watch Sean work it on ze rope.' (The Sean in question was of course Sean Villanueva O'Driscoll – regular climbing partner of Nico. On first meeting he came across even more off-kilter than Nico, and after getting to know Sean you realise that yes, yes he is.)

Pat appeared to think this was OK. So everyone was happy apart from me. I was the one now starting to feel nauseous.

After watching Sean and listening to the beta he relayed, Nico went for it. I had climbed *Left Wall* with my mate Dave Noddings, or Noddy as he is better known, to get a grandstand view, and with every move Nico made, fear increased. Not Nico's fear, no. The little Belgian whooped and joked and continued with something similar to suicidal abandon. No, *my* fear was increasing and about to hit overload. I knew Nico was a great climber, I had witnessed it and read about it, but bloody hell! This climb had never even had a ground-up attempt! It was really serious; the two climbers, Steve Mayers and Tim Emmett, who had climbed the route were so talented and fit, but neither had romped this climb. In fact, by all accounts, Tim had been almost a permanent feature hanging from a rope and working the climb before he eventually led it.

Nico continued to climb. He was now at the finger traverse, a third of the way up, and I knew there were some bold, hard moves to come, which were actually the crux moves of a climb called *The House of God,* which was a direct on *Lord of the Flies.* Nico twisted and turned and didn't really slow. I was impressed, but this was a warm-up in comparison to what was above. As he hung from the small ledge at about half height I shouted down, 'There's gear to your right and the left, make sure you get it.'

'Thank yoooo,' he sang back toward me, dwarfed in the middle of a vertical pocketed sea of rhyolite.

Oh, I thought, *what a nice person,* and turned to Noddy. 'He's about to die.'

When Nico continued, he had placed one wire in the halfway ledge behind a creaking flake and another a little higher on the left. Somewhere above him I knew was the fabled number-one keyhole which accepted the crucial piece to protect the very hard and run-out moves. The Belgian moved up and then up another move, fondling and caressing sharp edges. He placed another wire on the left rope, reversed and shook out.

'How's it looking?' I enquired.

'It loookz quite deefficult.'

Laying on my chest, filming from the top of *Left Wall,* I turned once again to Noddy.

'No shit … '

Fishing for edges – pockets, the correct sequence, the correct body position – Nico headed up and then right. He placed no more gear. Twisting, contorting.

'Go on; you can do it.'

He suddenly looked fallible, almost human.

'Come on … '

It was at this point I thought: nope, he can't. It was clear to see, and with one move in reverse, he let go.

The closest nut to protect his fall was so far away it would have taken a pair of binoculars to see, and this ripped cleanly from the rock. The little Belgian became even smaller as he shot down the wall. Five, ten, fifteen, twenty … and still he fell. Whizzing and tumbling, he plunged past the halfway ledge where the gear that was hopefully going to hold his fall was placed. He fell and fell, the speed of the flying Belgian increased. He fell past the finger traverse a third of the way up the face, or maybe it was two thirds of the way down the face.

'He's about to die … ' I was filming a snuff movie.

At last he slowed and stopped; he had fallen half the length of the forty-metre face.

'Are you alright?' I yelled.

'Whoooooooo!' was all he said before both he and Sean screamed and laughed.

It was then I knew the week was going to be brilliant, and that under the pale, innocent exterior of the little Belgian was a certifiable fucking nutter; life had suddenly become more carefree, crazy and uncertain.

After nearly killing the star of the meet on the first day, things settled down. Nico and I climbed together for the whole week and it turned into one of the most enjoyable and fun weeks of climbing in my life. *The Axe, Authentic Desire, The Purr-Spire, Me, Strawberries, Mister Softy, Blue Peter, Rust Never Sleeps, Tonight at Noon, Noble Savage, Byzantium* and *Direct Hit*. Each day we went out and each day I pointed him at choss and technical testpieces, and each day he lapped it up and revelled in it. The crux of the week though was staying up past 4 a.m. on the final night after two bottles of wine each and two shared bottles of single malt and hours of singing accompanied by Nico's mandolin and Sean's tin whistle.

17
the cathedral

Summer 2008
Llanberis, Wales

Graham Desroy was also on the BMC International Meet. Graham is known as 'Streaky', after Dennis Gray, the ex-general secretary of the BMC, said he was as thin as a piece of streaky bacon. Unofficially, Llanberis has been my home since 2004, about the same time as Streaky moved to the area from Yorkshire. The first and only time I had seen him before was in 1999 when I was being unceremoniously and repeatedly spat from an overhanging jamming crack at Curbar Edge called *Moonshine*. I was climbing with Jon Read at the time, and as I hung from a piece of gear, wasted, getting nowhere, Jon whispered, 'That's Graham Desroy.' Off to the side, I saw a thin gangly guy with long straight hair held in place with a bandana, and instead of blue jeans, his were white. I remember thinking how he must have thought we were punters, which, several years down the line and after getting to know Streaky, I'm sure that's *exactly* what he was thinking.

It took a year or so before our friendship was forged, mainly, I think, because I was still a little in awe. He is so old and has been a part of British climbing culture for so long, he is almost antique. He always climbs well despite decrepitude. I cycled down the Llanberis Pass one sunny evening and slowed to watch a raucous scene of shouting and top-off posturing beneath the famous *Jerry's Roof* boulder. Streaky had just climbed the 7c problem before his son Liam, and on his fiftieth birthday.

At the time, I didn't know how competitive Streaky was, even with both of his children, to whom he is a great and generous and loving father. But since getting to know him, I can safely say he could teach Lance Armstrong a thing or two about being competitive. Streaky has become one of my closest friends, even with his testosterone-fuelled competitiveness – something that used to wind me up so much that one day I had to deliver a few swift undercuts to his ribs, causing him to laugh and cry in equal amounts, which in turn, started everyone else at the crag laughing. I now call him The Hippy, which is actually a misnomer as he is really an old rocker: red bandana, tie-dye shirts, white trousers, and long, getting-a-tad-thin-and-grey, mousey-coloured hair. The Hippy is quite similar to Francis Rossi, the lead singer of Status Quo, but I would never tell him that because he would see it as a compliment.

On the North Anglesey coast, a large clean sweep of rock springs out from the hillside like a *Ramalina*-camouflaged World War II bunker. The sea laps the undercut seaward end of the cliff and a bluebell-entwined grass slope gives a steep but easy approach. Fishermen use this corrugated slice of quartzite as a navigation aid and call it Cathedral Rock. The Gogarth guidebook calls it Equestrian Wall. The Hippy had been kayaking around the north coast and took a few pictures, which he showed to me. This was a Hippy trait I was beginning to discover, although it had taken a while for me to catch on. If he saw a climb or a crag that he was afraid to climb, something that intimidated his dwindling bravery, he would plot a cunning strategy to capture my interest, and the next thing I'd know, I would be leading some hard and often run-out or crumbling line because The Hippy wanted to experience the climb with the safety of a top rope.

Captain Mark Phillips, once married to Princess Anne, is also quite old and getting thin on top, but unlike The Hippy, he was married to royalty. Never in a million years would The Hippy pull royalty. But *Captain Mark Phillips* is also an attractive E5 slash running the length of the Equestrian Wall, and it was because of this The Hippy and I first visited the north Anglesey coast together.

I could hardly move with the weight of several monster cams hanging from my harness. Holds creaked and flexed. 'I don't think anyone has climbed *Captain Mark Phillips* in years.'

'Really?' The Hippy replied, in an *are you surprised?* tone. He lit a cigarette, anticipating a long belay session. Smoke from his cigarette floated and wrapped around pennywort stalks in the back of the dark cleft. The smoke threaded spiders' webs spanning the dyke, the silk flapping and glistening in the breeze. I pushed myself into the confines of the crack. It smelled of earth and copper and damp insect life and Embassy Number 1. Embassy Number 1 had been Mum's choice of cigarette for a while and in some way The Hippy and his generous personality reminded me of Mum. Also like Mum, I suspected The Hippy – under that happy-go-lucky and generous exterior – if offended or upset could be quite ruthless in distancing people; but also like Mum, I suspected with family and close friends he would give away his last if he thought it would help.

The climbing had been physical, but the crux came near the top and I was shocked; I was shocked after so much climbing to find myself strenuously laybacking and smearing feet outside the crack – I was shocked to be so pumped. The wall looks like a slab from the side, but Equestrian Wall is an enigma and my arms were telling me this was no slab. A long ten minutes later I pulled on to the grassy crag top, hot and sweating, exhilarated but relieved. As I pulled in the ropes I knew we would both have to come back, because, like me, The Hippy loves an adventure.

My imagination had been opened with that first visit to Equestrian Wall, and The Hippy and I returned to climb a new route up an obvious wide and disintegrating crack which we called *Crazy Horse*. We gave it that illustrious grade of E3 5b.

Later in the summer I was fortunate enough to squeeze in another Equestrian day. A lone cormorant skimmed the sea and a porpoise jumped in the turning tide. The horses grazed contentedly in the field above. Daylight was shortening, a damp chill penetrated and dew lit the tips of the long grass. I had brought along Dan McManus, and in fact, I had pulled a Hippy sandbag myself by piquing Dan's interest for my own advantage.

Dan was twenty, talented and very bold; he was extremely driven with the touch of arrogance that is necessary to succeed. Although when we first talked I was the one being arrogant.

There had been a group of people bouldering on the Cromlech boulders in the Llanberis Pass. Dan approached me and asked if I needed a climbing partner.

'I can climb E3, maybe E4, and can follow anything.'

I looked at Dan with his unmuscled, skinny, bendy body and his pale face and fair hair. He had a strangely forward, but quirky and shy manner.

'I warm up at E3 and I don't need a partner,' I'd said. The truth was I really didn't need a partner, I had so many friends around Llanberis now and spending time with someone I didn't know held no interest. I certainly could have been more considerate and gentle though.

As always in these cases, when I am arrogant, it comes back to bite me on the arse and within a year Dan was climbing far better than me; he was bolder and a lot more talented. More importantly, Dan was different and interesting and very good company, so when we started to climb together, we discovered we could relate and chat about most subjects, and unlike many really good climbers, Dan liked to drink beer and wine and not take himself too seriously. One difference between Dan and me though, something I could not understand, was his reading material. Dan read classics between climbs: *Jane Eyre, Pride and Prejudice, The Mayor of Casterbridge* … I really don't like classics.

This was the second summer Dan and I had partnered up; the first summer had been full, we had climbed testpiece choss all over the North Wales coast: *The Enchanted Broccoli Garden, Conan the Librarian, Authentic Desire, The Clown, Rust Never Sleeps, Tonight at Noon, Rockin' in the Free World* and many more. Most of the time Dan was laid-back, but gently simmering underneath his pale and fair exterior was drive and determination; he really wanted to tick the hardest adventure climbs out there. I suppose he just hid and handled his ambition better than me.

Cilan was most definitely a Dan mission – most of them were, but this one appealed to the mountaineer and adventure rock climber in me. The abseil to the shelf where Dan sat was free-hanging. A rigging rope joined the marginal pieces of gear that anchored the abseil line; it twisted across the grassy headland running over rabbit holes and around dry tussocks. The only way out from the base of the cliff was to climb *Vulture,* a serious four-pitch E4 … or swim.

Littlejohn and White's *TerrorHawk,* a four-pitch E6 with a reputation for adventure, was our chosen climb. Neither of us feared it because James 'Caff' McHaffie had told us, 'It only has one hard move … just a bit of a pull near the top of the final pitch; you boys will cruise it.' Our egos lapped this up, forgetting who and what Caff was, which is one of the best traditional climbers in the world with a penchant for sandbagging.

Dan cleared rubble, making a space before sitting pixie-like on the large ledge just above the sea. Cilan Main Cliff is dauntingly isolated and bigger than anything at Gogarth. The pale bulbous rock is covered in bird shit, and looks like white graffiti-sprayed tombstones. A waterfall caught in a beam of sunlight poured out of a slimy gash in the clifftop and lit the crag with rainbow spectres. Apart from an occasional sailing boat drifting by, we were on our own.

Pulling the overhanging weather-worn teeth, height was quickly gained. The protection was abysmal but the climbing was relatively easy, as long as the thought of what could happen if a hold ripped off was shut away. Twenty overhanging metres later, I balanced on a ledge strewn with rubble. A corroded karabiner hung ten metres to my right, marking the first belay. A corner looked like it may have a gear placement, so I climbed to its top and nonchalantly grabbed a large hold. It broke. Still gripping the lump of rock, my arm swung like I was throwing a discus. As my body twisted I threw out the other hand. Fingers hit a ledge, clawing deep into mud. My twist slowed for a second ... just a second, before momentum and gravity took over and I dove head first down the cliff.

I filled my lungs and I screamed, tearing the skin at the back of my throat. My lungs emptied. Rock rushed past in a blur. The sea lapped indifferently and I screamed again. Dan's belay ledge hurtled toward me. I threw my arms above my head. Dan looked up before being plucked from the shelf with the tug of the rope. My fall stopped three metres above rock. I hung upside down looking into Dan's pale face, and laughed. Dan looked shocked.

Reclimbing the pitch was fine until I drew alongside the single wire nut that had held my fall. The nut was placed sideways into the lip of a crack and the rock surrounding the nut was splintered like a chicken bone. Feeling nauseous, I grovelled through the dirt to the old corroded karabiner and belayed.

The rest of the climb went: overhanging, technical, run-out, loose and wet. Our eyes grew wider and wilder with every move. The exposure crept into our minds. Our limbs worked, barely, pushing us higher as the worm of doubt wriggled deeper.

We pulled on to the grass headland a full seven hours after our abseil. A breeze blew through our sweat-soaked clothes. Exhausted, we collected the gear and staggered across the clifftops. Big round mushrooms glowed white in the evening gloom. Rabbits bolted into bushes. I imagined the moles that caused the dark bumps scattering the hill shuffling beneath our feet. Life flowed ...

Dan 'warmed up' throwing his bendy limbs all over the place while climbing a George Smith route called *Limpet Trip*. *Limpet Trip* is an oddity of the wall, in fact an oddity for George Smith, as for once it doesn't involve heel hooking, knee barring, grunting, swinging, slapping or jamming. It has no upside down and it doesn't follow one of the distinct features of the wall, which are striated lines running from left to right. *Limpet Trip* climbs the wall like a wall and because of three pegs it feels safe ... ish! Even the name is an oddity, as it has no horse connection like all others on the wall. I asked George where it originated and he told me it was from belaying a local who isn't the quickest, and as he had belayed, he had watched a limpet move from one side of a boulder to the other.

I seconded Dan, who climbs much quicker than a limpet, knowing my plan had worked: to warm up and check out the finishing moves of George's climb in preparation for a new route with the same finish. I was obviously learning a few tricks from The Hippy, but I also knew that someone as old as The Hippy had too many years' experience at being tricky for me to compete.

The planned new line followed a crack and three large distinct pods where owls roosted. After the pods the line continued direct, or it could be climbed the same as *Limpet Trip*. Dan is a tad crazy. His ability to see danger makes me appear considered. Dan thought my new line looked safe, and informed me that I wasn't allowed to practise but that I could have an abseil and a quick brush if I really thought it necessary! The direct finish from the top pod followed a small crease of friable rock. It looked like it would involve blind and strenuous laybacking with toes pressed to dirty friable smears. The protection was sparse. *Bugger that*, I thought, but the pods looked too good to be ignored.

Wedged into the long and narrow pod, the last in the line of three, the smell and feel was once again of damp rotten wood, earth, owls and elements. I buried my head amongst sand and guano and owl pellets containing tiny femurs, skulls and ribcages. Bundles of bones wrapped inside small packages of grey cotton wool. I placed a monster cam. Several failed attempts to escape the pod followed as I tried to reach a large round hole to the right. Then a chunk of rock resembling a piece of driftwood gave me an idea. Laybacking the driftwood, running my feet high, pushing toes to dusty smears, I crossed a left arm over the right and squeezed a sloping hold that looked like a bite out of a lump of two-by-four. Wafting blindly,

I scratched the inside of the round pod to the right and pulled myself into another fusty hole.

The top peg on *Limpet Trip* was still a way off, and with no more monster cams I hoped the climbing would be easy. But it wasn't. A long reach for a crimp. *Don't break, don't break.* Then a step right and the peg had me back on the familiar ground of *Limpet Trip*. Struggling, sweating, cursing – the finish of *Limpet Trip* was the crux of that route and this one also. Two moves from the top, a hold that I had used previously broke. Thrown from the cliff, I watched my clean first ascent disappear, but success came with the second, slightly soured, attempt.

Dan and I walked away from the cliff in the red and damp of the evening. A porpoise jumped waves and a breeze carried the smell of salt. Another summer was done. I was about to head off on an expedition to Nepal and then spend the winter in the Alps, but I knew in the spring I would return to this quirky deserted headland because it somehow fitted; it was an adventurous backwater, a place the crowds would never flock to. The north coast also felt wild, more so than the west, and the friends I had visited and climbed with added to this affinity; they enhanced my attachment and made the climbing there memorable.

18
trapped

December 2008
Fer à Cheval, France

We were trapped. One hundred and fifty metres of frozen stalactites hung on the cliffs to our left and above us. Neither Tim Emmett nor I had climbed here before, and I now realise that the Cirque du Fer à Cheval is virtually inescapable. A thick layer of snow covered stratified bands. Pine trees sagged with white. Ice gripped the limestone walls that wrapped around us: smears, drips, chandeliers, pillars, inverted unicorn horns. Some lines twisted grey and were barbed like wire. Others were not lines at all, just daffodil petals of ice that blossomed from bare rock. Blocks broke from the cliffs to our left, raking the lower half of the route we were climbing – the *Cascade de la Lyre*. No matter when we turned around, the outcome would be uncertain. Rappelling the line was the only possible descent. *Might as well continue,* I thought. *We've already experienced so much.*

That morning, I had waited in the dark centre of Cluses. It was the week between Christmas and New Year. Nothing moved until Tim's silver Subaru burbled into the dark car park. Forty-five minutes later when we reached the cirque, conditions appeared perfect: still and frigid. No human figures and no new snow. Stars dimmed as we skied the frozen riverbed. Red stratus whorls moved slowly across the sky. I hoped they'd keep the sun from the cliffs.

Tim sped up the first fifty metres: a freestanding pillar that glistened in glass ribbons and rainbow spectres like the rings of Saturn. Roped up, we shouted and joked for 350 metres more – not knowing that with each pick placement and each front-point kick, an invisible funnel tightened around us.

Before Thierry Renault made the first ascent of *Cascade de la Lyre* in 1992, he was an avid predator of hard new lines. Afterward, he turned to religion. And as I pulled on to the chandeliered wall, I was already praying to any god that would listen.

Tim dug into a snow cave and hid from the fusillade of ice. Occasionally, his blonde bouffant poked out and a high-pitched scream would instruct me to destroy it, to own it. Tim seemed to treat everything as a party. He was renowned for being psyched and 'mad for it'. He was the kind of climber who said things like 'Awesome, mate, wild, mate, let's crush it!' I didn't do *mad for it*. I certainly didn't do *crush it*. But when I finally met Tim, I couldn't help but enjoy his honest enthusiasm, even if he did use words that made me look over my shoulder to be certain no one else was listening.

Another squawk winged around the empty cirque.

'Kill it!'

Cleaning, leaning back, cleaning, swinging, kicking; I was getting more and more exhausted. I wished I'd trained more and pushed more weights in the cellar of Kenton's house in Mont-Saxonnex where I was living for the winter. The stress of the environment was also exhausting. My feet skittered on ice that resembled polished marble. Weak winter light shimmered across yellow scalloped ice like old memories.

I weaved, cut and ploughed a furrow through stalactites until at last I pulled into a groove beneath a giant thistle head.

'Mate, that's crazy!' Tim said, looking up at the next pitch. 'One of the maddest pieces of ice I've ever seen. It's like something from another planet. I'm going to kill it.'

I still didn't know Tim well, but was that a nervous flicker I saw, just for one second? A look of doubt in his shining eyes? Perhaps this outburst was a way of dealing with the tension, a way of fooling himself before getting involved with the monstrosity. Or, he may really just have been mad for it, I wasn't sure.

'Take a look around the back,' I said. 'There may be a way behind?'

Tim disappeared into a dark cave, half rock, half ice. A squeaky voice echoed.

'Yeah, mate, it'll go. It'll be easy.' Then a deeper, darker tone: 'It's avoiding the challenge, though, mate.' Then back to high-pitched and excitable: 'I'm going to have it straight up the front!'

It was then I realised that Tim's earlier expression may not have been one of fear, but the gaze of someone whose life was burning bright. I shivered and hoped Tim's fire wasn't about to be quelled.

Good to his word, Tim approached the thistle head at its steepest point. When he hit one of the smaller icicles, he set off a meteorite shower of blocks. I cowered, imagining what it would be like to be struck by the full force of the avalanches cascading down the line and our descent to the left.

'Tim, you're going to kill me,' I said. 'Go right, for fuck's sake.'

'OK, mate.'

He traversed beneath the roof with his body hanging at an angle of forty-five degrees. This was not the brash clown I'd mentally conjured from the magazine articles. This was a skilled, safe and considerate climber using all his ability to move with style and caution. Nearly horizontal, with his feet under the roof, he placed one ice screw, then another. His whole body twisted. A knee inverted. He hooked an ear of ice, pulled and locked. He was above the steepest ice I've ever seen anyone climb.

'Safe, mate!' he yelled.

The fuck we are. More blocks crashed down our descent route with a sound like exploding battleships. Tim rigged a fail-safe belay and, for the first time in a long while, but only briefly, I felt secure seconding a pitch.

Inching above the belay, my legs bridged wide between ice and dirty rock. Tim was safely hidden beneath a roof. A thin column rose up. Time was lost. It was almost night. I pressed my front points to small limestone edges.

'Go on, mate,' Tim shouted. 'Kill! Destroy!'

I faced out, looking into the darkening cirque. *THUNK* … I pulled into the dark. *THUNK* … Another life beckoned, a more gentle and considered life, a life where I did not want any destroying or killing.

I breathed deeply before grovelling from the top of the cleft. The massive shelf between the lower and upper cirques was a barren windswept moonscape, leading to a second tier of steep cliffs. Sweat-soaked clothes froze against my skin. Stars flickered. We were going to have to abseil back into the path of those avalanches. The ray of Tim's headlamp still swung within the bowels of the shaft. Pick, pick, grunt, kick. Another boom of crashing ice. I shivered.

Tim appeared and set about constructing a double V-thread into rotten ice.

'Here you go, mate.'

The light from my headlamp cut through the dark and the smattering of falling snow and caught a small, glittering package in the centre of Tim's hand. I unwrapped the foil from the outside of the chocolate before enveloping it in my mouth. The liquor inside swilled around my mouth and warmed my stomach.

The ropes were threaded through the abseil device in preparation for the descent. Two ends of rope faded into the gloom below me. In the incandescent beam, I looked up. Tim was smiling: white teeth, shining eyes, blonde curls. There was a soul ablaze, a strong pulsing heart, a life lived twice as bright. I released my grip on the rope and began to slide.

Three hours later, we touched down at the foot of the first pillar again. Millions of ice blocks glittered like neon lights embedded in the snow. But not once had they fallen during our descent. We dug out our rucksacks from beneath the debris of earlier avalanches and recovered the skis we'd stashed a safe distance from the base of the climb. But as we stamped into ski bindings, a roar of collapsing ice made us cower.

The day after mine and Tim's ascent of *La Lyre,* two French guides, Luc Avogadro and Eric Lazard, were killed when attempting the *Cascade du Folly,* a line to the right. Supposedly the pillar they were climbing collapsed and they both fell to their deaths. One week later, the French brothers Benoit and Vincent Drouillat also died, struck by falling ice as they descended *La Lyre.*

19
evening redness in the west

Summer 2009
Llanberis, Wales

The Hippy, Tim Neill and myself walked the exposed north Anglesey coastal path heading once again to Equestrian Wall. The day was bright. The sea's surface appeared almost glazed. The breeze blowing off the water was dense with salt and that salt caught my face. I stood and watched a gannet repeating a circular flight path across the sea's surface.

Warm-ups completed – although after *Crazy Horse* and *Captain Mark Phillips,* Tim looked more overdone than warm – I checked out the direct finish to the route I had climbed with Dan McManus last year, with fresh eyes. The gear still looked poor and the holds still looked limited. I brushed and cleaned a line, but it was impossible to see how I was going to join it together. The Hippy lowered me on a top rope and I stopped in the long narrow pod, the last in the line of three from *The Crossing* – the route from last year. Inside the pod, once again I became intimate with the rock and the earth. In a strange way, I felt at peace deep inside the ancient coastline. Something familiar stirred. The hollow echoes of the sea made me feel secure, almost like a child with his ear to a shell, hidden in the shadows beneath the stairs.

> As a child I used to sit and lean back against the old armchair between Dad's knees as he watched TV. Occasionally he would squeeze me with his knees and rub my head. These are the most affectionate and intimate moments I can remember with Dad. He has never told me he loves me. Dad's closeness moves in different ways.
>
> When I was eleven, I was a member of the Cheadle Health and Strength Club, a weights gym situated in an old chapel in the centre of Cheadle.

One year at the Cheadle Festival the club held a competition, something like the programme that was once on TV called *Superstars*. The competition had ten events over two days with the final event an 800-metre run around a track in the centre of the festival field. I was leading the overall competition. My friend Alan Johnson, who could not win the overall competition, but was by far the best runner, was also competing, as well as his cousin Pete, who *could* win the overall competition if he finished ahead of me. Dad came to me and said I should talk to Alan and ask him to run side by side to block his cousin from finishing in front of me. This was how Dad's mind worked; he would see an angle – go for the job with the most pay, sell at a good profit, do whatever is needed to make a profit. I was eleven and wanted to win so I talked to Alan and he refused. I wasn't really expecting him to do anything otherwise, especially as we were talking about blocking out a member of his family. I don't suppose Dad would have even thought of the family connection as a factor. He wouldn't see it as anything other than wheeling and dealing – there are only winners and losers. But the thought of this episode embarrasses me still.

Immediately, on leaving the calm inside the pod, the coast hammered home. The salty breeze quickened my pulse. The light from the sun defined the white cumulus. I climbed a different section of the wall than expected. My preference would have been to abseil and clean, so I could then try the line ground up. It feels more honest, it gives the rock a chance, it leaves a mystery element, but the blind nature and the insecurity of the route was convincing me I had made the right decision.

After a rest I set off once more: smearing and puzzling, attempting to work out what needed to be done. Gulls skimmed the sea. The wind stirred the grass. The Hippy sat content, a cigarette hung from his mouth, his white jeans smeared with dirt.

'How was that?' he mumbled through smoke.

'Desperate.'

Two more practice runs and I was now discovering the intricacies. There were several ways to complete a section as long as the feet could be trusted. Caff's words rang through my mind – *a weighted foot never slips* – but it wasn't just a case of hoping the feet didn't slip, and to be honest, Caff's saying was rubbish. It was having faith that the thin quartz veins that were crucial did not disintegrate.

The Hippy ended the day with what he later called *The Burghley Direct*, a new start to an Ed Stone E4 that is called *Three Day Event*. The new start was not intended, he just climbed where he thought the route began, which, quite clearly, was not where the route began. Tim and I looked on and shook our heads and laughed. The Hippy had written the description for this climb in the new Gogarth guidebook, but had still managed to sandbag himself. 'Watch me, watch me, ARGH, the foothold's crumbling, watch me!' Slapping, red bandana slipping, breaking holds, old creased eyes on stalks, more slapping, white knees rubbing, splinters flying and catching on the wind.

Eventually, shaking and sweating, scared senseless – bandana nearly over his eyes – The Hippy lunged for the top in a sort of reverse stage dive. White jeans slithered out of sight. I must admit to feeling a warm glow inside after watching him sandbag himself. But it was great to see him try hard and use years of experience to get himself up the climb, even if he did almost have a coronary.

I refer to The Hippy as my secret technical weapon, because whenever I fall from a climb or we work a climb and I can't fathom a sequence, I lower him or ask what he thinks. More often than not, his years of climbing and natural ability find a way, and because he is getting old, it makes him feel appreciated. The Hippy was becoming a great friend – his generosity was astounding; but at times his seriously competitive nature and his savage piss-taking border on hurtful. On occasion I have taken myself away and had a quiet talk to myself. My sensitivity is a gift from Mum and it's a gift for which I do not apologise, although it has taken me many years to grow comfortable with it. One day The Hippy called me a technical dunce. I boiled inside. *Technical dunce or not, I have climbed loads more difficult and bold routes than you, Hippy!* ... was what I thought at the time.

I know it isn't worth becoming upset with a close friend over something so trivial, something that just dented my ego, and – truth be told – in comparison to The Hippy, I *am* a technical dunce. Generally, I only feel upset when close friends say hurtful things, because close friends are the people I respect and value and rely on in life to keep me going. The Hippy, Neil Brodie, Tim Neill, they can all be quite cutting and at times I feel their banter touches on deeper, more complex insecurities. I have tried to move on from this type of competitive and cutting banter; it doesn't sit that well with me. But I can't help feeling that life is too short to be too bothered. Having friends like The Hippy, Brodie and Tim, all strong complex characters, is more important than losing their friendship over the odd thoughtless comment.

Half submerged, the blazing sun lit the sea with fiery reflections. The crag glowed vermilion. Shadows caught behind flakes, and I imagined the pods being indifferent to the passing of another day. In the glow, the three of us – Tim, The Hippy and me – packed ropes and cams and extenders and listened to the cry of the oystercatcher. The clock on the Bull Bay church tower struck seven. Another day was almost over.

The style of climbing on Equestrian Wall is my favourite: run-out, technical, uncertain, but with time for contemplation between moves. I knew I could climb this route, but due to the nature of the rock, success was never going to be certain. I liked this, it reminded me of a John Redhead quote from one of his North Stack routes called *Birth Trauma*: 'Those attempting this climb should give themselves to karma.' I had long passed the stage in climbing where getting to the top was the be all and end all; although a difficult lesson, the experience is more important. The experience of living in Llanberis, of being close to the coast and away from the intensity of what some perceive as success, of making money and being a professional, is also important to me.

The Hippy and I drove once again along the north Anglesey coast and parked outside the pub at Bull Bay. On my first attempt to lead the climb I had worked on the previous visit, The Hippy – cigarette drooping – was taking notice for once.

I came second in the competition behind my friend Alan, meaning I won overall. I won fair and square, and that honesty felt good. I can't remember if Dad was watching the race. He probably wasn't. I came second in this race also. *A weighted foot never slips* … I focused on a thin quartz vein and pressed my toe firmly against it. A cracking sound reverberated. The quartz my toe was pressed into broke, and I was thrown. My neck snapped back: twisting, cartwheeling, bumping, jarring – crispy *Ramalina* floating in a cloud of silver-green. The Hippy lowered me into the soft grass on the steep slope.

Chemically numbed, the second attempt finished with a new direct finish to *The Crossing* and a swollen elbow, and I called the climb *All the Pretty Horses* after Cormac McCarthy's first book of the Border Trilogy.

After leaving school and home at the age of sixteen I became a gamekeeper in North Wales. I left the job after about two years because I was being treated terribly by my boss's wife. Two weeks after leaving the job, Dad and I returned to the estate near Porthmadog in my mate's white Morris Marina van to collect my motorbike and my ferrets. Dad and I both met the head gamekeeper who was a tough man, but he appeared upset that I had left. I still felt upset, I felt like I had let him down. His wife, who had treated me terribly, did not make an appearance.

Dad and I stopped in Llangollen for a cup of tea and fish and chips, which Dad paid for, and as we sat eating, a fire engine sped past. Someone walked into the chippy and said there was a van on fire. Dad and I looked at each other, before popping our heads outside. The white van with my ferrets and motorbike inside it was on fire. We left our chips and ran towards the van, which was being hosed down. A brake cylinder had caught fire, but apart from replacing the cylinder and a tyre, everything was OK. The van was parked outside a garage and fixed for £90 before we carefully made our way back to Staffordshire. When we arrived home I sat with Dad as he recounted the adventure we had both been through to Mum.

Glistening *Ramalina,* spiders' webs, flowering pennywort and rock the texture of wood – it was not always the obvious that brought comfort and closeness. The draw of this deserted coastline was strong. Bright sun, scudding cumulus, then bright sun. Shadows moved between green and white waves. The troughs between the waves were at times dark and in an instant, illuminated. Reflections crossed the wall. The weather was forecast to be much worse on the mainland, but here on the north Anglesey coast a microcosm of better weather added to the whole esoteric experience. Equestrian Wall had a pioneering feel. It was never going to be popular or well used and I was glad about that; I liked taking something from very little and making it my own, making it important to me.

Climbing the cliffs of North Wales was starting to become a deeply profound part of my psyche. The Hippy and I went on to climb together for most of the summer. *Hysteresis* was all soft rock and streaks of bird shit. *Primate,* a crumbling arête above the sea and a Joe Brown E2, was all exposure. The climbing in Wales was taking the place of, and becoming almost as important to me as, a relationship. Except this relationship, physical and elemental, at times appeared simpler and less challenging than one of flesh and heartache. On rainy days I would climb indoors at the climbing wall, where on occasion I would climb with Jenny, a woman I had first seen in the arms of her boyfriend near the Cromlech boulders in 2004 – my first summer in Llanberis. She was obviously a little older now and in a long-term relationship with a friend. The age gap between us was large, although I could not help but be drawn to her and her fragility. Occasionally at the climbing wall she would bound downstairs and machine-gun me with conversation. And occasionally, in contrast, she would appear a little lost and unhappy. At times my climbing relationship felt similar.

Peregrines screaming above the warm stalks of swaying grass of Gogarth's Upper Tier. The fluttering North Stack carpet of pinks in the wind. Simple is what is needed. The prison had affected me over the years. In life it is easy to get drawn into situations that are not correct, but maybe this *is* life?

Scimitar Ridge, a curving crag of steepness situated high in the Llanberis Pass, has difficult technical climbing that has always spoken and appealed to the part of me that needs challenge. It gets the morning sun, a slice of glowing corrugated rhyolite cut from the steep heather of the Llanberis Pass. Scimitar is concave like a wooden rowing boat tipped on to its gunwale, and below, twisting through the boggy valley base, a stream of clear mountain water slowly flows, reflecting the sun and the mountains. It is as a glittering artery feeding the dark earth, and the earth is made up of lives blown on the wind of years – desiccated skin, blood, bone, sinew – lives lived, lives lost, love lost.

Scimitar is the home of hard climbing, thanks to the nature of the rock itself. There are very few crimps and holds to pull on – it is all open-handed, side-pulling, smearing feet and palming. Spotting protection from below is difficult and reading the rock even more so. Scimitar hides its secrets well. Scimitar rewards the confident.

Jenny couldn't commit. She couldn't commit. I stood on the steep grass slope below and looked up, sensing her internal dialogue. She was filled with doubt. It was a blind and bold pull into the groove on a climb called *The Roc-Nest Monster*, a committing move, one that took belief, and this was testing her. She lowered off. Climbing at times reveals the raw; climbing can cut to the quick. I felt disappointed for her. Even in those days when we were just friends – I say 'just' but I suppose it was never really 'just' for me, because somewhere under all of life's layers, she had always been more than 'just', more than 'just' since the first time I had seen her. And for some reason it was important to me that she succeed and be happy. I should not have cared, she was destined for someone else, she was *with* someone else, but I wanted her to be happy. Climbing can be cruel, but it is always honest.

Another day and back to Scimitar. A route called *Surgical Lust*, first climbed by Paul Pritchard, had entered my dreams long ago. It was fantasy. Longing. I wanted the intensity, to succeed over the possible damage I knew it could inflict. The simple natural beauty intertwined with complexity. Was I ready? It was almost the end of August, nearing the end of my summer – I was about to go away once again on an expedition to Nepal and a mountain called Chang Himal. The Hippy held my ropes on a third attempt to climb *Surgical Lust*. Time was running out. The previous two attempts had both been forced – the weather had been wrong, the friction poor and both had ended in failure. Climbing is nothing but honest and to the point. I wanted this climb but twice I was spurned.

Everything fell into place on the third attempt: the partner, the weather, the condition of the rock, the climbing – I opened myself totally. I became almost free of ego and constraints. I understood what may happen and accepted it. And later, sitting on top of the crag having at last committed and experienced, I almost understood. I almost felt honest, I almost felt whole, and this life, my climbing life, almost felt as though it were everything.

Almost.

20
into the shadow

October 2009
Chang Himal, Nepal

Stars flicker in a slow-spinning sky. Old snow crackles. The moraine – a rubble-strewn lunar surface – creaks under our feet. A sickly yellow moon lights our path. Ice gleams. Andy Houseman and I are creeping like thieves; we're scared that the mountain might hear our approach. Eighteen hundred metres of snow, cold, rotten granite, thin ice skin, fluted sugar spines, and a pointed summit so far above, the north face of Chang Himal seemed to penetrate the mist of the Milky Way.

Each day in our countdown to the climb, a cold wind had blasted. Ghostly reefs of snow tumbled down Kangchenjunga. Spirits tore from Chang Himal's summit crest. A week before, I had stared up at Chang Himal. I could picture my small figure on the north face, where the shadows curled from spines of snow.

'I can't imagine setting off to climb something so big and unknown,' my friend Tom Briggs had said.

We were sitting in chairs, side by side at Base Camp. Tom was a bold British trad climber, and had joined us for the trek in, as had The Hippy and Mandi, The Hippy's partner. The routes Tom climbed intimidated me.

'It scares me just looking and imagining being up there, in the middle of that,' Tom said. 'What makes you want to put yourself in that position?'

Looking up, my eyes watered with the intensity of the sun. Brown grass withered around us. Wallowing yaks cut crescent trenches into the earth. High above, séracs tilted and tottered, just enough to warn and tempt. Black rock, overhanging rock, serrated ridges, scalloped snowfields – all wavered across a vast white sheet. Shade and light arced over it, with the sweeping of the day. Ravens circled. The wind dug the trenches deeper. I wanted Tom to stop talking. *How do you prepare yourself for the invisible, the unknown?* But then I thought: *how do you prepare yourself for life, for love, for loss, for death?*

Now, twisting and turning into the dark entrance gully, I think of Eric Escoffier, blown without a trace from Broad Peak in 1998. And in that same evening, from our cornice bivvy high on Savoia Kangri, Paul Schweizer and I could see a plume of snow and cloud lift off K2's summit and vanish into the fading sky – and we tried not to think about the darkness beneath us.

The wind is an unknown, unseen quantity: how do you prepare for the invisible? 'Write a will, mate,' Stevie Haston had told me before I left Llanberis.

Houseman and I reach the snow cone at the base of what we've christened the Narrows. Relief floods in; the snow pack is hard. I look behind and find Houseman is retching.

'That's not in the plan,' I say.

He vomits again.

'Do you want to go down, try again in a few days?'

'No.' His voice is strained and I imagine his mind twisting with doubt, with guilt. 'I feel really weak, but if you don't mind leading, I'll keep going. I don't feel sick enough to justify going down.'

His gaunt face and dark, intense eyes remind me of Pete Boardman who was lost on the North-East Ridge of Everest in 1982. Ten years later, Boardman's body was found near the top of a black tower. Houseman has become one of my most trusted and respected partners for this type of thing and one of the few climbers with whom I'd want to be on this face. What a difference from the first impression I had formed when we met in the Café Andino in Peru and I took his talk as boastful bravado.

Stars dim. Snow ripples like sand. Flotsam emerges above the white sea, a black boulder, a corniced crest, the detritus of mountain fall. I dreamt about these fragments when they were just small forms of dark and light through my binoculars. Close up, they feel familiar. Much imagined, they are now real.

Youth follows, haggard. He leans on his axe. The boyish smile is missing. *Would I still be climbing if I were this ill?* We've left behind the séracs that may or may not pour down our line. The angle of the face tilts upward. Under a shallow crust, our crampons spark on rock. The plan had been to abseil the line on V-threads. I push it to the back of my mind.

'I'm feeling weak,' Houseman says again.

I stop and turn: grey light unveils snow-covered mountains – hard ribs and hollow shadows, sharp radiating patterns, a vast coral skeleton – against an oceanic sky. There's the jumbled moraine, there's our single convoluted track cutting toward the dots of Base Camp tents and the small stone huts of Pangpema.

Houseman is the same age as I was when I first started to climb. It doesn't seem that long ago, but it's been fifteen years. Time on a mountain is unearthly time, inexplicably slowed. Still, it does not stop. Ever since my twenties I've imagined so many out-of-reach scenarios. Each daydream chilled me. I knew that one day I'd attempt to act them out – whatever the cost. But sometimes that cost feels too high. Sometimes in the small hours, inside this dream, I have other dreams.

Houseman and I reach the first in a series of questions: the lower and smaller of the two rock bands.

'Do you mind leading this?' Youth says.

'Neither a borrower, nor a lender be,' Grandad would quote to me regularly. I can hear his honest northern childhood almost choking him. In the pub, Youth liked to tell stories of breaking trail for me, or catching my fall as I reversed over that crevasse as we downclimbed the Tacul in a white-out. If I lead for a whole day, he might be quiet in the future – at times, his focusing on my weaknesses annoys me. Perhaps I still have an ego to contend with?

But soon I am adding up rotten snow, thin ice, limited protection, exposure and a big pack.

No rescue ... No rescue ...

Nine days of walking lies behind us: green, tangled forests and flowing water; rough-turned patches of dark earth; flooded rice fields, bright with reflected sky; spiders' webs that stretched from bamboo stalk to bamboo stalk, thick with cadavers; icefalls slithering above a village of weathered wood, and those yak bells that made our base camp feel at once like home.

No rescue. Write a will, mate. Home is a lifetime away.

A block, flat-topped, gives respite. I stand on my frozen island and try to swing the blood back into my wooden hands.

Control yourself, warm fingers, place a piece of protection, swing your arms. Swap feet, hook a glass-thin piece of ice, a lump of rotten snow.

An hour later, we are digging into the centre of the face. I'd imagined our first bivvy in my dreams back in Base Camp, while I lay warmly wrapped, listening to the yak bells. I dreamt of it during the hike in, I dreamt of it before we even reached Nepal. In dreams from a different life, I saw us settling in for the night on a snow step, our words hushed, our minds excited. The wind and the warmth of partnership would weave closeness around us and the step would give a feeling of belonging more than any brick house or profession could.

Here, snow sloughs, and the wind blows only cold. Mick Fowler grades his bivvies for comfort. Five is a lie down. One is hell. I zip up my two jackets and pull the sleeping bag around my shoulders. Base Camp is a glowing dot. *Three, definitely three.* Chang Himal's summit cuts the grey clouds into pieces as they stream and swirl about the face, covering the stars, then hiding Base Camp.

'I don't like the look of the weather,' Houseman says. 'It'll be desperate if the weather craps out.'

His face is pale. I think of the inmates I have fought, pressing their heads against the cold floor until the blood drained from their cheeks.

'Stop being negative,' I say. With 1,000 metres already behind us, I don't want to contemplate bailing. 'Or at least keep the obvious to yourself.'

Sitting on the snow step, my mind is soon dragging me again into fiery depths of red, yellow and grey quartzite, of walls sprayed with white guano and rippled with grey mud.

Last summer in North Wales, my sixth summer since quitting the prison service, Tim Neill and I were attempting *Helmet Boiler*, a Mick Fowler route in Mousetrap Zawn at Gogarth. *Helmet Boiler* was a route most climbers wouldn't even consider. Only a handful of people knew its run-out horror and the grade wouldn't impress anyone. Another kick against a certain outcome.

The ropes ran in a long, traversing arc below me, held only by a quartz protrusion with a sling around it and a rotting twenty-five-year-old peg. I stood on an island of relatively good rock in a sea of softness, digging and scratching, scraping mud from more mud, searching for something solid.

I excavated a crack, and it crumbled. In the midst of the overhanging mud, a quartz hold jutted like a glass doorknob; I'd have to use it to escape this wall, but quartz has a tendency to snap. I climbed towards it and reversed back to my island several times. At last I wrapped a hand around the doorknob. Seagulls shrieked on the wind, flight feathers ripping. Waves washed in

> fishing floats, tangled orange nets, yellow-bubbled scum, plastic bottles, and memories.
>
> The hold didn't break. Yet higher up, a smooth quartz band did.
>
> The clock hands spun and I fell – mud, madness and pain, that crusty, twenty-five-year-old peg wouldn't catch me – and just as quickly, I slapped for the doorknob and caught it. Once more, it didn't tear. I screamed at Tim, and he screamed back. The sea swept into the zawn, and the seagulls cried freely. The clock hands slowed … and minutes became hours again.
>
> By the time I slithered from the mud runnel's exit, I was beaming with light, overflowing with energy.

At Base Camp I'd dreamt about the second rock band of Chang Himal, picturing the fragile snow. It rattled my mind. We'd told Buddy, our cook, not to send for porters until we were above it. Buddy had a proud paunch and he would lift his shirt and stroke it when he laughed. We couldn't help laughing with him. He'd been on many expeditions, but mostly to large, non-technical peaks. The only one to a small, difficult mountain had ended with the team running away. Buddy recounted this story frequently, between bouts of laughter. Houseman and I had failed twice on our warm-up peak, an easy plod opposite Chang Himal; we didn't think Buddy had much faith in our abilities.

'It looks OK,' Houseman says, as he climbs from the snow ledge where we spent the night.

I think the rock band looks steep and difficult. After about an hour, Houseman agrees with me. Following him, the hot aches burn in my hands.

'You're obviously feeling OK now?' I shout, between screams from the thawing of my fingers.

Youth laughs atop the overhanging runnel. His face is ruddy with wind and health. He points with one of his massive red mittens.

'One of three ways, I reckon?'

Above, three thinly iced corners invert. I don't like the look of any of them, but eventually I decide to take the left-hand line. It's going to be OK. But after the first thirty metres of good ice, my fingers are wooden again, my calves burn, and the voice in my head screams …

You're going to fall. It's miles from anywhere. Write a will, mate.

The angle of the face now bulges. The ice turns thin and hollow. It squeaks. I need to trust it, but I imagine it detaching in a sheet, both my picks ripping out, my body falling, bouncing, crampons catching, knee joints rupturing, before a final menacing *thud*.

I wedge myself into an overhanging corner and slot a large blue hex into a wide crack. Spindrift starts to pour. I swing left into a trough and tap at a greasy millimetre-thin sheen. Flakes of green ice spin, catching on the wind.

'Watch me, Youth.'

Fucking ridiculous. A normal phrase heard and shouted all the time across low, sunny cliffs. Up here it is the scariest phrase imaginable. Houseman, tied to the poor belay, must be willing me on.

'Watch me, Youth.'

Houseman and I try to climb everything free. It's our upbringing. My grandad's voice echoes in my head, and I'm sure Houseman can hear it, too.

If a job's worth doing, it's worth doing well.

I need to work hard to make up for lost time. Time, that most important commodity. My picks are less than a centimetre in. The bulge pushes back. More than a thousand metres of air below us. *The ice was an oil slick on the surface of the sea, and the snow was yellow-bubbled scum washing into the shingle beneath Mousetrap Zawn and once again, just for a fleeting moment, there was Helen belaying with scuffed hands, hands that once held my heart.* Time is a healer. Are we all just commodities?

Screwed against tiny rock edges, my front points teeter. The ice skin peels. Snow lumps rip. We're over a week's walk and a two-day drive from anywhere. With each move, I expect the ice to break, feet to sheer, picks to tear, my body to drop. Time would slow at first, then after ten, twenty, thirty, forty, fifty metres, the speed would increase to a blur, like an accelerating motorbike. With numb fingers, wide eyes, burning arms, I tap. I hold my breath, before tap, tap, tapping again.

When I first started to climb I would open climbing magazines and books and I kept seeing one of the first ascensionists, Paul Pritchard, his thin Lycra-clad legs tucked into socks pulled high, with dyed blonde hair or a black Mohican or a giant rhubarb-leaf hat. I saw him in pictures that shouted: skin-of-the-teeth, bold, crazy, thrilling, life-on-the-cusp-of-society, an individual's own rules, imagination, fun. The sea frothed white below him, the rock crumbled red, grey, clay. He climbed the lines that others called 'unjustifiable'. He lived a life that others called 'unjustifiable'.

In 1997 I met Paul in a pub on the outskirts of Llanberis. Jules, Jamie Fisher, Owain Jones and I were about to travel to India to attempt the Shark's Fin on Meru Central, a climb Pritchard had tried in 1993 with Johnny Dawes, Noel Craine and Philip Lloyd. Rain ran down the windows and the wind shook the privet hedge that bordered the dark lane. I'd only been climbing for four years, and I was so in awe of Pritchard, I couldn't speak.

In the summer, I'd seen a line like an overhanging razor-blade welt of pebble that sliced the far wall of Wen Zawn, cutting directly through the obvious, classic climbs. The line was a climb called *Rubble*. The guidebook named it 'the softest line in the world' and 'the best line at Gogarth'. Only four people had ever climbed it. From the viewing promontory opposite, the salt wind and the crashing sea seemed to speak.

Paul had returned to Llanberis, and I had the courage to ask, 'Tell me about *Rubble*, Paul?'

Paul's suntanned face cracked into a cheeky grin. Beneath the stubble, the laughter lines grew. Crow's feet deepened. Bleached by the sun, feathered with blonde streaks, his hair jutted out in all directions. His eyes burned bright. And he was back in Wen Zawn, a place he'd made his own, an amphitheatre lined with his routes, echoing with his fall. On the boulders the shadow of his body still seemed to lie unconscious as the sea rushed in. And just for a second I could see he was there, he was there and truly living, truly alive, totally awake.

In that second I was there with him, in a dark space lit by his stories. Salt stuck to my skin. The wind ripped through the zawn with the smell of seaweed. Grey seals circled beneath the white and turquoise eddies. The sea crashed like rockfall. My hands touched greasy stone. My heart pulsed, almost beating from my chest.

Then we were back in the packed Gallt y Glyn, jostling and shouting, feet sticking to the carpet, in a fug of music, swaying bodies and sweat. Paul stood off balance. A large support brace wrapped around his ankle. A sling cradled his arm. And the rain ran down the window.

'It's HVS ... except for the E7 bits!' Laughing, he limped away, his pint sloshing as he bumped and merged into the pizza-eating throng.

Far away, in the dark, a light flashes on and off, on and off – yellow against the dark and silver. Buddy is signalling us from our base camp as he has done every night. I stand still, belaying Houseman. The cold eats into my skin, but the small bright light warms me. I imagine Buddy's laughter ringing toward us. Youth climbs alongside me, and together, side by side, young and old, we begin to dig and chop. We've made it; we are above the second rock band.

The wind throws spindrift down on to us. The stars flicker, the black sky slowly turning. After only a few minutes of chopping, we hit ice. A small shelf, probably one-and-a-half on the Fowler scale.

'This is going to be comfy,' Houseman says. I laugh; he has tried to sound positive ever since I bickered with him.

'Only another 600 metres,' I say.

'Two days, then?'

Two days? It's already day three. Light and wind and shadow sweep across a frigid sea. Peruvian-style flutings, walls of unconsolidated snow curve above us and on into the sky. Rock interlaces arabesques of exfoliating and compact granite, and for an instant I'm back on *Rubble*, tearing at the zawn's quartzite fascia, delving deep beneath what had first appeared solid. Guts, pebbledash and veins.

Mid-afternoon, 300 metres below the summit of Chang Himal, we dig in and begin to worry. The flutings between us and the west ridge are convoluted monsters with seams of rotten snow. We opt for a more direct approach. Just above our bivvy, a peak of aerated snow rises ten metres and, like sand, gives no support. I don't fancy climbing it so far from Houseman's belay. We have no clue any more whether we can continue or not. In my mind I see us on some false summit, separated from the real one by a thousand unconsolidated metres of snow, unable to cross the void.

We've made a mistake. I know we've made a mistake.

It's possible we're going to fail. We're so near and failure is going to tear my heart out. I've started climbing so late. How many ascents like this do I have left? I have sacrificed so much.

Spindrift slices into our small cave. Drohma Peak glows close by, a sharp red outline. I sit holding the stove. The surface of the gas canister frosts.

All night in our small cave, while Houseman appears to sleep, I make conversation in my head.

'Why did you fail?'

We failed because of bad conditions, poor weather, dangerous climbing, sickness; because we went the wrong way, because the gear was stolen. Because we weren't strong enough, hard enough, good enough; because we are useless dreamers.

For once, after a trip, all I want is to answer the question, 'Did you summit?' with a simple 'Yes'.

I imagine myself on the summit, content and smiling.

The night wears through me. Tired from thin air and the sense of impending failure, I start the stove early. Gas fumes choke. The light from the stars quivers and bends. I shout at Houseman. He mumbles and shuffles – neither of us are good at rising from bivvies. I shout again. We'll need all the time the day will allow. We have one day of food left, but we'll spend two or three days more if necessary.

I plunge arms and legs into the snow dune above our bivvy before climbing to a crest. Relief at last. A steep sidewall leads into another runnel system. The line wavers slightly and then straightens out to the summit.

It's on. It really is on. I think of teasing Youth by keeping the good news to myself. But then I shout, 'It's on, mate, it's fucking on!'

I return to the bivvy where our packs are pushed into the back of the cave, the cold ripping my lungs. I try to take my mind off the pain.

Jules Cartwright and Jamie Fisher are gone. In the valley, the losses make no sense. But up high, surrounded by thousands of mountains, something seems to expand, briefly; minutes swell to contain hours. Infinity bursts within an instant; one life holds many lives, many possible ascents; one existence races along several paths, each way leading to liberation; and nothing good or bad ever ends. In such moments, mountaineering and my life make plenty of sense.

Houseman leads out of the fluting and on to a broad, dazzling crest. We meet at a snow bollard. Youth is silent, his eyes hidden – but I know they are shining.

Taking no gear apart from what I have collected on the way, I continue. The sun lights my soul. Snow crystals catch on the wind, sparking with light, before blowing out into the clear blue sky, never to return. I try to continually move, but the gusts push me back. I've been here before, battling the wind, driving the shaft of the axe. The light, the emptiness, the solitude. Ice granules scour. Images pierce my mind. I pray for no false summits. Kick, breathe, pray, kick.

It's HVS … except for the E7 bits! Someone else has taken your place, someone who may live to old age.

Crystals fly like spume. The sun refracts into rainbows. Just a few more metres, and all that I dreamt from the shadows will take form. My axe cuts the final crest, and through the slot Kangchenjunga's huge sérac-strewn north face and its three summits appear. To the right, Jannu is a dark gravestone. I turn and shout to Houseman, but he doesn't hear. A thousand days of despair catch on the wind, but in an instant, the hands of the clock quicken even before we sit and celebrate a summit.

The next evening, during the long descent, I stand waiting for Houseman to set up the last abseil anchor. He searches for solid amid the crumbling rock. Somehow, he always finds them.

I look up and once again, in a slow-spinning sky, infinite stars twinkle. And from below in the still night, the soft jangle of yak bells floats across the creaking moraine. Even before we reach the ground, Chang Himal has dimmed into the past. Dreams dissolve into shadows. And with the door about to shut, the key unlocks another image. I see Youth fantasise with his new success behind him: *where do I go from here?*

And then I hear myself ask the same.

21 similar to a scottish quarry

January 2010
Rive Gauche, France

Kenton Cool abseiled into the Rive Gauche looking for a climb called *Home Wet Home*. He stood beneath a thinly iced cleft he originally thought was the climb. But it wasn't. Removing a glove, he pulled his mobile phone from a pocket and called Jon Griffith who was stood next to me on top of the crag. His opinion was delivered in the typical reserved Cool style.

'It looks shit, mate.'

I said I would abseil anyway and as I slid down the rope I became more excited by the metre. The climb looked steep, a tad loose in parts, a paint-streak of ice, not a lot in the way of protection. *Brilliant, brilliant, brilliant, what a line.* Lowering into the snow next to Kenton, I voiced my opinion.

'It looks amazing!'

'You're a fucking nutter.'

I set off and after one false start, got going properly. Kenton was not attached to anything as Jon Griffith, who wanted to take pictures, had pulled the abseil rope which would have been the sensible thing to belay from. The prospect of me falling and ripping us both down the crag was playing on everybody's mind, so I shouted to Jon who was hanging above and asked him to drop the rope with a loop. I clipped a runner to the loop and climbed past the first unprotected bulge. Once past the bulge, I placed the first piece of gear and everyone relaxed. Everyone except me, because looking up this thinly iced V-groove, it was not going to be easy or particularly safe.

I climbed, backfooting, tapping, cautiously tapping, udging, almost crawling. The intensity grew and as the intensity grew, the gear placements became fewer. The snout of the Argentière Glacier to our left inched forward and a frozen petal crumbled. In my dark cleft, the crash echoed. I really didn't want to repeat the episode from last year, which happened a little right of where I was ...

Tequila Stuntman is a modern mixed climb just to the left of the even better-known climb, *Nuit Blanche*. It was first climbed by Andy Parkin, Dave Hesleden and Neil Gresham. Unlike *Nuit Blanche*, *Tequila Stuntman* climbs steep ice on to a section of steep rock that leads to an ice dagger. Like *Nuit Blanche* it starts from a ledge halfway up the cliff and the approach is by abseil. I had climbed *Tequila Stuntman* a few days earlier with Pete Benson and Andy Houseman. When an ever-keen-to-climb Steve House had appeared in the valley and sent me a message, I suggested we go to climb both *Nuit Blanche* and *Tequila Stuntman* one after the other. Steve lapped it up. And standing on the ledge, having abseiled, my head was spinning a little.

Fuck, how did I get here?

By 'here' I didn't mean a little ledge halfway up a cliff about to climb *Tequila Stuntman*. What I *meant* was, 'How the hell did my life lead to climbing with Steve House?!' THE Steve House! This was the man who had climbed the *Slovak Direct* on Denali in a single sixty-hour push alongside Mark Twight and Scott Backes. This was the man who had climbed the Rupal Face on Nanga Parbat with Vince Anderson, one of the greatest alpine ascents ever. He had climbed *M16* on Howse Peak in winter with Barry Blanchard and Scott Backes, *North Twin* in winter with Marko Prezelj, Mount Alberta's north face in winter ... his regular climbing partners were a list of the most inspirational climbers that had ever walked the planet. He was a part of the brotherhood, he was the prophet, and his word was THE WAY!

WHAT THE FUCK?! STEVE FUCKING HOUSE!

'I'll start; I climbed it last week and the second pitch is the meat.'

'OK, Nick.'

Steve was attached to a screw with a loop of rope to allow him freedom to move around on the small and airy ledge. I quietly fluffed up my chest: Steve, THE Steve House, had used my first name.

I set off and immediately something felt wrong. I was climbing a thin thread of brittle. *Shit, wrong place.* Only I could be climbing for the first time with a god of alpinism and set off in the wrong place.

Ah well, keep going, in a few moves I'll be into the line, no problem.

The climbing was technical because of the nature of the icicle, but I had been climbing loads, it'd be OK, and I didn't want to faff about because this was THE Steve House belaying me – he had climbed the *Slovak* in less time than I had climbed the first few moves of *Tequila Stuntman*. But the moves were trickier and more pumpy than anything on the Rupal Face, I told myself. *Everything is fine, I'm cruising.*

Better put in a screw.

I normally wouldn't have bothered, but I didn't want THE Steve House to think he was climbing with a reckless fool. The ice in front of my face was only just thick enough for a screw and my feet were still on the thin thread. To place my body into a balanced position, I flagged the right leg behind the left.

Stylish. That'll impress Steve!

Hanging from one axe feeling very relaxed, I removed a screw and began to place it into the thicker dribbles in front of my face. I was hanging from my right arm and placing the screw left-handed.

Get this, I bet Steve is really impressed now, placing a screw left-handed.

The added pressure of pushing and twisting placed more force on the one front point that was placed into the icicle, holding my body in a tensed, strenuous position. Too much so in fact, and with one push and one twist, the icicle that my front point was placed into exploded, as did my grip. I shot from the climb quicker than you can say 'Slovak Direct' and hit the ledge at Steve's boots with a thud.

For a second, just one quick second, I thought of rolling over and kissing his boots and saying, 'I am not worthy', but I'm sure he would have rather I didn't, so I turned and looked up, up into the horror-stricken face of my hero, and in that face I could see a million thoughts, but the biggest and easiest-to-read thought was: *Who the fuck is this punter?*

In a flash, in an attempt to ease the situation, I said, 'Don't worry, Steve, it'll be fine, all my mates are used to me falling off.'

After a dusting down and Steve adding another three screws to the belay and shortening the rope between himself and the screws so it was now tight enough to play the 'Star-Spangled Banner', I set off again without any repercussions and afterwards we climbed *Nuit Blanche*.

A few days later Steve and I travelled to Kandersteg for more ice climbing, so I guess he must have decided I wasn't a total punter after all, or maybe he just couldn't find anyone else …

In a way, the climb that I was now attempting just to the left of *Tequila Stuntman* – this overhanging V-groove, this temptation with only just enough ice for progression – was perfect. It was everything I loved about climbing. The climbing was technical, but the psychology was intense. My back pushed against the overhanging groove and to the side I could press a thigh against rock and squirm, and in doing this, the weight reduced from my picks. At one point I had to commit both feet and both picks to the ice on the right wall. All of my weight now relied on a frozen mist that adhered so beautifully, it was almost illusion. Jon, hanging above taking pictures, screamed:

'Nick, for fuck's sake, stop it, you're terrifying me! I'll throw a rope!'

Generally, I'm not one of those climbers who needs quiet. On scary rock climbs, I prefer talk and banter; it takes my mind away from the possible consequences. On this occasion, the climbing was so intense and multi-dimensional, I needed to concentrate – to plan, spy, plot; this climb had all the elements of a John le Carré novel. If I committed before weighting a point, or knowing where to move, I would almost certainly fall, and the last runner was so far below anyway, it was almost in Italy.

'Jon, please be quiet.'

A few hours later, the first ascent of *Homeward Bound* was climbed. Kenton seconded the seventy-metre pitch and by the top had changed his opinion on the quality of the climb, though he nodded knowingly, convinced his judgement on my mental state was correct.

22
best before

Summer 2010
Llanberis, Wales

Through the drizzle, the upper levels of Vivian Quarry form a thin gash. The old mineworks – sheds made from hewn slate blocks, cutting tools, a narrow-gauge railway, ornate iron gates and a stone clock tower – are below the quarry, next to a modern visitor centre, a museum and gift shops selling slate trinkets and ice cream. At Christmas, a train takes children to visit Santa in a slate grotto. Middle-aged men in boiler suits and flat caps paint railway fences. They remind me of Dad.

I drive a little further before turning toward the centre of Llanberis town. The pebbledashed council house estate, the litter-strewn bus stop, and the telephone box with a broken window. A youth, who looks about sixteen years old, maybe seventeen, walks along the wet pavement. He walks behind others. All of them wear black uniform trousers and uniform blazers with Snowdon Railway badges sewn to the chest pocket. Seasonal, going-nowhere jobs. They look like pictures of workers walking the cobbled streets and red-brick alleyways of 1960s Manchester. The youth at the back of the group, his uniform hanging from a skinny frame, removes a cigarette from his mouth. Smoke billows about his young face. The youth reminds me of myself from the time I worked a dead-end, seasonal job at Alton Towers, but also from a time when life was fresh and work was grown-up and the world was big and there was so much time it didn't matter if the work I was doing wasted a week or a year or four years. Life was a seascape, a disappearing bird on the horizon. Real life was tomorrow, next month, next year.

The Hippy and I are on the hunt; we have high hopes that dry, unexplored rock can be found. Parking in front of the Rhoscolyn church we pack bags, but as the lid shuts tight, a cloud of drizzly fret blows in on a westerly.

What to do?

The Hippy and I sit in his car listening to the rain and Johnny Cash while watching the old folk, even older than The Hippy, huddle beneath umbrellas or scuttle into the church.

'It was better this time last year, eh?'

Almost a year ago to the day and in perfect weather, The Hippy and I had climbed a new route in Fallen Block Zawn. Climbing, especially new routing, always takes me back to the two-stroke motorbike stench from my teenage years. Never quite knowing how it was all going to turn out, sliding down the road, exploring a piece of the unexplored, tearing clothes, touching the untouched, ripping lumps of flesh out of my legs, wondering, dreaming, imagining. And after each fall on the bike, each fall from a climb, I'd pick myself up, get back on and kick down on the starter.

Earlier that morning an impromptu gathering at The Hippy's place found four of us – Hippy, Geordie Gary, Dave Simpson and me – drinking coffee.

'I paddled past an interesting-looking cliff, somewhat reminiscent of Mousetrap Zawn, the other day, Nick – just your kind of thing I reckon, loads of potential,' Dave said.

'Where was that then?'

It turned out that this mini Mousetrap was on the north coast of Anglesey and only had one established route, called *The Lost Pillar of Scheiser*. Now call me weird, but this was actually a route I knew about. I can't remember what it was that had originally drawn me to this climb, but words like *decomposing, rotting quartz vein, George Smith* and *XS* were all words that had been used and these are words I find inspiring. Only just warmed up for summer, still in the month of July – which was a month too early for adventure choss, as the bird bans didn't come off until August – The Hippy and I, bored of sitting in the rain, decided to 'go have a look'.

It was only going to be a look. Even though the bird bans were not applicable to the Anglesey north coast, The Hippy had a glint in his 'let's be mellow, man' eyes. Wheels spinning away I thought we might crash as the red bandana fell in front of his eyes, but he recovered and continued to drive in his somewhat aggressive and erratic style while weaving around the grass growing in the middle of the single track lane. After just minutes of looking down and reading the map I was ready to barf. But within about the same time it took The Man in Black to sing 'A Boy Named Sue', we were there.

Waves whipped by, the wind crashed and gulls screamed. Believe it or not as we walked and the sheep nuzzled grass on the deserted headland, the sun came out. Timing the dash between waves over swathes of popping seaweed, we came to a stop beneath a quartz pillar that cut the only semi-solid path through guano, mud and sand.

'Guess this is it then?'

The sea arch and the shingle beach would have made this an idyllic spot, but I was starting to sense enthusiasm sprouting from my old-enough-to-know-better climbing partner. Sitting down, still feeling carsick, the tune 'Don't Take Your Guns to Town' floated through my mind.

For once I was happy just to look around and chill, but I could sense trouble brewing. *Well, bugger that!* The Hippy could take on this overhanging tottering pile if he must, and for once I would take the soft option of the second.

'Shall we do it then?' I asked with trepidation, not wanting to sound like a lightweight and hoping The Hippy would see sense.

'We might as well as we are here.' The Red Bandana spurted enthusiasm, knowing he had a get-out clause.

'Who's going to do it then?' Big trepidation, knowing I didn't have a get-out clause.

'I'll give it a go.' The Hippy enthused even more, touched with blissful ignorance.

'OK.'

Big relief. Finally, I thought, *finally an easy ride up some chossy horror show.*

Riding my motorbike and long before The Man in Black, I wore red jeans, a wispy mohair jumper and Dr Martens, with the Sex Pistols providing my soundtrack. The revving engine screamed in time with Johnny Rotten and 'Anarchy in the UK'. I was free to choose, free to steer the direction my life would take.

I was free to walk away from this situation too, and as the ropes were laid at the base of the pillar, doubt reared its ugly head in the form of a line from the Tenpole Tudor song, 'Who Killed Bambi?': 'Never trust a hippy'. All I could envisage was The Hippy getting a little way up, filling the climb full of my gear and deciding it wasn't for him, and so leaving me in my delicate state of barfdom to take on the choss.

Shaking my head clear of this pessimistic punk-rock scenario, I settled in for a relaxing belay. The Hippy pootled off, a couple of metres and rising, nonchalantly pulling his white-jeaned form upward.

My, what bravery, what bottle … what foolishness. A foothold snapped leaving him hanging from one arm, but still he continued in the direction of imminent doom.

'Great, keep going, Hippy.'

Amazing, I thought, *this is actually going to happen.* For once I was on the sensible end of the rope while the nutter above skittered and pulled lumps and looked at a ground fall. My imagination pictured exploding gear and rock and The Hippy ricocheting all around.

So this is what it's like?

Another pull, a lump flew. Another pull, a foot skittered. And then it happened … for the first time since starting on this teetering journey of quartzite uncertainty, The Hippy started to thump the rock to test his holds. For the first time, he came out from his happy hippy place and realised that the whole pillar was detached …

'Shit! That hold I just banged above my head caused the rock I'm stood on to vibrate!'

Still feeling like I was going to barf and not feeling mentally prepared to take on this horror show, I offered kind words of encouragement – the kind of words your belayer often offers when they don't want to try the route.

'Go on, you're doing great! Keep it going, I'm with you all the way.'

… Which of course I wasn't, and I didn't really care if he was doing well or even if he landed with a mighty splatter among the seaweed at my feet. I just didn't want him to realise his mistake and back off.

The Hippy slowed, and pulled up and tested. He reversed, slowed some more and pulled up and tested some more. At last he pulled up one more move while smearing as much of his cheesecloth on as much decomposing rock as possible.

'Ahhh, ooooh, ahhhhhhh, ooooh … this whole pillar is moving! It's loose blocks piled on loose blocks, piled on the loose blocks that my gear is in … I don't like this any more … Your go.'

'Wanker.'

Yet again, in an attempt to escape the rain, The Hippy and I kick the starter and leave Llanberis and drive even further west. Heavy squalls hit the car as we head toward the Llŷn Peninsula. White horses riding the Irish Sea gallop alongside a westerly and mount the coast. The peninsula narrows. The sense that sea is all around is prevalent.

Driving through the popular holiday town of Abersoch, the semicircular bay is made up of fishing boats, speedboats, blue polypropylene nets and stationary Fordson Major tractors – the same make and model I remember from the hayfields of Staffordshire. The tractors are used for towing boats – boats worth more than several years' income for the farmers I used to work for. The relaxed and privileged holiday atmosphere always appears out of sync with the choice of our final destination.

Craig Dorys, Craig Dorys, Craig Dorys ... like a chant for the doomed. These are words that bring terror into the eyes of adults who wished they were still children. The Hippy and I are not children, but no matter how much we try to believe there are not bogeymen beneath the Craig Dorys stairs, we both know there are.

When we park in the farmyard at the top of the headland, the cows in the tin shed rub against rattling gates and the Jack Russell runs toward us, shaking her whole back end. Birds flit in the green hedgerow. But beneath the bright day, I feel the stirring of a storm.

The grass meadow with grazing stock is tranquil and the walk toward the headland is slow. The Hippy appears to be slowing his normal slowness, which is very slow. Eventually we reach the top of the crag where a gentle breeze blows in from the sea, hitting the crag and lifting. Standing on top of the cliff facing the full flow, I imagine clouds pouring over an escarpment. And in the breeze, in these imagined wind-clouds, the torture and wails of the insane can be heard.

'It feels early for this, Hippy.'

'Yes.'

Talk is at a minimum; we both have bad things on our minds.

Dorys comes in different scales of badness depending on which facet of the crag you are going to climb. Stigmata Buttress is bad. In fact, Stigmata is more bad than the baddest bad out there, but the lines are strong and as long as your will is as strong as the lines, or you lack imagination, you may stand a chance. Moving along the crag, the Upper Facet is actually very solid, the surface of the rock is a skin of quartz with pockets and breaks and gear and pegs. However, it is very steep with a chance the crag may get steeper as the whole rock face is a ginormous flake resembling a climbing wall that can be set at different angles. Byzantium Wall, a reasonably solid and imposing forty-metre wall of breaks and crimps, is next, and around the corner is the orange sheet of the Golden Wall. A slightly snappy, run-out, beautiful – in a femme fatale kind of way – vertical sheet of quartz, sand and clay. We are aiming for the femme fatale.

Warm-up done, this is a day for The Hippy, who for some reason has his sideways head attached, and before long, he begins shuffling following the first of two HVSs, *Scintillating Stitches*, complaining that his Tesco £1 reading glasses are not working and he can't see his feet … and all without the aid of a Zimmer frame! Naturally I am impressed. We finish going sideways and top out happy with our day of climbing, but mostly feeling happy to be alive, and so we run away, although of course, The Hippy's run is a slow-to-moderate walk.

18

19

18 Rob Greenwood aka Loud-Young-Youth on the crux of *The Citadel* on the Shelter Stone. It took Rob's enthusiasm and determination – but most of all the DMM credit card – to get me out climbing two days in a row on the Shelter Stone.

19 Christmas Day/birthday climb. The second ascent of *Terminator* on Craig Ddu, Llanberis Pass. Photo: Ray Wood.

20 *Byzantium* on Craig Dorys. One of the more standard and solid climbs on Stigmata Buttress. **Photo:** Ray Wood.

21 Guy Robertson on the first ascent of *Godzilla*, Coire Nan Fhamair, Beinn Bhàn, Applecross. This place always reminds me of Toscaig pier, handlining for crabs with Tami.

22 Me on the first winter ascent of *Central Route* on Llech Ddu. It snowed and snowed. After being isolated for fourteen hours while climbing we returned to Llanberis and entered a winter wonderland of abandoned cars. Fortunately the Berlingo had snow tyres fitted. **Photo:** Tim Neill.

23

24

23 Andy Houseman, early morning on Kyashar after a bit of a battle the night and day before. We traversed waist-deep snow and gained the crest and decided with one day of food we couldn't be bothered! Reaching Base Camp later that same day was very pleasant.

24 This ridge on Kyashar was the fun before the horror. Andy Houseman climbed a fantastic and bold lead on terrible rock soon after. **Photo**: Andy Houseman.

25

26

25 With the second ascent of *Guerdon Grooves* on the Slime Wall of Buachaille Etive Mòr, a climb that had a mythical status, I felt I could give up Scottish winter climbing. I didn't though. **Photo:** Colin Threlfall.
26 The *Slovak Direct*, Denali. Another mythical route with a big reputation. Climbing this settled me for quite a while. Mark Twight sent me a message congratulating us on our ascent, especially given the poor weather. Thanks Mark, that meant a lot. **Photo:** Andy Houseman.
27 Almost on the summit ridge of Denali. Relief. **Photo:** Andy Houseman.
28 Denali summit. Words cannot express the feeling of reaching this summit after some of the most sustained climbing while in such a serious situation. **Photo:** Andy Houseman.

29 The north face of Mount Alberta, Canada. It's my problem, but once a route, mountain or area becomes popular, it detracts from the experience and makes me want to look for something a little different. Photo: Bob Sandford.

30 Will Sim high on Alberta's north face. And the climbing just kept on coming.

31 Day three, retracing steps in an attempt to find the way off Alberta. After a forced bivouac on the eastern slopes, I thought I was going to die of hypothermia. Photo: Will Sim.

32

32 Will Sim leaves the cave bivouac on Alberta. It was a strange feeling being enclosed before stepping out once again into the exposure and hard climbing.
33 Paul Ramsden in our second bivouac on the North Buttress of Nyainqentangla South East. Paul was very happy with the 'snow nappy' that his mother-in-law had made for him … and so was I.
34 Me at the start of day two on Nyainqentangla. **Photo**: Paul Ramsden.
35 The liaison officer, me, the village leader, Paul, and the driver. This was taken after the climb. We were back in Lhasa later that same day. **Photo**: A local!

36

37

36 Day three and almost on the ridge of the North Buttress of Nyainqentangla South East. We dug a bivvy ledge soon after even though it was only 1 p.m. – we were knackered! **Photo**: Paul Ramsden.

37 Dad, *Jasper* and me. A surreal experience. This journey with my dearest friends Mark and Nikki and then my nephew Jake will remain with me for the rest of my life. Almost as intense an experience as any climb. **Photo**: Nikki Clayton.

23
death of paradise

Summer 2010
Craig Dorys, Wales

Spark plug flashes erupt from the Irish Sea and in the distance the Cardigan coastline is a blur. Standing at the top of Stigmata Buttress, Craig Dorys, I face into the breeze and watch a solitary gannet circling far out to sea; black pointed wing tips cut the salty air. The waves like the years roll on and never stop. Small pebbles at the edge of the sea are panned like gold. Large rocks with veins of quartz like Saturn's rings are rumbled, but like some people, the rocks remain stationary. Craig Dorys, a crumbling sea crag washed up on the Llŷn Peninsula, offers hope to the climber in search of more than just a grade.

Grey sealskin breaks the surface and sparkles silver. Porpoise fins slice the waves. The waves roll and pull the smooth grey pebbles. The sun's heat cracks the earth. Wire fencing is strung between old wooden posts. Rusty barbs wrapped with wool rock in the wind and the fence creaks. Clay bands between crumble-rock are sticky. The sun moves and once again warms the cliff. Joyous with the return of the sun, the rock lightens and the clay turns to dust. The dust catches in the breeze. And in the breeze, the dust sails over the sea.

Standing beneath Stigmata, it's all corners, overhangs and folds. A wave of crumbling choss bursts upward. This is about as steep as it gets on Dorys. My back faces west towards Ireland, toward the sun and the sea. Is life just flotsam, just a collection of experiences to be snatched up or left to drift away, forgotten? Standing in the dust and the rock chippings, forty-four years old, I still remember lying with a girl on a patterned carpet, enjoying teenage fumbles that feel as familiar as yesterday. Kick down on that starter motor, begin and challenge predestination; give the rapidly racing years a swift kick into tomorrow and make today last forever.

My back feels the warm sun, but my neck is in the shade. I stand beneath a Stevie Haston and Leigh McGinley climb called *Bam, Bam*. I have stood here many times and many times I have looked up. On one of those many occasions I belayed Dan McManus who was attempting an on-sight, but that was back before there was even a route here. At that time there was just one rusty wire poking from an exfoliating crack in the back of a corner, and there was much speculation of what would come above. Folklore said the wire belonged to Pat Littlejohn who had placed it on a ground-up attempt before lowering off. Caff had also attempted the line, but similar to the day I held Dan's ropes, had not climbed above the rusty wire, which was actually not high at all.

Like some mountain summits, does every piece of rock need to be touched by man or woman? I'm not sure it does, but be it from ego or desire to experience the euphoria of pushing oneself beyond what was once imagined possible, I become entranced. I am guilty. But the game we climbers play is trivial. It is not poverty, famine, homelessness, war, destitution or hopelessness. Sometimes we forget this and place too much importance on our personal endeavours, endeavours that actually mean very little to the majority of humanity. And as time passes and I become older, style and ethics in British rock climbing still remain important, but honesty and treating fellow human beings with empathy and compassion and understanding becomes more important to me, as it should.

The line with the one rusty wire became the route called *Bam, Bam* in 2009. 'We cleaned it on an abseil first; we must have removed a mini-skip's worth of loose rock,' Leigh McGinley explained about his and Stevie Haston's cleaning of the line before the first ascent. Jack Geldard climbed the first on-sight and second ascent, and I seconded Caff in 2009 on the third ascent three weeks later.

I look up. I want to try and lead *Bam, Bam*. It is nearly a year since I followed Caff and even though the rock is so steep as to never see rain, it is close to the sea. It has felt the full force of winter storms and the lingering sea fret. The holds are no longer chalky. The three previous ascensionists had intimate knowledge of which holds to use – or, more importantly, the best holds to avoid – either by cleaning and inspecting and preplacing gear in the initial groove, or by using chalked holds. When I followed Caff,

I climbed quick and snatched the gear without stopping. I noticed very little of the climb and remember nothing, apart from how tired my arms had been at the top and how the only holds I had touched glowed white with chalk.

After Haston and McGinley's cleaning and ascent of *Bam, Bam* there had been internet musings about the tactics that had been used. Haston answered the question, 'Is there a ground-up ethic on the Llŷn?' with 'Some people say there is but I have never been part of it, or agreed with it, or forced people to it. I have actually disagreed with it several times.'

The day I seconded *Bam, Bam,* Caff had mentioned a line to the right, which was also a Haston line. I do not know the name of the climb, the description or the exact line but I remember what Caff said.

'Haston told me never to try to on-sight the line because I would die.'

I walk to the right and stand beneath the cliff and I imagine Haston at the base grabbing handfuls of rock and grinding them to dust.

'Wake up, Hippy, and give me a belay.'

I lower a rope down the crag in what I think is the approximate location of the climb to the right of *Bam, Bam*. The end touches on to the wasteland at the base and is so far out, it appears to be some kind of rope trick.

'I'm going to take some gear to clip the rope as I abseil, it's the only way to be near the rock.'

The day passes. The sun sweeps the blue. Gin palace yachts rumble through the smooth water. We could be in the Mediterranean, but the cliff at which we have set our stall might have been in the mines of Llanberis, so dark its mood. But *my* mood is one of vibrancy and hunger. The climb is called *Melody* and the thought of pulling on those first holds with the intention of continuing on lead is both horrifying and thrilling.

After the dark, quarried slate and the rain, the now arid atmosphere of the Llŷn feels like an illusion. But when I look out past the water-worn boulders, I realise that this is real, this is now. The waves lapping the tessellated rock shelf mark this time, my time. The next wave arrives and washes my thoughts out to sea, and the clock keeps moving forward.

On top rope, I climb the whole forty metres of *Melody* twice. It's a route of two halves: the first consists of overhanging waves and lumps of compressed and creaking mudstone, threaded with seams of orange fudge and quartz. Nearly all the rock shifts, and anything can break at any time. For protection, the lower wall has three in-situ pegs. The first peg is part of *Rust Never Sleeps,* which traverses right, but it's too low to be of much use for *Melody*. The second and third are low and close together – thin, flaking, tied off. Should the rock break, there's not much hope of walking away.

If the rock doesn't break, you climb up and up without protection until the base of a hanging corner and a small exfoliating moon crater. Grey, orange, dust and clay – you make an awkward squirm pushing your back to the moving wall of the left side of the hanging corner and a high foot smeared to an unreliable, nasty mound of dirt. At last there is a cam and the first protection since the pegs almost at the start of the climb. At the top of the corner there are scabs of damp quartz that fingers have to wrap and a sticky crack in a fold that takes another cam. Capping the corner is an overhang that fingers can spider around before pulling and crawling to the ledge that marks the halfway point of the climb.

With the breeze ruffling my clothes and puckering the forty-four-year-old skin of my face, I sit on that halfway ledge with the earth behind and the water in front and the brackish air all around, and I remember a young man straddling a motorbike with his life ahead of him. I remember the blurred hues of flowers in the hedgerow. Fear threads my thoughts and entwines with other feelings that loiter just beneath the surface: excitement, the unknown, destiny. An inner voice tries to convince me that I will be bold enough, good enough. It also speaks of opportunity and lost chances, of the then and the now and maybe the never.

The second half of *Melody* is like a painted canvas: orange with patches of silver moss, pocked, fallible edges, exfoliating seams, dusty brown scallops. A hand-placed peg and a tiny cam in a thin, shallow, fragile seam provide nearly the only protection for about ten metres until you reach the end of the orange section, and then two deep breaks take good cams.

I climb a metre and a half to the right from the highest of the two breaks and follow a series of holds that lead to the top. I shout to The Hippy. He pops his red bandana head over the edge, rubs his sleepy eyes, and agrees this looks like the most obvious way. At this point, neither The Hippy nor I know the line or even the name of the climb, but later I read the route description on the internet. I realise that Haston must have continued direct using a small, slug-shaped crimp to make a long stretch across blank stone followed by a lunge. It would be so easy to miss that lunge. It would be heartbreaking to fall after surviving everything below.

Climbing is a strange activity. We persuade ourselves to choose this or that piece of rock when we could walk to the top or take an easier route. The original finishing move of *Melody* feels forced to me, so I decide, if and when the time comes to lead the climb, I will follow the way that I have on first inspection. This way appears to make sense; it is more certain.

Two days pass before I stand in the sun on top of the pillar at the start of *Melody*.

'You OK, Hippy? You're not going to fall asleep?'

A loose stone has just hit the earth, bounced and rolled away. *That'll keep him alert.* The dark, creaking face towers overhead. I'm here because I have to be. I've decided that this is for me and that's all there is. I grip the untrust-worthy holds, arms held aloft, surrendering. The Hippy shuffles to avoid more flying rock, and I wonder if in some way he *has to be here* also. It's as if he still has to be involved in this motorbike ride, at whatever speed and in whatever format.

I decide to place my own pegs alongside the original pegs. I don't consider mine to be any better or worse than Haston's, but at least they aren't rusty and I know exactly how fallible they are. I don't question my ethics; the pegs only protect the first few moves, and pegs are common at Craig Dorys because the protection on the steeper sections is almost non-existent.

I pull up and begin to climb, and possibly, for the first time since I started to climb in 1991, my mind is quiet, almost numb. Cutting loose, heel-hooking, pulling rock so steep as to feel like an indoor wall, I try not to think of what would happen should a hold break. But when I reach the halfway ledge, I can't believe I'm already here. Where did the time go? *Seven years have passed since I left the prison service. What have I done in all that time? Where will I be in another nine years?* The orange wall above looks down with a creaking brow. 'Come up here and challenge your future,' it calls.

I step up, squeezing a crumbling edge, and eyeball the hand-placed peg and the very small cam. Life has become simple. I press my fingertips on small edges that bow like springy wood. Cam lobes brushing crunchy fins a little higher give no confidence, but it looks good to have the ropes running through something. A friend, Ray Wood, watches from the edge of the cliff, his mop of hair dark against the bright sky. The wall bulges between us, and the toeholds decrease; it looks as if it will take a lifetime to reach him.

I hope The Hippy is awake. My mind is close to shutting down. Quickly, I enter a practised sequence of crumbling finger pockets and sandy toeholds, and then I'm through and nearly out to the other side. Ahead, there's one more section of difficult moves, carbon-like columns that have visited me like ghosts in the night. But I feel good. I have strength in my arms, and the boldest part is below me. Clinging to edges, I imagine hanging from the deep crack above and placing the large cam that will give me belief to continue. But I'll have to use holds that might break. The rubber of my shoes pressed to smooth rock stabilises. I think of the rubber-nobbled back wheel of my motorbike, and for just a second it's gripping, gripping the road … my fingers grip, grip the creaking flakes … the wall blurs … both finger holds have snapped. I scream and scream and fall and scream …

Cat-sitting, I spend three days and three nights in my ex-partner Helen's house near Llanberis. I drink red wine and try not to think about what would have happened if the hand-placed peg and the small cam had failed. I'd fallen, but been saved by the most slender of margins.

It's strange to be here in this house and not really feel any connection or loss, how I've changed or how time has eased the pain. It feels good to be friends with Helen once again, and as I lie I thank her for this; it was her insistence and persistence that encouraged the renewed friendship. Life really is too short. It's been three years since we broke up. Time doesn't stop – well, not until that inevitable final moment. Are all relationships like this – illusions of love? Will time always heal and will someone else always come along to take my place or her place?

I walk the length of the kitchen, the wooden floor bows, and I look through a rain-streaked window at wet mounds of discarded slate. The back garden is overgrown: silver birch, thick fibrous marsh grass, bramble and slate miners' sheds. Water drips. The dark slate heaps look darker still …

Three days later I'm back at Craig Dorys.

'We may have a problem,' Ray Wood says, as we draw into the farmyard and see the car of Stevie's regular partner, Leigh McGinley.

Stevie lives in the French Pyrenees, but he is visiting. Twin ropes, taut with bodyweight, run down the line of *Melody*. The Hippy lies on his stomach. Rock crunches as he drags his old body forward. He stops with his head just over the cliff.

Haston is hanging from the ropes in space, swinging and twisting and shouting. 'Hi Stevie!' The Hippy says. The Hippy is always friendly.

A burst of adjectives rises like the sound of a motorbike accelerating. Haston abseils, hits the dirt and sprints like a cheetah, heading for the path to the top of the cliff.

'Shall we go?' Ray says.

Shuffling and jittery, flicking stones with shoes, we stand nervously. It has been seven years since I left the prison service but almost immediately I am transported back to the dark days. The sparkling sea, the green fields, the cows and sheep, the distant beaches – they all close in, become grey, confining walls. A sprinting dot appears on the horizon. I imagine I am at a door telling someone they cannot come in or go out, knowing there will be no compromise, just aggression. My stomach twists.

'Maybe he's just pleased that someone is showing an interest in his route?' I say to the other two, in an attempt to lighten the mood.

In shouting distance now, Haston yells, 'DON'T YOU DARE SMILE, DON'T YOU *DARE* FUCKING SMILE.' I quickly surmise he isn't happy at all.

I think that it is an interesting thing to shout at someone standing very near the edge of a cliff, when confronted by an angry man. The last thing I can think of doing at this moment is smiling. I recall some of the folklore that surrounds this man and his ferocious reputation. I have friends that have been on the receiving end of some of it. I also think of all of the climbs … a solo of the *Walker Spur* in winter, *Nuit Blanche, Terminator, Angel Dust, Me, Isis is Angry* and *The Empire Strikes Back*. I respect this man and his achievements within climbing; he uses imagination and courage. To me, his faults are obvious and visible, but climbing needs individuals and characters, and all of the stories of aggression have been blown out of proportion, surely?

'DON'T YOU DARE FUCKING SMILE.'

This peaceful area has suddenly become a prison. Seven years have passed. Seven years and within seconds I feel the bile rising … no; smiling is the last thing I am going to do.

'YOU'RE NOT GOOD ENOUGH. WHO GAVE YOU PERMISSION TO PUT PEGS INTO MY ROUTE?'

'The pegs are old, Stevie, they're rusty, I've just backed up the old with new.'

Suddenly I remember there are three of us, three against one, what are we playing at? I turn to see Ray, who is very thin, attempting to hide by squeezing his very thin frame in a very small horizontal crack.

The Hippy has been slowly easing his aged body from its lying position into a sitting position. I think *this is it, this is it, The Hippy is coming to my rescue, here he comes, here he comes …* but all he does is sit there. He tells me later he thought Stevie may find his lying down disrespectful, hence the careful easing to a sitting position.

With the movement, Haston jumps at The Hippy and shouts into his face.

'YOU'RE OLD ENOUGH TO KNOW BETTER; THOSE PEGS ARE PERFECT.'

I think about sprinting at this point – fuck The Hippy, fuck Ray, every man for themselves. But then I remember Stevie has been training for an ultramarathon and I imagine myself days later, still running with Stevie still fuming and angry, slowly catching up.

'YOU'RE NOT GOOD ENOUGH, YOU'RE NOT EVEN USING THE CORRECT HOLDS, AND YOU'RE USING THE LEDGE: ONE OF THE HARDEST MOVES IS CLIMBING PAST THE LEDGE WITHOUT USING IT.'

His argument doesn't make sense; how can I not be using the correct holds? And as for not using the ledge that *has* to be climbed on to and past, it is unimaginable. I also recall the statement he had made the previous year about not making anyone abide by 'his' rules or crag ethics, but choose to keep it to myself. I stand and listen and apologise, not wanting to inflame the situation, but I feel my self-respect diminishing.

'I'm sorry, Stevie; I didn't mean to upset you.'

'UPSET ME? UPSET ME? I'M MORE THAN FUCKING UPSET! YOU'RE LUCKY I'M MELLOW NOW. I'M TAKING YOUR PEGS OUT.'

We wait, and when Stevie slides down the rope, we run away.

The Hippy and I returned later that summer to Craig Dorys and climbed a new route which we called *Blood Meridian*, but as the days turned to weeks and the summer turned to winter, I felt bullied and robbed of an experience; my new-found life in Llanberis was tainted.

24

the pitfalls of a peroni supermodel

December 2010
Llanberis, Wales

I could not believe it: winter weather had attacked Wales and for once I had decided to stay. Wales had become a frozen wasteland. The multicoloured Llanberis shopfronts aged – silver eyelashes adorned window sills, gutters wept icicles, Llyn Padarn had cellophane stretched around its edge. A cormorant was perched on the edge of the rowing boat, webbed feet slipping on icy wood. People walked down the centre of Llanberis wearing wellington boots with skis or snowboards over their shoulders. A muffled stillness had hit the Llanberis Pass. Streams, hidden beneath the snow, gurgled like crevasses. The slate molehills surrounding the town resembled moguls.

Christmas approached and I wrapped new routes like proverbial presents. The second ascent of Haston's *Terminator* on Christmas morning brought back some bad summer memories, so I refused to be drawn into saying anything about the climb apart from how good it was. The biggest gift of the Welsh winter was a fourteen-hour outing on Llech Ddu in the Carneddau with Tim Neill. A persistent snowstorm added to the memory as we climbed the summer line of *Central Route* and afterwards, as we returned to Llanberis, we found it now resembled an alpine village.

Come the New Year, Scotland was also in good shape.

January 2011
Aviemore, Scotland

The Glenmore Lodge bar heaved a fusty fug. The throng swayed. Beer flowed.

Driving builds a thirst and having driven from Llanberis my thirst was overwhelming. Dougal Haston looked down from behind his glass frame hanging high on the panelled wall, and winked. Primarily I had driven to Scotland to present a lecture to the Association of Mountaineering Instructors (AMI) on the Saturday evening, but climbing was also high on my agenda. Andy Houseman, my climbing partner for Saturday, stood next to me chatting and drinking and being his usual charming self.

'On no account can I miss this lecture, Youth! I need a short day. We will have to climb in the Northern Corries.'

I had arranged to climb on Sunday also, but this time with DMM rep Rob Greenwood. Rob, super-psyched, super-fit, super-loud, super-young (in fact, younger than Youth) Greenwood.

I lifted the long, slim, supermodel-shaped glass. The glass had a swirling Italian pattern and the word Peroni etched into the side. The glass oozed sex appeal. It fitted my hand perfectly as I grabbed it suggestively. Even better, it was three-quarters full of strong lager. I smacked my lips. I was happy with my lot; this winter was already turning into one of the best.

Houseman leant toward me. The hubbub increased. For a second, big dark eyes locked mine and he wore a concerned expression. To be heard above the beer-fuelled revelling, he leant even closer. The smell of temptation and corruption and intrigue wafted on his persuasive Yorkshire baritone and crawled into my ear.

The Peroni supermodel was now wearing a long yellow skirt with only a frothy blouse to cover her curvaceous bosom.

'Benson reckons the Shelter Stone is plastered. Guy Robertson and Pete Macpherson did a new route there yesterday ... ' Youth schemed.

'Really ... ?'

'Really!'

'Really!'

Houseman, who knew exactly what he was doing, continued conspiratorially.

'I'd love to climb *The Citadel*.'

'Fuck. Dammit. *The Citadel!*' I cried, vulnerable to his coercion.

The Peroni supermodel was now indecent. A short pair of yellow socks was all she sported.

My head swam with opportunities and possibilities. My head swam with consequences. My employer for the lecture was DMM; they had paid for my fuel and were paying a wage. Chris Rowland, DMM's brand manager, was soft and fluffy, the laughing policeman of the outdoor business. Chris loved the fact that I climbed and climbed and climbed ... If I missed the lecture, Chris would not be the problem.

Ed Chard, head of AMI training, was an ex-guardsman. Ed had a shaved head, tattoos, was seven feet tall in his wool socks and had a frame that would scare pissed-off polar bears. Ed was not called Big Ed for nothing! The whole weekend was Ed's baby. Ed had asked me in the summer if I was available for the lecture, and confidently, I had said, 'Ed, no worries, you can rely on me.' Now, standing in this sweaty bar, I knew if I let Ed down, the consequences would have painful repercussions. Ed would be the problem!

'Fuck it, OK, Youth, let's climb *The Citadel*.'

Just at this moment, my climbing partner for Sunday pressed another fully dressed Italian supermodel into my hand. I lifted her to my lips ... She was gorgeous. She was tall and sleek and cool to the touch. I took off her top in one quick manoeuvre.

'Houseman and I are going to climb *The Citadel* tomorrow, Rob.'

'NOOOO, YOU CAN'T, BECAUSE THAT'S WHAT I WANT TO CLIMB WITH YOU ON SUNDAY, ON SUNDAY ... THIS SUNDAY!' He delivered his dismay in a tenor/counter-tenor.

Rob's young, fresh face dropped. Blue eyes brimmed. Bottom lip quivered. I had the feeling I had just entered the cast of a tragic Italian opera and I was now playing the lead role of drunken jester. I really hate letting folk down, especially when they are about to collapse and cry in front of me. But what was I to do? And then, in one swift moment of un-thought-out inspiration, my mouth sang, 'OK, no problem. Andy and I can climb *The Needle* tomorrow, then you and I will climb *The Citadel* on Sunday. On Sunday, on Sunday we can climb *The Citadel*! Yes, on Sunday ... '

I looked left at Not-So-Youth and then right at Loud-Young-Youth, and both were nodding their heads vigorously.

Shit.

Walking the length of the bar, or what had now transformed into a stage,

I began to feel concerned.

'Hi Ed … '

Ed unfolded from his chair and stood up and enveloped my hand inside a great paw and proceeded to crush it.

I looked a long way up in an attempt to see Ed's face. When I eventually focused on his features I could see they were rimed.

'Erm, what is the latest time I can start the lecture tomorrow?'

'Eight thirty … why do you ask, Nick?' His voice boomed a low and manly bass. Then he stepped one massive step nearer. I stood in his shade and icicles formed. My mouth puckered, and I nervously quaffed the supermodel's skirt from the second – or was it the third? – Peroni fling I was having. Instantly I wished I'd had another.

'Well, I was thinking of climbing *The Needle* on the Shelter Stone tomorrow. Yes, before the lecture.'

'Better not drink any more of those then. It wouldn't be good if you missed the lecture – if you missed the lecture it could prove painful, oh yes, very painful if you missed the lecture … '

Not-So-Youth swung his van into the car park at 6 a.m. It was snowing. Cloud and spindrift swirled the tarmac. I had the feeling that the crescendo was about to unfold.

'OK, let's go,' I said, sounding confident, but secretly hoping the weather would stop us in the Northern Corries. My hand still ached from Big Ed's grip, and his booming voice Pavarottied through my mind …

It wouldn't be good if you missed the lecture, no, it wouldn't be good, oh no, not good, not good.

Some time later, at a flattening, we stood in the rain. A steep slope led into the Loch Avon basin. The cloud obscured everything, then it didn't, then it did … and the rain immediately turned all it touched to verglas. My rucksack had a clean clear sheen covering it like cling film. My walking poles glittered.

'How about sacking it off and dropping in to Coire an Lochain?' I suggested, trying not to sound too enthusiastic.

'Yeah, it is bad, isn't it?'

Team Sheffield, a group of four climbers, two of whom were friends, stood huddled nearby. We had mercifully bumped into them just as our map had caught on the wind and flown away into the murk.

'What were you thinking of doing?' Nick Wallace asked.

'*The Needle*, but it's looking doubtful now, so we may just go into Coire an Lochain.' I could read his mind: *That Bullock talks a good climb, but he is just an impostor, a pretender!*

One of Team Sheffield, whom I had only just met, swung to face me. He looked at my boots and, ever so slowly, passed a withering stare over the length of my body before finishing at my hooded head.

'We are going to go and have a look anyway,' he added.

And with that, Youth and I swam down into the wind, rain and cloud, down into the Loch Avon basin. Down into the wind tearing up the slope, down into what was becoming a complicated maelstrom of my own making. It was everything that made the storyline of an opera: lust and greed, love and desire, and with every step I could hear a booming bass.

It wouldn't be good if you missed the lecture, oh no, not good, not good, especially not good for yoooooooou …

Youth and I stood beneath the Shelter Stone. The crag rose out of the snow as stern and upright and as solid as Big Ed on duty outside Buckingham Palace.

'Where does the route start?'

It was then that I realised I knew nothing about this climb apart from the name. I didn't know the grade, the length, the history, the line, the first ascensionists … All I knew was that I had some recollection from distant memory that it was hard and someone had bivvied on the first winter ascent that wasn't very long ago.

Not good for yooooooou …

We rock-paper-scissored for who would go first. Not-So-Youth won …

That evening, standing in the dark and wind at the top of the goat track before dropping into Sneachda, spindrift slapped my face. The sodium glow of Aviemore spread orange across the horizon; it reminded me of looking down to Courmayeur from the Grandes Jorasses. I felt like singing. I called Loud-Young-Youth and left a voicemail message on his phone …

'Tell Ed not to worry, it's six o'clock now, I'll be at the lodge at seven. You don't fancy a short day in the Corries tomorrow, do you?'

As I stumbled and ran and skated from Coire an t-Sneachda, I wondered what spin I could put on it to convince Loud-Young-Youth that it made sense to climb in the Northern Corries on Sunday.

The bar, if anything, was even more of a steam and sweat and fug than the previous evening. The framed picture of Dougal Haston flooded with condensation. My lecture was about to start and I had hit Loud-Young-Youth with every excuse and every reason why it would be better to convenience climb tomorrow and have an adventure the day after. Dougal, looking down through streaming condensation, raised both eyebrows and shook his woolly hatted head disapprovingly.

'I'll check the weather,' said Loud-Young-Youth.

I knew this reprieve was only for a matter of seconds, as unbeknown to Rob I had already checked the forecast and Sunday was OK apart from the possibility of high wind. Monday was looking bad.

I held tonight's supermodel. She sported an even more alluring yellow number than the night before. I lifted her, and winked at Dougal.

Loud-Young-Youth returned.

'Tomorrow is definitely the day, Nick!' his young chirpy voice chirped.

My legs almost buckled with fatigue.

But as quick as my delicious supermodel was undressing, I played my trump card.

'All the gear is soaking and hanging in the chalet, and the lodge folk say I have to empty my room by 5 p.m., and I have to do my lecture now, and it's going to be too late to sort it all before an early start, and I haven't sharpened my picks, and I need to change my underpants, and I need to wash my hair, and, and, and … '

Loud-Young-Youth, obviously a better card player than I and obviously a fan of the ongoing opera, chose to play his trump card in a perfect tenor pitch ….

'I have the DMM credit card. I'll see if I can book us into a room tomorrow night, and get your stuff moved into it while we are climbing.'

Bollocks.

Standing on a chair, swinging my arms around reliving some Gogarth falling-down horror show, I turned toward the audience. My next Peroni supermodel was being graciously helped down the staircase on a conveyor belt of hands. Loud-Young-Youth stood at the top of the lecture theatre stairs. He had a wide smile running from young ear to young ear and his big blue eyes sparkled. Both thumbs were up …

25

what were his dreams?

March 2011
Llanberis, Wales

Rich Sawbridge had been one of my fellow PE instructors from HMP Welford Road in Leicester, and he still had some of my belongings stored at his house. I drove from Luton Airport after a trip to climb new routes on the Lofoten Islands in Norway and called him.

'Long time and all of that.' I started the conversation.

'Yeah, how are things?'

'Good.'

'Hey, you won't have heard about Bob, will you?'

'No, what has he done now?' I asked.

'A few months after retiring, just after you left the prison, he was diagnosed with stomach cancer and died three months later.'

I became interested in training as a PE instructor after two and a half years on the landings of B Wing in Gartree Prison. Two and a half years of opening and closing, opening and closing. The steel door would bang, the air inside the cell displaced, the door's locking mechanism would clunk, and the round tally on the outside of the door with its white-painted groove would turn from vertical to horizontal to show the lock had slid home and the door was secure.

After two and a half years I had had enough. It took another two years before I was physically fit and had the experience to begin the PE instructor training, but my life had focus. It was on a visit to HMP Welford Road – the Victorian prison in the centre of Leicester – with Tony Buckle, another trainee PE instructor, that I first met Bob McFadden.

Bob was a member of the three-man PE instructor team at Welford Road, and something of an enigma. Steve Brown, the senior PE instructor, and Nige Masters, also a PE instructor, were both friendly, fun and easy to be around. Bob, on the other hand, was a wiry Yorkshireman who blew hot or cold; there was very little moderation in Bob. He was a Marmite man. People loved him or hated him, and when they hated him, they hated him with a passion. When in full flow, which was more often than not, he held nothing back, not an ounce; he was combustible. I grew to know Bob well and spent quite a lot of time in his company, and in that time I watched him fight on the rugby pitch, fight on the basketball court, fight on the five-a-side football pitch, fight on the gym floor, fight on dance floors, fight in car parks, pubs, weight-training rooms. When Bob became my boss at the Welford Road gym he was facing disciplinary charges after complaints from inmates and even members of staff.

Bob was a very knowledgeable basketball and rugby coach, but his delivery and ability to get his knowledge across were often lost on a large proportion of the people he instructed because his manner was blunt and aggressive. As a boss he was hell to work with because Tony and Rich, the two other PE instructors, and I, did not know from one hour to the next Bob's mood or motivations. One day he could be very conscientious and the next we could be shutting the gym and heading to the pub, where at some point we would possibly have to pull Bob from a fight.

I first met Bob in 1990, and soon after we played on the same rugby team, and we drank together; he taught, trained and helped. And even with his massive character faults and inconsistencies, I thought the world of Bob. He was extremely generous, so much so that when I applied for the PE instructor job at Welford Road and Bob was the boss, I knew the job was mine before it was advertised. Somewhere underneath and inside that wiry, complex and fragile Yorkshireman was a very lovable, very generous and large-hearted person.

In 2003, when I handed in my resignation from the prison service it was into Bob's hand that I passed the letter. I dreaded giving my resignation to Bob because I knew he would take it personally; he would have seen it as me deserting him, letting the side down. But it was OK in the end, because Bob was fifty-five and he was about to retire, so it wasn't a problem. He was happy for me and I was happy for him, and when I left the prison for the last time in October 2003, I hadn't seen Bob in weeks because he was using up his annual leave before he retired.

Ensconced in Ynys Ettws, winter had left Wales. Snow had been replaced by rain, and as I sat looking through the windows at a rain-soaked Llanberis Pass, I thought about Bob and how unfair and delicately balanced life was and how easy it would be to miss out on much it had to offer.

My phone rang, breaking my thoughts.

Guy Robertson's zeal travelled across the airwaves and bellowed when I answered.

'Now then, Bullhorn, are you coming climbing with Benson and me at Applecross on Monday?'

I held the phone at a distance from my ear. In some broad Scottish blather I could hardly understand, Robbo continued, but I did catch the words: Godfather, Applecross, new direct, raving Sassenach.

The first time I met Guy was at about 6 a.m. on a clear and crisp morning outside a tent shared with Pete Benson and pitched near the CIC Hut beneath Ben Nevis's north face. Pete and I had flown from poor conditions in Chamonix to Scotland. The tent unzipped, and the raging ball of stick-thin Highland fury that is Guy Robertson was there in the flesh – but not that much flesh.

Robbo and I immediately bonded and soon after the three of us set off to attempt the first winter ascent of the four-star summer E1, *Minus One Direct*. Robbo and Pete had tried the line several years before but were forced to retreat in a sudden thaw. There was no thaw on that day, and in the dark we returned to the tent with the first winter ascent completed.

Since *Minus One Direct* Robbo has become a great mate, but he is someone with whom I occasionally bicker and argue, possibly because I see a lot of myself in him. I recognise the conflict, the anger, the frustration. Some young climbers today, in my mind, appear to lack humility and are full of hubris. But maybe this is an age-difference thing, maybe this is my fragility, because beneath it all, I think both Guy and I dislike ageing and we want to continue in a similar vein to that we have already experienced.

I could say the opportunity to eventually climb on Beinn Bhàn, near Applecross, was what pushed me into driving north. I could say 'life is short and opportunities have to be taken', but it wasn't that either. The warm thought of placing some English blood in the middle of all of that rich Celtic goop was what eventually did it. It was also the thought of how I would feel if I didn't go and they nailed some great big new route without me. FOMO – fear of missing out – was all the extra encouragement I needed to spend eleven hours behind the wheel and £120 on fuel. It was also these occasions I loved the most. This, being able to get up and go, drop anything, this was the thing that made my roaming, and at times my being on my own, worth it.

April 2011
Applecross, Scotland

Sun-wind-rain. Sun-wind-rain. Cloud-rain-sleet. Snow-white-out-dark. Deer stood at the side of the road trembling. I pulled into the parking spot just before the stone bridge at the start of the steep and winding Bealach na Bà and waited, while memories drifted by me.

> Mum, Dad, my sister Lesley, me and Tami, our golden Labrador, had travelled from Cheadle to Applecross for a camping holiday. It felt like Dad had transported us to another planet. Thirteen out of fourteen days it rained. To fill the days we would head to the shop in Lochcarron, tracing the bends and hairpins down the Bealach na Bà, or, as it translates in English, the Pass of the Cattle. Dad loved driving that road. There were many days we ended up handline fishing in the rain on the deserted Toscaig pier. Eagles glided over the cliffs – cliffs that thirty-five years later I would climb. Tami gobbled mussels quicker than we could clear them of their purple shell. The mussel, pierced by a three-barb hook, all slippery and orange and salt-smelling, was good bait for catching crabs. But on one occasion, we swung the mussels pierced by hooks and Tami – quick as a greedy Labrador – dashed out, snapping her jaws shut around it. We had caught a Labrador. The barb was lodged deep inside her cheek. Dad was careful and gentle as he removed the hook, and Tami trusted him implicitly.

At 10 p.m. a car pulled up behind my van and illuminated the Bealach na Bà sign. I opened the back doors and peered out into the night that was now lit with yellow. The blue Peugeot parked next to my Berlingo rocked with Scottish determination.

'Ach, look, Bullhorn is all wrapped up in his festering love pit.'

Pete, as intelligent and articulate as he was, always managed to surprise me with his Glaswegian gutter.

'Piglet, how are you? And where is the saviour of Scottish winter climbing?'

The passenger door burst open and ejected into the Highland emptiness was enthusiasm, hope and success; a powerball of skinny Scottish energy. Balanced somewhere, just above his head, I imagined a halo made of glowing purple thistle, blazing a message into the dark that read 'NO SURRENDER'.

I knew that no matter what, tomorrow was going to be memorable.

The following night, I drove towards the CC Hut, Riasg, at Roybridge. It was midnight and throughout the two-hour drive I stopped and jumped several times from the van. My legs were wracked with cramps, but I was happy: Pete, Robbo and I had climbed a new six-pitch route we later called *Godzilla,* and the cliffs from my childhood had brought back many memories.

Packed inside the maroon Austin Maxi with Lesley at my side and Mum in the passenger seat, Dad drove along the narrow lane in Applecross leading to the campsite. The rain constantly fell and the tunnel of trees dripped heavily. Slowing to negotiate the narrow entrance to the campsite, Dad slammed the brakes on as a stag broke out from the trees. The creature hesitated, billowing steam and flashing dark eyes before vaulting the fence and the bonnet of the car in one. Antlers like weapons, red, rippled muscles, a smoke of breath from an open mouth. And then he was gone, lost to the mist and dark hanging between the trunks of pine – just a ghost, a memory.

I drove into the night with legs cramping and jumping, a grown man with the dreams and aspirations of a younger man. In that night, with the snow on the side of the road, I followed the tyre tracks of a maroon Austin Maxi that was driven by a man, younger than I was then. *What were his dreams, his aspirations?*

Mum had owned two Morris Minor Travellers; Dad had lovingly and meticulously renovated both. The Morris Minor Traveller was the forerunner of the modern estate car, and had an exposed wooden frame. Dad spent hours every weekend working on the first of Mum's Travellers, a green one. And then when they sold that one – probably because someone offered

> Dad a good profit – he did an even bigger restoration job on the second, grey one. He replaced, sanded, polished and eventually varnished the wood; he completely resprayed the whole of the bodywork with hand-held spray cans. I remember looking through the glass windows in the wooden doors of the asbestos garage, watching Dad sand, spray, sand, spray … the wood was covered by newspaper held in place with masking tape, and Dad only came out from the garage to receive a fresh cuppa when Mum made one. He put hours and hours into restoring that car for Mum and when it was done it shone. Mum loved it.
>
> One weekend I went out early hunting rabbits with my ferrets and when I returned the police were at the house. The Morris Traveller had been stolen and later it was found burnt out. Mum was in the kitchen crying. She had always left the keys in the car ignition, so it had just been a case of pushing it from the drive and starting it up. Mum was so upset. 'Oh, love, it's all the work your Dad put into doing it up.'
>
> *What were his dreams?*

Driving south, I was headed to my nephew's wedding, and later in the day I sat inside a stone church in the middle of Harpenden. Dad was sitting next to me, his face ravaged by alcoholism, his nose orange peel. The service running order was printed on a piece of yellow card balanced on the wooden shelf in front. I looked at the hymns and saw one was *Jerusalem,* written by the poet William Blake. I turned to Dad.

'Look at this; *Jerusalem* was written by William Blake, I didn't know that.'

Dad turned to me for a second and said, 'So what? A mate of yours, is he?' and turned away.

26
balloons

April 2011
Kathmandu, Nepal

The plane jetted Andy Houseman and me east via India and now we are in Kathmandu. All of the baggage, the food, the tents, climbing gear, boots, sleeping bags, the coffee pot and so on are heading toward Lukla, and tomorrow we will leave Kathmandu and follow our gear. The Hinku Valley, a valley I have travelled through twice before, will be familiar but the experience will be different and the mountain we are hoping to attempt will certainly be different; it's almost impossible to say what will happen.

I wake and walk along the early morning Thamel streets heading toward Java, the cafe with my preferred brand of coffee. Between Thamel buildings, an early morning slice of sun reflects shoals of silver. The smell of the night is heavy in the gutter. A woman squats. Fingers break the surface of the water that is held inside a blue bucket. Tears dampening dust.

A smear of blood on the pavement. The smell of stale piss. Sun-dried vomit. Rotting vegetables wrapped in see-through plastic. The pavement supports a bundle of sleeping lads. Skinny chaffinch-legs and grass-stalk arms poke out from this mound of rags, boys and dogs.

A mop of black matted hair, punk-spiky, belongs to one boy who is striking in a grubby, town-fox kind of way. His eyes are brooding, bloodshot, old and young all at once. This lad never begs. He plays, he fights, he sleeps, he forages for food, or scavenges, taking the food wrapped and rotting in see-through plastic. He gets high. Breathing in chemicals. In and out, in and out. An inflating and deflating toxic balloon. His face hides behind the balloon and then shows. He's just a child.

April 2011
Lukla, Nepal

Houseman and I, having caught the early flight, sit outside Paradise Lodge in the early morning cold. This place holds so many memories. I see ghosts. The last time I sat here with Houseman we had been attempting a new route on Peak 41. The trip had been cut short when our whole base camp, and everything in it, had been robbed. Sitting here, I remember waking on that morning in the bedroom above …

A cloud of condensation crawled from my mouth. The condensation wet the fabric near my face. I rolled and pulled the sleeping bag around my shoulders and stared at the plywood. Outside the window, feet shuffled in the dirt and a cockerel crowed his wake-up. A screech of rubber hitting the runway and the roar of an engine drowned the crow of the cockerel.

I lay on the narrow bed in Paradise Lodge feeling robbed – robbed of all our gear and robbed of the chance to climb a new route on Peak 41; robbed of an experience. I rolled again, pulling the bag over my head in an attempt to delay. Houseman, lying in the bed next to me, also wrapped against the cold, shuffled. A voice outside, out on the lodge veranda, pulled me from my lethargy. The voice was English. I couldn't place the accent but it was broad and friendly and welcoming.

I pulled myself up, turned and looked down to the white plastic table that filled the veranda near the entrance to the lodge. And for a moment, I had returned in time to my first visit to Lukla in 2003, five years before, and sitting in the thin, smoke-filled air, at that very table with Jules and Al Powell, that very table where the English guy now sat smoking a cigarette and drinking a mug of milky tea. He reminded me so much of Cartwright, all tall and gangly with an unruly clump of hair, unshaven, smoking and emanating an air of 'this is where I belong'. I pulled myself out of the sleeping bag, grabbed a cuppa and went to speak to the guy outside.

His name was Chris Walker and he was guiding a group, but unlike some of the 'guides' I had encountered in the Khumbu, it was obvious that Chris was very much at home and experienced – in the place he wanted to be. We gelled immediately – shared stories, another brew and more stories. Houseman turned up and joined in. It turned out we had mutual friends and had climbed some of the same climbs. Houseman and I were both fed up

> having had most of our gear robbed from our base camp, but talking to Chris, his enthusiasm and excitement at being in the mountains rubbed off. It reminded us that we would be back; we would once again feel a similar excitement.

I never met Chris Walker again. Chris died while walking down the spur to the right of the gully on Buachaille Etive Mòr, Glen Coe – the gully that Michael Tweedley and I had climbed on the approach before Michael's near-fatal fall after our ascent of *Raven's Edge*. I remember when I heard about the accident; it took me back immediately to that morning in Lukla and how speaking to him had lifted both Houseman and me. But this time, instead of gear, something so easy to replace, I knew the world had been robbed. Whenever I think of that morning, I still feel robbed of the chance to get to know Chris, but I know my loss can be nothing to that of those who knew and loved him.

April 2011
Tagnag, Nepal

The snow fell every afternoon during mine and Andy's attempt to climb the south pillar of Kyashar, a rock route in the upper section. The weather was disappointing, but base camp times were fun as The Hippy and Ben O'Connor Croft had turned up to share the camp and attempt to climb Kusum Kanguru. After a few weeks, Houseman and I decided to change objectives to the west ridge – a striking line that had only been climbed once before.

Leaving Tagnag at midnight, the threatening approach was climbed without incident until about eleven in the morning when we straddled the snowed-up rock ridge running between Kusum Kanguru and Kyashar at a height of 5,800 metres. To either side, snow-covered cliffs dropped to green meadows. Looking ahead at the snowed-up, tottering pile of rock buttress guarding the west ridge, we hoped there was something easier, or at least something more in keeping with the conditions, around the corner.

Around the corner, snow and hail poured down the face. Mist swirled, drips of water dropped from overhanging rock and soaked into clothing. There was no ice. The snow covering the rock was powder, not a single patch of névé. The rock was loose. It was impossible to say whether the hooks or torques were going to hold. At one point, belaying, I leant my back against a large, person-sized spike of rock and it tumbled down the face leaving me tight on the anchors. The ropes beneath were still in one piece but my nerves were frayed.

Traversing on to the west face, looking into the deep cloud-filled valley of the Khumbu kilometres away, the air was empty. Houseman led the final two pitches to the snowy west ridge while I planned. I planned how to get us off the face. I planned for the time when Houseman might rip a block and his fall strip half a pitch. I planned for the boulders following in his wake. After a while of standing, belaying, shivering, thinking, I stopped planning. It was eight hours since we had traversed on to the west face and nineteen hours since leaving Base Camp – 1,600 metres of vertical ascent into our lightweight quick push; eventually we were above the technical difficulties. At seven in the evening we dug into snow beneath a boulder. We were travelling light, but not that fast. The hill was winning.

A few hours of digging was followed by a few minutes of eating. The crescent moon gleamed. Stars that make up the Plough blinked.

We woke at 3 a.m. and by 5 a.m. had begun traversing to the west ridge. Our single day of rations had been eaten. All that remained – a few gels and bars – felt pretty insubstantial. I waded thigh-deep snow and knew that the summit of Kyashar was not going to happen.

Returning to Kathmandu the failure is not easy. I question my abilities, determination and drive. But the style of the climbing, be it successful or a failure, is the most important thing. I reconcile with myself. I am, after all, searching for experiences and not just a summit. Or am I fooling myself with platitudes, and really do I just crave the admiration a successful summit gives? As a PE instructor I was taught that strength is admirable, but strength without skill is nothing. I take a similar philosophy to the mountains and say: to climb a mountain is admirable, but to climb a mountain using a whole host of techniques, gear, gadgets and human support is nothing.

The street boys in Kathmandu lie baking on the pavement. As I walk in the afternoon sun, I think about our climb, about our style of ascent and what it all means … and in the end I come up with the answer: it means nothing.

Once again I fly from Kathmandu leaving behind the complexities of life on the pavement and escape back to my Llanberis.

June 2011
Llanberis, Wales

Living in the Llanberis Pass is an escape ... but escape is the wrong word. It isn't an escape; it is real. It is real life: real memories in the making, a simple existence. Rock climbing on a daily basis, watching the weather and the sheep. This is my existence at the moment and the simplicity suits and relaxes me. Finding sequences to enable passage through folds of rock means nothing, solves nothing and cures nothing. It doesn't help fight injustice and inequality. It doesn't help the homeless or the starving. It does not end war.

I sit and wonder. I wonder if there really is a choice for everyone and I come to the conclusion there isn't, there really isn't! Not everyone is fortunate or lucky or brave or healthy enough to make the leap, whatever the leap may be. Many will not have had the upbringing to give the confidence that is needed to take chances and to make the choices they may have preferred. I'm sure to many people my writing and view on life sounds at times like I'm haughty and looking down from my climbing castle and gloating. This has never been my intention. Did I set out to inspire? No, not really, because when I left the prison I set out to have the best life for me, a life that would help me and my situation; I did not take a chance for anyone else.

Not everyone who would like to has the option to be able to climb for weeks at a time. But I do think it is an option within reach of some, though certainly not all. But there may be opportunities for many to take that first step and move into the unknown. It could be stepping out of a front door, a walk around the park, or accepting that life means different things to different people, and acquiring an understanding that not everyone can do what they want to do all the time. But for the people who are unhappy with their 'regular' lives – and I know many people are *not* unhappy with their 'regular' lives, people who make scathing comments about the life I have chosen, I do wonder if they act this way because they feel held back, not bold enough to take a chance for themselves?

August 2011
Anglesey, Wales

I spotted a space last year – a space on the overhanging fin that has the climbs *Godzilla, The Jub-Jub Bird* and *The Trail of Tears* at Rhoscolyn, Anglesey. The Hippy and I had walked the grass until we stood above the fin. The Hippy's thinning hair poking out from beneath his woollen beanie flicked into his eyes. The sea shimmered. I abseiled, but oh my god was it steep. So steep in fact that inspecting was almost impossible. But as I slid into the orange depths, I could see holds … holds of a sort, although they looked more like something you find in a foil packet and dip into a jar of salsa. Gear? Yes, there looked to be some of that also. Sliding lower and lower, down and down, it pumped my forearms just looking. We ran away. But after looking again this year, the Hippy and I accepted the challenge.

The first dabble on a top rope was fun. No. No, I lie. The first dabble was *terrifying*. Lowering into that place, lowering into the overhanging space beneath the fin, felt like a Salvador Dali painting. My mind howled, but down I went, totally in The Hippy's hands. Down into the fiery depths. Being the first ever to pull on those flakes, flakes I expected to burst like a boil, I felt close to madness itself. But I pulled anyway and immediately pumped out. The rope pulled me upward; The Hippy above sitting in his blissfully ignorant world of sun and cigarettes and whatever else, took in the rope too tight and I wanted to reverse but the rope pulled and pulled and pulled, and I swung to lunge for a manky piece of tat threaded through the eye of the ancient peg in *Godzilla*, the climb to my right. And the rope pulled and I hung in space, surfing like Superman (but not feeling like Superman), while all the time I was clutching, gripping, squeezing a flake in one hand and the tat in the other. And The Hippy, The Bloody Hippy, was sitting above smoking and sunbathing and half asleep.

FOR GOD'S SAKE, HIPPY.

Desperate, desperate, I wanted down, but I was flying and surfing up … and as I jerkily went up in my flying position I prayed. Oh did I pray …

Oh Lord, if I ever get out of here, I promise to be good. But only after I punch seven shades of shit out of The Hippy.

'Slack, slack, slack, slack, SLACK!' I chanted.

The Hippy awoke from his sun-induced coma and eventually lowered me. I stuffed a cam into the offwidth crack of *Godzilla* and clipped to it –

hopefully now the old duffer above wouldn't rip me clean from the face once again. Eventually I managed to commit and tentatively, ever so tentatively, I pulled on the undercut flakes. The world turned black.

Upon reaching a rail in the middle of the fin, try and try and try as I did, I couldn't fathom a way to continue, and eventually I let go and swung, ready to unleash the secret technical weapon.

The Hippy lowered, not really looking like the secret technical weapon; he looked more like the secret technical wimp as he wittered on about being scared. His red bandana fell in front of his reading glasses and he used that as an excuse to delay. I fed rope out quickly and jerkily, making him squeak. Eventually he swung into the flake of *Godzilla* and attempted to climb the undercut traverse that leads into the middle of the overhanging fin … and the rail where he had a technical whitey and refused to move.

'I'M SCARED.'

Eventually he established himself above the undercut flake moves, without actually pulling on any holds, and set to solving the mystery of the top. And eventually he did solve the puzzle, by using some really small things.

Fuck; it's a boulder problem!

Six visits later, we had many memories, a new pair of rock shoes, the loss of skin, a monster lob and many, many funny hours stored. The best moment being from The Hippy, whimpering and begging me not to lower him.

'I don't want to go down there, it's a scary place! No, no, please don't make me go down there!'

'Shut up, Hippy, get on with it!'

The route was climbed and *The Frumious Bandersnatch* was its name.

September 2011
Craig Dorys, Wales

A year has passed since my encounter with Stevie at the top of his route, and with the fitness that has come from climbing *The Frumious Bandersnatch* – and unfortunately with a mind that does not easily let things go – I check easyJet to make sure there is not a Mr Haston travelling to Britain. When it appears there isn't, it feels as good a time as any to return to Craig Dorys for another attempt at *Melody*.

It's too late. It's too warm. Forty metres is such a small distance, but forty metres at this moment feels so far – it could be a lifetime.

I imagine once more: cutting loose, lifting feet, clinging to crunchy flakes and picking quartz scabs. I imagine fingers probing orange, creaking crimps and fingering collapsing pockets ... and imagine is all there is today.

Leaving the crag, The Hippy and I decide on an early start the next day in an attempt to beat the heat.

An alpine start sorts it and it is a terrifying yet freeing day. I successfully climb *Melody*. The original pegs that Haston placed in 2005 are the only pegs I use and the holds are the same finishing holds as on the first ascent. I stand at the top of the crag looking out to sea and think: possibly I am good enough, after all.

27
that's rowdy, dude

January 2012
Scotland

I walk through Glenmore Lodge's double doors and immediately I breathe the familiar air, thick with anticipation. The air clings to the wood, it clings to the leather sofas, the cushioned chairs and the reception counter. It fills my nostrils and crawls through the veins that make up my body.

Having attended two summer BMC International Meets but never a winter meet, I know roughly what to expect but winter climbing is so much more involved than summer cragging in Wales. The thought of being strapped to a wad for a week of rain takes more courage than I have possessed in the past. In the weeks running up to the meet, I had winter climbed in Scotland plenty, but I had found myself getting nervous, I dreaded my international partner saying the words, 'Take me to the Shelter Stone.' I imagined wandering with some superstar in a white-out, lost, walking like souls in Dante's Inferno on the Cairngorm plateau. I imagined the universal internet lynching of a supposedly competent mountaineer. I was sure I would be strapped to someone who could actually climb a bit, and when it was revealed I was pretty average, I would be called a fraud and ostracised and sent to the dark lonely place that pretenders go to – and *boy* do pretenders get short shrift from behind the computer keyboards in today's society.

'We've put you for the week with a nice New England, East-Coast American, Nick,' Becky McGovern says in her northern way. *Great,* I think, although because of Becky and her track record for sandbagging, I'm not sure. At least he will speak English though; result! Well, a kind of English, and he will no doubt know my friends Freddie Wilkinson, Kev Mahoney and Ben Gilmore, who at the drop of a hat will forgo climbing for drinking.

Brilliant. One quick route each day in the Northern Corries and then the bar. No chance to get him, or myself, lost. Maybe I can hold it together on one short route and not give the game away about my lack of climbing ability.

I shook Bayard Russell's hand, my partner for the coming week: he had a firm grip and his stature resembled a small but solid freight train. And what a relief; he had that New Hampshire laid-back accent, the same as Freddie, Kev and Ben – this could work!

Walking into the Northern Corries on day one didn't go to plan. Floundering about in a white-out, I appeared to have lost the Lochain, the easiest place to find in the whole of Scotland. Bayard was talking and laughing while I quietly stressed because the corrie didn't look like the corrie. The cloud thinned for a second and I spotted a spur.

'Right, let's look over there.'

Relief was the sound of someone shouting and the clank of a hex.

'Wow, it's out of condition, hey?'

'Whatdoyoumean?' I gabbled, surprised.

'Well, dude, it's all white and covered in snow.'

'Yeah, that's how it should be.'

'WHAT? ... Really? ... Man, that's rad!'

OK, I thought, *I might stand a chance.*

Once we'd found the climbing, the next thing to do was find a climb. The Lochain was swarming with bods from the meet; they looked surprised when I asked them where the climb *Pic 'n' Mix* was. Their surprise, I felt, was not because of the route I sought, but more because I didn't know where it was. Once I was pointed in the direction of the climb, I front-pointed towards the huge finger-pinnacle that was materialising from the mist.

All around me were folk I knew. Dave Garry was on *The Hoarmaster* and Si Frost was climbing *Hooker's Corner*. Perfect; both Dave and Si had climbed *Pic 'n' Mix* so I yelled and asked them where it went. Other climbers looked aghast that I appeared to know nothing about the climb. And they were right; I didn't even know the grade, but in the fog of my mind I remembered Tim Emmett thrashing away in some film alongside Ian Parnell who looked up and laughed his demented laugh. Someone had also told me it was all on good hooks and had gear. Perfect.

Bayard cruised the first pitch, which was good; one more pitch and we could go drink beer and be awesome in the bar.

Dave yelled across from his climb. 'When you leave the belay, pull into the crack, and if you want to go straight up, it's never been done in winter – the original goes around to the right.'

Always looking for simple, I thanked Dave and left the belay. Yes, there was a crack and it looked OK. A few moves and I had turned from the bumbly punter who couldn't find the crag into Ueli Steck – in my mind, anyway. God I was good, it was easy! What was Tim thinking going around the corner and not finishing the job? He must have been having a bad day. A few more moves and the verglas increased, along with the wind, the spiky hoar and the steepness.

It's OK, I'm Ueli.

A few more moves and still no gear.

Perched high on the front face of the pinnacle the wind beat my body; my jacket flapped like a sparrow's feathers. I locked off with one arm and faffed around with the other to get protection: a nut, a cam, a bigger cam, a bigger nut, but eventually I dropped a hook into the hole made by my pick. And then I dropped another hook into another hole alongside the first and continued. Bayard, a long way below, was huddled in his jacket thinking this was normal. I flapped and swung my arms to encourage blood and scratted to find a good torque, good feet, good anything.

In a few short metres my Ueli Steck bubble burst. The left pick was placed into a rounded crack and repeatedly snatched free. Feet skittered. I brushed big ears of hoar from the surface of the rock. The snow covered me. I looked wistfully to a sloping ledge on my left. I had to move, but there was nothing obvious for the feet and it also meant leaving my one good hook and I really didn't want to do that.

Bayard looked up. 'Go on, send it, dude!' But the only thing I was going to be sending, if I blew this, was for a helicopter.

A head popped over the top of the crag.

'Hey, Nick, I'm just going to set up and film.'

It was James Dunn, the cameraman for the meet. *Great,* I thought. Now my ineptitude at climbing, followed by my blood-curdling scream ending in a messy death, was going to be watched by millions and they will all sit together in the theatre saying stuff like, 'It doesn't look that hard' and 'I thought he was meant to be good?'

I leant left and fished and scraped but found nothing positive. In desperation, I reverted to my hard-won Canadian tactic and dragged the pick down the slab above until it caught on what I can only imagine was a ripple. Swap feet, right pick into the rounded crack, flag left leg.

Holy shit, what am I doing here?

James, above me, looked happy. No, actually he looked ecstatic; I could see the pound signs rolling in his eyes. It was on the tip of my tongue and I nearly said it. I nearly said those immortal words: *Throw me a fucking rope.* But suddenly I was pulling. And then the right pick blew. My body barn-doored. I was twisting and swinging. The good foothold popped. I was twisting, pivoting. Three points of contact, I was hinging on two that so easily could be one that would then in turn be none. I threw a glance at the left pick holding me and I imagined the ripple it snagged. I looked into the air that I would no doubt be tasting.

Holding the barn door, hyperventilating, I replaced the right pick and the right foot. I leant and matched, placing both picks on the ripple. Inside my creaking head there was the sound of ravens pecking. I pulled up, smeared a foot and threw a leg on top of the sloping ledge and as I did my left pick blew.

'ARGHHH!'

Taking as much weight with my leg as I could, I fished above for a pick placement in the small roof of a groove. There was nothing good, but I pulled anyway. James turned away; even he had lost the stomach, although his camera remained pointed. The upside-down pick held and I kneeled on the ledge, dry heaving, lungs on fire.

'Dude, that was rowdy … '

All I could think was how I had nearly killed Nico Favresse on day one of the summer meet and now I was doing the same to myself.

The meet continued in a slightly more controlled way after that. The next day I followed Jen Olson and Bayard on *Daddy Longlegs,* also in the Northern Corries, and we took a rest the day after. Lochnagar and *Trail of Tears* was the climb the day after and, being old, we rested on Friday in anticipation of a big final Saturday, when Bayard and I would be teaming up with the Scottish messiah of psyche, Guy Robertson. I emailed Robbo to ask the plan and the response was disturbing.

'Nick, I've been training hard and climbing easy routes and I'm getting nervous and jittery; I'm borderline ANGRY! We will go to the Buachaille … '

Walking in in the dark on Saturday morning past Lagangarbh over iced puddles, we looked up and, like a vision from a dream, there was a white wave running down Slime Wall. Robbo turned to me.

'It's on, it's on, MY GOD, IT'S ON!'

As Robbo had not actually said what the plan was I could only guess that whatever it was, it was *on*.

I had always dreamed of climbing the mythical *Guerdon Grooves*. *Guerdon Grooves* was first climbed in winter by Dave Cuthbertson and Arthur Paul in 1984 and had never had a second ascent. Climbers whispered when they spoke of it. At the start of each winter, internet forums would always have a thread guessing the grade of *Guerdon Grooves* and ruminating on whether it would ever be climbed in winter again. *Guerdon* was mythical, a dream, a magician's trick. And with every step up the hill, the anticipation increased – well, for Robbo and me; Bayard just thought it was another day on the hill in Scotland.

We started to climb at approximately 10 a.m. and with each move, the anticipation and history and myth intensified. The crux of this climb was coping with the folklore. I could see Cubby teetering and run out, creeping up snow-covered slabs. I could see Dai Lampard trudging up the approach slopes four times. I could see MacInnes, Bonington and Patey just across the way in *Raven's Gully*.

At 6 p.m., all three of us stood on the top; the route was climbed. Robbo's anger was quelled. Bayard, knowing nothing about the history of the climb, thought it had been 'an awesome outing, dude', but I could tell it was lost on him. And for me? Well, I thought I could now give up Scottish winter climbing.

28
over the top

May 2012
Llanberis, Wales

I was adamant that I would stay in North Wales climbing rock for the summer. Twice I refused Andy Houseman's plea to be his partner and go climbing in Alaska. Andy, being a Yorkshireman, drives a hard bargain.

On the first phone call he told me his sponsors would fund the park and peak fee and the accommodation in Anchorage. I turned him down.

On the second phone call he told me his sponsors would fund the park and peak fee, the accommodation in Anchorage, the food and the flight. I turned him down – I really wanted to climb rock in Wales.

On the third phone call I asked him what it was he wanted to climb in Alaska, and he replied the *Slovak Direct* on Denali.

June arrived, and instead of climbing rock in Wales, I sat alongside Andy on a plane flying over the Atlantic heading towards Alaska.

June 2012
Denali, Alaska, USA

Shadows of familiar things – walls made from sawn snow blocks, tents dug into drifts, skis standing to attention – stretched across the snow in the glare of the mid-morning sun. Rucksacks packed, Houseman and I left Denali's camp at 14,000 feet (4,270 metres) and headed for a prominent spur – the West Rib – high above the village of tents that had been our home for the last three weeks.

Following the well-trodden furrow, we walked past the board with the weather forecast, and the ranger station with its ice-encrusted cables hanging from solar panels. I looked to the left; the Denali West Buttress human train was heading to Camp 17,000. Since arriving on the Kahiltna Glacier I had encountered some strange people: a guy intent on soloing the West Buttress with long bamboo poles in the shape of a cross strapped to his body; a middle-aged woman who wanted to become the first Indian female soloist; a guy with chain mail draped over his tent and a large pole sporting flags from several countries with which he had no connection ... the list was nearly as long as the line of people. It never failed to amaze me how a mountain attached to a significant altitude or designation attracted so many trophy hunters.

Reaching the West Rib, we started downclimbing, abseiling and jumping the numerous crevasses; our tracks were a spider silk sticking a thousand holes and we felt like flies. Colin Haley had suggested the Seattle 72 Ramp for approaching the *Slovak Direct*, our intended climb, but climbing into and out of the Northeast Fork, I was beginning to wonder if Colin had a different take on what was acceptable. The *Slovak Direct* had seen five ascents since 1984, but this was the first time anyone had started the climb by this approach. I jumped down a three-metre ice wall, having thrown my rucksack first, and cursed Colin. The approach was an expedition in its own right.

Sprinting beneath séracs loosely bonded on to the cliffs, the skin of my lungs shredded. Houseman out front continued to jog and I, attached to him by the rope, continued to gasp. Clearing the embedded debris from previous sérac falls, I collapsed and quickly untied: at forty-six years old I was more in fear of further running attached to the incredibly 'off-the-couch fit, but also getting older' Youth ... than falling down a slot.

We ate while sitting on a snow step cut into the slope beneath the Japanese Couloir at the start of the Cassin Ridge. I stared into the maw of the Kahiltna's Northeast Fork, also known as the Valley of Death, the 'usual' approach for Denali's West Rib and the Cassin. The corridor was threatened by large ice slugs clinging to the steep sides of the valley, and in my mind they were slipping, slowly slipping until they'd fall and crash, filling the valley below.

The sun waned and clouds began to creep along the capillary of glaciers. Foraker's bulk poked from the cloud, a thick finger pointing to stars – stars that we would never see in the twenty-four-hour daylight. I sat, and as I sat, I quietly prayed that this mythical route – a route Steve House was quoted as saying was his first world-class climb – would happen. It had to happen;

I didn't want to dwell on the consequences of failure in such a remote place.

Two in the morning. Emptiness. We climbed on to the crest of the Cassin before several abseils down the original start landed us on the East Fork Glacier. Cracks split the ice. I felt the tension in the glacier transmit up through the soles of my boots, running into my legs and finally into my mind. *This climb is a space walk.* Our heads tilted. Transfixed, we watched the sun escape the grip of the mountain and we began to warm to our route. Shadows of two lonely people smeared the creaking glacier. This was to be the final day of the settled weather, but we didn't know this at the time. If the forecast had been correct, if we had known that the day after would be unsettled, would we have set off or would we have run off?

Having studied the sérac hanging over the start of the route and the second sérac to the right – a monster called Big Bertha that separates the fifty-eight technical pitches of the *Slovak* from the then 'easy' 1,000 metres of the Cassin – we decided to wait until evening and cold. Houseman erected the little tent while I lay on my mat.

Surrounded by a semicircle of some of the largest and most sheer mountain cliffs in the world, we lay and waited. And waited and waited. And eventually wilted like freshly cut flowers. Rocks rattled. Séracs released. The glacier groaned. I groaned, but sitting up and looking, *really* looking, I reminded myself of the special emptiness that engulfed us.

In the night, which was of course part of the twenty-four-hour day, feeling sucked dry and jaded, it took us a while to remember how privileged we were to be in this lonely place. Packing rucksacks, Big Bertha decided it was her time. An echoing boom and then icebergs exploding down the face. The collapsing sérac filled the cirque with sound.

'Shall we run?'

'Damn right!'

Grabbing bags, crampons, water bottle and boots – all arms and gear – Houseman being younger got the better start. I stood watching the snow-cloud eating the glacier and I stopped trying to collect, and just accepted. Bertha's freshly cut finger clipping lost power, but the wind and the crystals, like the shockwave of a blown-up tower block, dusted my clothes, covering me in perfect frozen stars.

Once again, setting out, the sérac directly above the beginning of the climb crumbled. We decided to give it an hour more.

The wall is big. Mark Westman had made the fifth ascent of the *Slovak* with Jesse Huey, whose words sliced my brain:

'From halfway it's only one way: over the top. Reverse is not an option.'

I imagined it, over the top. Over the top … the top felt like another life. I recalled Mark Twight's writing:

'Twenty-four hours into it, and almost 4,000' up the route, we passed the point of no return. The Czechs had climbed forty-three pitches to reach the same spot. We didn't have enough anchors to retreat, the terrain would have swallowed us.'

Over the top I imagined us knackered, battling a storm, out of food, out of energy … over the top of the highest summit in North America. Were we good enough? Maybe this whole outing was over the top? After all, approaching the climb had already taken two days. But the wall was quiet now and running away would make us no different to many of the people we had met on the glacier – people who had escaped the city in search of a trophy. People who in my mind had no right to be on a mountain with the reputation that Denali holds. But were Houseman and I any different?

Crossing the bergschrund, I snatched a glance at Houseman and caught him looking at the horizon. *Bloody hell, I now trust this man that was once The Youth. We have shared so much.* The clear blue sky from the past six days had disappeared; it was now strangled by grey. We were in for some weather. I turned and continued, swinging and kicking, the barrier in my mind had been crossed; it was similar to beginning a workout in the gym, knowing that you are about to give everything. I accepted all of it, but still I felt nauseous. The door was open with only one exit: 2,800 metres of climbing. At that point it would still be easy to turn, to take the sensible option given the imminent bad weather, but I kept on plugging without saying a word.

Four meals and five days of gels and bars – the sum of the food we had left Camp 14,000 with. Already two of the meals and two days of bars and gels had been eaten. Sheer and intimidating granite cliffs enticed us, stabbing the mist that engulfed everything. The emptiness, the loneliness – it had presence. I thought of the Slovenians on the first ascent and the eleven days this climb had taken. Mahoney and Gilmore on the second ascent had taken seven days. Who the hell did we think we were to get on this with so little food?

Climbing rotten rock, bubbled water-ice, rotten ice, an overhanging ice chimney, torquing picks into cracks and joined by the rope, we moved together and pitched. Large fat flakes of snow filled the sky. I zipped up my hood and swore. Sometimes it doesn't feel right to push, but this time I felt angry, angry like my friend Robbo had been, and I let the anger feed my body and fuel my drive. Reaching a bergschrund splitting the first ice field we decided to stop. Huey had told us this was the only good bivvy site on the whole of the route, so after nine hours, a quarter of the way, we took it in preparation for a big second day.

'It's really windy up high,' Andy said, looking up.

Setting out at 3 a.m., we traversed the ice slope and followed thinly iced gutters. Like entering an underpass in the city, the half light ignited my imagination: will we reach the steps that lead to the daylight on the other side of the road or will the mountain mug us? Tower blocks twisted. The sky between these monoliths was streaked with red. Plumes of spindrift ripped from the summit slopes and flushed the gutters between the skyscrapers.

Houseman led us deeper still, until he was beneath a huge corner with continuous dribbles and overhanging blossoms of ice. Seventy metres below, I couldn't see into the corner.

'What's it look like?'

Houseman's answer was succinct. 'Scary.'

One hundred metres up the corner, I took the lead – forty metres remained. The wall to my left, a sheet of the most perfect granite, blushed and covered me in a vale of spindrift as if embarrassed by my floundering human effort. I pulled around an ice bulge, pushing a front point into a small imperfection on the left wall, and felt like a blot on the most beautiful feature I had had the fortune to taint.

As I sat in the wind and the sun having escaped the corner, Houseman was still below being pounded by snow, still sucking skinny, robbed-of-oxygen air. The powder clouds exploded all around him. We were getting somewhere, but behind me, a porcelain arête pointed the way to the most technical pitch of the route.

I've never really understood rock, paper, scissors, and stood next to Houseman, beneath the crux wall, it was obvious he didn't either. Like gunslingers, three times we had drawn gloved hands and three times we had pointed smoking scissors. I didn't know how a stone or a piece of paper was expressed, so on the fourth draw, I pulled scissors again, and Houseman pulled a clenched fist, a rock, and we both concluded I had won. It wasn't until I was about to set off we realised that a rock blunts scissors. Oh well …

Rumour had it that this A2 pitch would go free at about M8. I stepped from the snow without wearing my pack.

Sketching, breathing deep, picks twisted in flared cracks, crampon points sparking, I was still climbing without resting or a fall; biceps began to cramp, drained of energy from the corner below. Nearly at the top of the wall, a few metres of hard climbing remained, but looking up, I saw there were going to be several more difficult moves with very few footholds. I was out of cams to protect the climbing to come. My mind screamed, *Do it! Do it, get on with it!*

And then in a flash, another voice shouted, *What the fuck are you trying to prove?*

I had spent too long on this pitch already. I had pushed, run it out, I had already risked breaking an ankle or worse, and we were now at the point where getting off the climb would turn into an epic – especially if injured. I reversed to my last piece of gear.

'Take.'

Almost immediately I felt like a let-down – not good enough. The mindset to be able to push in good style a million miles from anywhere is what makes the difference, and on this occasion I had found myself lacking. But in another moment, I felt good about not pushing on: it didn't matter, we were still there, still climbing … maybe not only Houseman had grown over the years?

Houseman lowered me and took over using whatever style he could to get us back on track, and in an hour or so we were both above the crux, heading into a deeper wilderness, heading into the grey of what would have been night, if night was something that happened there. More than at any other time on the climb, I accepted that we had now reached the point where it would be better to go up and over than to reverse. Over the top. Over the top. Twists and turns.

Houseman, battling, was out front. Spindrift clouds wrapped around and blinded. Having tried so hard to climb the crux pitch, my energy levels were low. I cursed my stupidity. Huddling beneath a boulder, fighting sleep and cramp and cold, I belayed. Houseman fought avalanches pouring down the final technical pitch. We had been on the go for about twenty-two hours; there were still thousands of feet to climb. And for the first time in nearly twenty years, the thought that something could go seriously wrong haunted me.

At 6 a.m., twenty-seven hours in, and on day two, my feet were blocks of ice; I had had enough. I *needed* to stop and warm them. Having reached the avalanche-threatened slopes of the Cassin Ridge, we found a flat spot behind a large boulder and crawled into the bag that should have been a tent, had the wind not made it impossible to thread the poles. Six hours later, in what was now thigh-deep snow, we set out again. Three thousand feet remained. Up and over the top in one final push, that's what we wanted, but we were shut down at 1,800 by gales. With me holding the tent, Houseman threaded the poles – it flapped like a kite. I envisaged it lifting and taking me with it and flying over Denali's summit to join the streams of snow arcing from its highest ridge.

Sixteen hours passed, and in those sixteen hours, neither Houseman nor I talked about being pinned down until weakness had taken over. I lay in the little single-skinned tent – it buckled.

I thought of Al Rouse who died of exhaustion on K2 and Iñaki Ochoa de Olza who died high on Annapurna. This isn't a game we play, it isn't sport. Mountaineering for me will never be about beating the clock or breaking records; my climbing is about personal experience, it is the reason I get out of bed in the morning; it is not an updated status.

Twight, House and Backes' single push of the *Slovak* was such a leap, even though it was not the first time single-push tactics had been brought to a major climb. It was about commitment and style and personal challenge; it was not about setting records for speed or making headlines. The experience on a testing, committing climb, the self-questioning, the ability to survive on the brink with no guarantees, this is what it is about for me, and when I begin to race the clock or attempt to break records, that will be the time to give up.

'Listen.'

I pulled my head from the frozen sleeping bag. The wind had dropped. It was now or maybe never.

Thigh-deep, avalanche-prone snow made the 'easy' part of this climb anything but easy, but there we were, six days after leaving Camp 14,000, slowly balancing on Denali's summit ridge. Cloud filled the valleys. The afternoon sun, low in the sky, reflected from snow scallops. Denali floated on an untamed sea of cloud. Later, we found out the weather had been so poor that no one had attempted to reach the summit for two days.

As I stepped on to the highest point in North America, I thought of something Ian Parnell once said to me: 'We both know that the crux of any route in the mountains is the final step on to the summit.'

Stepping on to that summit I knew he was right, and it is often the 'easy and normal' things in life that are the most challenging.

29
flames

April 2013
Lake District, England

Spring is an in-between time, an awakening. Fresh growth and waxy buds glistening in the weak sun. Lambs balance on shaky legs, not yet used to their routine. See-through, wrap-around plastic jackets to save the lambs from perishing in the winter's cold have been removed.

Fingers wrap cold rock. Tendons, not yet conditioned, crimp. The rock holds the winter within its heart. The wind flows from the north. Cold fingers thread a hand through clothes. Blackbirds sing a 4.30 a.m. alarm. Pheasants *cock-cock.*

I feel little loss with this winter's end. Life has moved on – from cold to warm. Once again the tide has turned and I have not only a new van, but also a new relationship. With Jenny. The Jenny from the Cromlech boulders, the Jenny from Scimitar Ridge. Life is now driving my new red van between North Wales and North Cumbria.

Last year was long and cold – Alaska, Nepal, Canada, Scotland, America and once again Scotland. And after prolonged cold comes warm expectations. Is this the year? This is always the year though, isn't it? But this is THE year.

For only the second time in sixteen years I'm not going on an expedition to the greater ranges. The thoughts of alpinism and rock climbing spin through my mind at an ever-increasing rate. A blackbird balances on the stone wall that surrounds the old school house in Grange, Borrowdale. And beneath the twigs of blackbird legs, the outline of the stone wall mirrors the skyline of the fells. The rocks from the wall are matted with moss. Rain beads on the blackbird's feathers. The mature hardwoods surrounding the hut sway. Blue tits and chaffinches flit between swaying branches.

I lie on the bunk in one of two bedrooms. Stained and varnished boarding wraps around the walls and the ceiling. Foam mattress, sleeping bags zipped together, two more sleeping bags twisted into a synthetic plait seconding as a sheet. Jenny is on the bunk opposite, riffling through a bag of clothes. She looks as fresh as the day I first saw her leaning against the Cromlech boulders in the arms of someone who was not me. High cheekbones supporting a pale complexion are hidden by long red hair; her hair is straight apart from the occasional wave. Her lips are full. Her blue intense eyes are locked with concentration while hunting for clean clothes.

Apart from a woollen pullover, she crouches naked. The pullover accentuates her defined shoulders. The lime spotlights the red of her hair. A rib of wool caresses a flat stomach just below her belly button. Her thighs are pulled together, staggered, one knee in front of another like a sprinter locked to starting blocks.

In the hall outside the bedroom, the sun shines through a skylight. It seems to be magnified by the recent snow that has hit Britain and the Lake District. It gives an autumnal glow to the building, as does Jenny's presence. She emanates autumnal hues, harvesting, hayfields – she takes me back to working in the fields and pinpricks of sweat breaking the skin of a teenage boy, a boy with his whole life ahead of him ... she reminds me this is now lost, never to be again.

I stare. I want to lock away this image because I fear at some point I will once again be on my own and this eight-year-old dream to be with her will be gone. In my life, moments like this are rare. Moments like we had shared together earlier in the morning are also rare. 'Tell me if there is anything you want,' she had said.

I discovered that until that morning, I had never truly let go. I had always been outside looking in, calculating, assessing, trying my best to please someone else. And for the first time, I really began to relax and feel at ease with someone else. I know this sounds unbelievable – how do you reach forty-seven without truly letting go and feeling at ease in someone else's presence?

Jenny and I had known each other for several years, although only as friends until now. But there *had* always been a connection. For me the connection felt as shocking as a hold snapping and being catapulted from a climb. I still remember Stu McAleese driving us towards Llanberis after a day climbing at Gogarth. I looked from the passenger window and saw her, red-faced, jogging up the slate steps leading from the old railway. She looked at me and I stared back; it felt like a coincidence, but in some way it felt like a nudge, some crazy timing to remind us both of the other person's existence. Total crap, I'm sure, but dreams on occasion come true.

'Take me winter climbing,' she had once demanded in her forceful but amusing way. A way I found endearing, but also sad because she often appeared to struggle to keep friends. But we never did go, not until recently anyway – I thought she would surely drive me mad with her bounciness, her ups and downs, and I would most certainly drive her mad with my impatience.

My lifestyle doesn't lend itself to relationships. It is a hazard I hadn't envisaged when walking out of the gates of full-time employment and leaving a fixed base. And it was only when I met her that it dawned on me that it truly was a hazard. Solitude gives strength, protection, safety, dreams; solitude at times can be the easy option. Solitude is an open door leading wherever you would like it to lead. But I do enjoy sharing.

On the surface she was strong, outspoken, confident, opinionated, sociable – some people found her difficult. She could speak her mind. But beneath this exterior, there was a vulnerability.

Long ago during a relationship break-up, someone shouted at me, 'You've never been in love!' At the time of the argument I took no notice. It was absurd; of course I *had* been in love. But now, lying on a bunk amid a pile of twisted sleeping bags in the Lake District, I realise that maybe she had shouted the truth – or at least, if I had been in love, it was never as unconditional and deep as the feelings I now have.

The night before, Jenny and I had sat facing each other in front of the open fire.

'Have you ever had your heart broken?' she said.

The old school was lit by two lamps, a yellow glow from street lamps shining through the windows and the flickering coals from the open fire. My immediate reaction was to say no, not really, not properly, how could I have if I hadn't been in love? But what was heartbreak, what was love? The more I thought about her question, the more I grew to know myself, and in those few seconds the answer became obvious.

'Since a certain time in my life, I have had my heart broken with the ending of every relationship.'

It was the most honest answer I could give, and an answer she quietly processed. I looked into her face. A pale mask. And on her skin, the glow of the fire dappled orange. Large eyes, unblinking, processing, blue. She stared into the fire, another time, another relationship, another life. Then with hardly a motion, her head nodded.

We jog the fell above Ullswater – a gentle, rising expanse. The wind slices the skin on our faces. Rock pokes through the earth's grassy covering, which is also covered by a layer of compacted snow. Carved snow crescents wrap the rocks like mini glaciers around mini mountains. We pass over peat sculpted by the hooves of sheep. Beneath our feet, jogging through the squelch of snow and bog, frozen tears dribble down the stems of marsh grass. A buzzard cries.

Later, as we drove back to the hut from Keswick, a deer walked the white line in the middle of the road. Ears erect, fragile legs; the stone wall was cleared in one jump. The night and the woods cloaked the deer until it melted between the trees almost as if it were a dream.

'At some point I will suffer insecurity,' she had said as we lay together on the sofa in front of the coal fire.

'Insecurity is sneaky; it enters the mind when least expected. It is insipid and irrational,' I said, without letting on that I had already fought insecurity of my own and I would no doubt suffer more.

When will she realise I am old? When will she realise she is beautiful?

Trainers dab at the snow. We struggle to run the steep hill, clouds of breath smoking from our mouths. Large rotting bales of barley straw lie around, mould threading its way between the golden stalks, aiming for the heart of the bale.

There is a twenty-year age gap between Jenny and me, and the ticking of the clock is a constant reminder that we are mortal. Rivers flow, birds migrate and the tides reach their highest level before turning twice a day, every day, of every week, of every year.

30

dreams and screams

June–August 2013
France and Spain

Jenny and I drove south to Europe for three months over the summer. The Ariège, with its steep valleys and even steeper limestone, was the starting point of our time away. It was idyllic, except for the thunderstorms high in the Pyrenees – the source of the wide river that ran next to the campsite. The storms in the mountains changed the character of the river in an instant. One moment the deep water was still and calm, and then in a second, unpredictable, angry, agitated – a boiling spate of panic and emotion that washed away the cheese and the beer and the butter and all of my dreams. I began to fear the storms and fear the evenings after climbing. The river cut into my security.

Many evenings Jenny said she was leaving me in the morning to jump on a bus, a train, hitch a ride, go anywhere. Anywhere away from me and climbing, because she was not a climber, she was useless, she was not as good as the others she compared herself to. And with her self-loathing I felt a failure. I grew weary and with that weariness came guilt. I should have driven us away, as far away from that angry river and climbing as quickly as I could, but I didn't.

The next stop, Rodellar, was full of people, and like the Ariège there was a river, which flowed through the bottom of the gorge. There were many people climbing, but even with the crowds the river could disguise its danger by disappearing into underground passages.

Jenny's climbing progressed and she climbed well, but it wasn't enough – I suspected it would never be enough. I tried to understand, but I didn't – I didn't understand at all. Even the slackline became a whip with which to open old wounds. I despaired. I grew angry. I was sad and exhausted. I felt guilty and useless. I was flawed. Found out. A dreamer. A hunter of the impossible.

The towers of Riglos provided some release. I drove my red van away from the intensity of Rodellar and the crowds, aiming towards the conglomerate towers that stood like giant orange cacti. There was no river. We parked and explored and made a plan.

To beat the heat, we rose at four, and in the dark I started to climb the first pitch of *Fiesta de los Biceps*. Together, we meandered a chalked and cobbled line. The day warmed and, with no expectation and only the watching eyes of vultures, we climbed and laughed. The weeks of intensity fell away from us and once again we were together and happy; this was my dream. One pitch from the summit, at the steepest section of the climb, the wind rushed by us dramatically as a base jumper accelerated past, speeding towards the earth.

We walked from the summit of La Visera in the sun and later, sitting in the shade outside the refuge, drank a beer. The owner of the refuge owned a large and slobbering bulldog we christened Poirot. Poirot drooled and attempted to hump my leg. Which Jenny found hilarious.

We drove away from Riglos, heading north to France, to Millau with its bridge and north to Gorges du Tarn with its slow, wide and clear river. Our sabbatical was over; once again the climbing became like a measuring stick to use as a punishment.

In the evening, leaving the campsite and crossing the bridge in the centre of Les Vignes, we stopped and hung over the metal railings to count the brown trout silvering in the eddies. Brown rippling bodies in the current; beautiful brilliant creatures battled against the flow. One by one the lights of the street turned on and spotlit us standing there together.

With only one week before the ferry returned us across the Channel, we drove to Chamonix for Jenny's birthday. I presented her with an eight-pitch climb, high above the Vallée de l'Arve on Les Vuardes, called *Plénitude*.

For three months we had climbed pockets and tufas, and here, separated from the eyes of the world, shrouded in mist, high above the valley and the trees, we were faced with smooth limestone and water-worn tears and grey ripples and technical grooves and run-outs. The climb should have been a disaster, but it wasn't. No aspiration or expectation, no onlookers, no ego or ambition. To reach the base of the climb, we abseiled in from the top of the crag, before struggling to be once again back on the top. And once we were back on top, at eight in the evening, back into the damp and boggy forest with its giant rhubarb, we stood together shivering and laughing at our ineptitude on *Plénitude*.

But way down below, down beneath the clouds, beneath the both of us, was the fast-flowing river, and this river calmed for no one.

November 2013
Banff, Canada

I had been invited to the Banff Mountain Film and Book Festival to present a lecture about *Echoes*, my first book, and after the festival I was staying on to climb with Greg Boswell. This was my fifth ice-climbing trip to Alberta and I was sitting talking to Steve Swenson about some of the local climbs while a group of us from the festival ate in a restaurant in the centre of Banff. Steve sat close to me; his black hair, sharp eyes and slim athletic frame belied his years.

Outside, the wind scythed the street. Snow scuffed the road. But sitting in the warm, I could smell the damp of the forest above the Vallée de l'Arve and the earthiness of giant rhubarb after Jenny and I had climbed that massive sandbag *Plénitude*. Jenny could change the direction of my life – in fact she had. But our dream of 'together' was becoming increasingly complicated and exhausting. We had spent the summer together and every good day felt more precious because I was never sure when our relationship would end. Being in Canada was a relief, and that filled me with guilt.

A few days later, sitting in a large brown leather chair in the Alpine Club of Canada in Canmore, I stared at the sparkling snow weighing on the branches of pines and hiding the bands of strata on the Three Sisters. Tomorrow I would drive to Calgary to pick up Greg from the airport. Three coyotes – puffed, grey, red and black – slunk past the window. They miss nothing. They see everything. Later, I sat and watched a pine marten, his back arched and his thick jumper puffed. He bounced across the wooden patio on the hunt for something that he would possibly never find.

31
just beneath the surface

December 2013
Chamonix, France

It was just before Christmas and I hadn't long returned from Canada and a successful trip with Greg: *The Maul* on Wedge Peak, the third ascent of *Man Yoga*, the third and fourth ascents of *Victoria's Secret Deviation*, and *Rocket Man* and *Nemesis*. A great trip; the tide had been full, masking my problems, but I was sitting alongside Jenny driving the little red van to Chamonix and once again I was exposed.

I had booked the ferry for the two of us a week before, but with each day closer to departing, I didn't know if I would be on my own. But against all odds, we sat together covering mile upon mile of familiar road. My phone chirped text messages for some of the way and in those messages I recognised some of the feelings of desperation.

Guy Robertson's text messages pumped out a *need* ... 'I need. I want. I have to have.'

I sent a text back. 'Chill, Robbo.'

He continued to send texts, becoming steadily more desperate, each including bigger and bigger and more complex adjectives.

I replied, ' ... are you drunk?'

The self-flagellation we appear to inflict on ourselves in our modern world of constant information is, I find at times, debilitating and torturous. I've always worried about Robbo's sanity, because like me he also appears to struggle with the constant social media boasting. But he is a Scot, he has fire running through his thin body, and on occasion, his frustration will turn to anger. But on this occasion he was worrying me more than usual.

Jenny and I spent two weeks climbing ice and training over Christmas and

New Year and for most of the time it was extremely difficult. I returned from Chamonix keen to drive straight to Scotland to meet Robbo, to run away. I had to rest to build resilience, didn't I? Christmas and New Year had been bruising and upsetting and feeling this way – needing escape – led to guilt, because my pain was selfish. My pain was something I could walk away from and after a time feel healed. The complications within the relationship between Jenny and me were building to an almost impossible and certainly exhausting situation. We clung to each other and fought for survival because the relationship was something we both wanted, but the difficulties inside the relationship were becoming destructive.

January 2014
Scotland

Two weeks had passed since the original texts from Robbo and he still hadn't claimed his first success of the Scottish winter season. As I drove north I expected more sense from a daffodil, and at that moment, I decided we probably made a good match.

The weather came good to allow a couple of new routes – one in Creag an Dubh Loch in the east, and one on Stob Coire nan Lochan in Glen Coe, but the clear spell was over now. I returned to Roybridge to sleep alone on my bare mattress in the back of my little red van, to eat alone in the hut while looking out of the window with a million thoughts and emotions – hardly seeing the rain at all.

The rain ... the bloody rain ... it poured. And poured. And poured. The bloody permanent dark. The dark was smothering. Depressing. Invasive.

Through the day, I ran the narrow lonely lane from Roybridge that headed towards Glen Roy, undulating, winding. The rain bounced from the surface of the road. Ancient trees lined the lane and growing on their trunks was glowing moss. The brown peaty river – frothing white and bubbly – churned its twisting way around mossy boulders. Running, sweating, steaming. The deserted lay-by. Empty bottles – Glen's Vodka, J.P. Chenet Blanc – and discarded pink toilet paper, a soggy rosy pile. I imagined I was running along Cormac McCarthy's *The Road*. I felt separated in these post-apocalyptic highlands with only my thoughts for company. No one has a monopoly on misery ...

I had walked into four different crags in the week and then walked out again. My rucksack remained unpacked. The most memorable and inspiring part of the week's failures had been the 5 a.m. battle to reach the Cairngorm plateau. Snow, gales, a white-out. What the fuck had Robbo and I been thinking?

In the beam of the head torch, I picked out a white carrier bag blowing in my direction. It was only when it tumbled nearer that I realised it was a ptarmigan, being beaten by the wind. Her wings, so used to being strong and carrying her body, flapped around like polythene. She clawed the snow with broad feathery legs and at last found purchase, hunkering about a metre away from me. My torch shone into her dark eyes, and they blazed.

Sitting in the Wetherspoons pub down the far end of Fort William High Street, the rain hit the outside of the windows. After an aggressive email I decided no more. I ended mine and Jenny's relationship with an email. I felt alone.

Another day of rain. I sat in my van in Morrisons car park watching people leaving the train station and meeting loved ones. I sat and watched people embracing in the pouring rain. I wondered how long it would be before they hated each other and didn't speak.

Heading for the underpass toward Fort William town centre, I avoided the large puddles rippled by the wind. The waves on the surface of the puddles washed up on a beach of pavement. My mood was dark. It had been too long since the last numbing climb and waiting in wet Scotland made me miserable; I had too much time to think, I had too many conversations with myself. I was pitiful! I attempted to reason with myself. I attempted to see the truth and what was rational, but all I could see in the heavy drops of rain was loss.

Streams of water poured down the tiles on the front face of the underpass. The inside was lit, almost dazzling compared to the world outside. Music echoed and filtered begrudgingly into the damp gloom. The busker was in his fifties, a medium-sized man – wax jacket, bit of a belly, tweed flat cap, grey complexion and a worn and weary face. He played an acoustic guitar and his singing and playing were good. Emotion stirred deep inside the pit of my stomach. *Why did he need to busk, what had gone wrong? Was he on his own?* His eyes were sharp, they stirred something in me – something that punched me in my hollow self-pitying gut. I placed a few coins in his guitar case and looked at him, deep into those eyes. Swinging the guitar from side to side – strumming and singing – he looked up and gave me a nod.

Walking from the underpass and back into the rain, my mood felt lighter. I made a pact with myself to stop wallowing in self-pity and to try to cheer up. There was always a glimmer of hope in the small unnoticed things of life, like a busker's nod.

I drove to Aviemore and Glenmore Lodge on Sunday and on Monday morning, the first day of the BMC Winter International Meet, the forecast was atrocious. What to do? My mood was once again sliding, but I thought of the busker, music, life, love and the ptarmigan. I decided that Jon Walsh – the Canadian climber I was partnered up with for the meet – and I should walk in to Creag Meggie just to check out conditions, put in a track and if it was anything like suitable, we would stash the gear ready for the following day – which had a slightly better forecast.

The following day Jon and I started walking in the dark. The snow fell in large wet flakes. And in the dark and the wind, the drifting snow filled *Raeburn's Gully* and sloughed from Pinnacle Buttress. Our tracks from the day before were only just visible as we approached our intended climb, a climb called *Extasy* that had only seen two previous ascents.

Raeburn's Gully felt dangerous with the massive amount of snow. As Jon and I geared up beneath the cliff that was covered with gobs of ice, I could not stop thinking of the time I had been here just over a year before with Jenny – the start of our relationship. *'Take me winter climbing.'* On that occasion we had climbed *Smith's Gully* and afterwards we had walked out in training shoes, chatting and excited to be in each other's company. It had been so warm. Little birds flitted in the trees and spring felt close.

Jon and I battled the snow and the difficult conditions, and later topped out after completing the third ascent of *Extasy*. Neither of us fancied crawling on to the plateau because the wind howled, driving the snow to white-out, so we abseiled until we stood on the Appollyon Ledge where we traversed to *Smith's Gully*. Immediately I recognised the belay where I had stood and watched Jenny climb towards me just over a year ago – she had been so happy and full of life.

After the final day of the meet, when all of the visitors had gone, I decided to head south to Cumbria. I wanted to meet Jenny and attempt to resurrect our relationship.

Loch Linnhe, the black pool, the sea loch that follows the great fault, was on my right. A fishing boat, strong, but so easy for the sea to wreck, rolled on the swell. Rusting angle iron covered in seaweed with bobbing car tyres and blue polypropylene. Bubbled brown scum washed up on to the pebbled shore. An oystercatcher with his long orange beak skittered amongst the green probing cockles. Dark clouds passed across the surface of the loch. A rain squall troubled. And beneath, hidden out of sight in the deep, the wrasse and whiting threaded the kelp while somehow maintaining their position amongst the cold currents.

32
the light of the moon

April 2014
Llanberis, Wales

The wind blew down the Llanberis Pass. It was the Saturday of the Easter weekend. The Cromlech lay-by, opposite the boulders – where I had first seen Jenny – was full of cars, and in between the wheels of the cars, empty drink cans, plastic bottles, Mars bar wrappers, newspaper pages, cigarette packets and carrier bags, all danced down the road to a Caribbean soundtrack. Detritus blown west by the wind – west, just like my thirteen-month relationship. A brief relationship resurrection had imploded after Jenny had failed on a climb on Scimitar Ridge, and that had turned into self-hate. I was not strong enough to cope or help with this kind of illness.

'You've got it sorted,' one of the folk staying at Ynys Ettws said a few days after the break-up. I wasn't sure I had anything sorted.

May Day bank holiday weekend came; it was Friday. I lay in my van at 11.15 p.m. listening to cars turning into the hut entrance and the barrier clanging and the gravel crunching beneath wheels. A VW Transporter parked next to my van. The occupants disembarked. Talking, slamming doors, bumping into my van.

April is the cruellest month. The Great Orme poked into the troubled sea. The sky was solid grey. On the horizon a thousand newly constructed wind turbines turned. I had just finished climbing for the day. I drove my little red van, who was still without a name, around the narrow one-way road. The wall on my right, constructed from limestone blocks, turned and twisted, following the pavement and the road's edge. The wall separated us from the dark green sea.

The male kestrel hung on the wind; he glided a metre above the top of the wall. I checked the van's wing mirror and there was no traffic behind, so I stopped and opened the window. Close enough to touch, or so it seemed, the kestrel didn't hover – his wings, taut and braced, tilted at the correct angle to manage his solo performance. Bernoulli's principle or something along those lines, although I'm sure the kestrel wasn't up to scratch on aerodynamics. The wind took hold of his small, fragile body and puckered the soft surface. Burnt red, black flecks, a blue tinge to the ruffle of long wing feathers. His feet, just visible, were bunched yellow fists pulled into milky down. Streaks of black ran from just above his feet to the speckling of his throat. And above the throaty speckled ruff, his head was stationary. Large eyes, as big as pomegranates, ringed with yellow, locked on the long grass.

I rock-climbed every day: *King Wad, Chreon, Killerkranky, Romany Soup, Warpath, Big Boys, Centrefold, The Mask of the Red Death, The Moon, Perygl, Oriole, Skylark, Mayfair, Contusion, The Enemy Direct, North by Northwest, Agamemnon*. Climbing climbing climbing. The cold wind carried images and memories and conversation. Sadness and regret. And the climbing covered all that up.

From the side of the stream near the hut a heron lifted, folded and flopped, all awkward angles and pointed elbows, her legs and undercarriage yet to be lifted and her politician's chin sagging. The wind caught her canvas and she once again became a ballerina. And beneath the humped bridge crossing the stream, a dipper bobbed; rock to water to rock to water to rock.

Tears flowed. How do you do? *I've been better actually.*

At Gogarth's Yellow Wall I sat buried inside my hood, belaying on top of the crag facing the choppy Irish Sea. The tide was full. Behind, tourists passed me all wrapped up. Turbo-charged great black-backed gulls wailed. Fingers and feet numbed; my mind alert.

It was early morning; inside the hut everyone had already left. One fully charged bluebottle was my companion. The fly jerked and buzzed and popped as it repeatedly hit the windowpane. I hated the bluebottle. On the outside of the window, in the top right corner, the fat and speckled spider, sitting in the centre of her web, caught the breeze. The web contracted like a diaphragm. I wished she was inside. Ted Hughes was also my companion: *Birthday Letters*, a book Jenny gave me as a gift. Did she realise the content, the meaning? I expect she did.

The groove of *Nexus Direct* on Dinas Mot hangs high above the hut – it hangs high, as high as it has in the eleven years I have known it. In the winter, water funnels between its rough rhyolite, and in summer, the muck bakes to a crispy bran flake. Until two days ago it had been just a groove – an open book – one possibly as raw as *Birthday Letters*. And if you had asked me where it was situated a day or two ago, I would not have been able to tell you. 'Somewhere up there,' I would have said. 'Somewhere up there, high on Dinas Mot, somewhere among all of those corners, folds, grass, slabs and sheep.'

'No, I haven't done it.'

And if you had asked me its character, I would not have been able to answer. But, since that Sunday, since I failed to unlock its dimensions and see the pain behind its smooth curves, I now know where trouble lies. And now, like the moon, like my memories, like the tides, it looks at me before I close the red doors and it welcomes me as I wake in the morning. And like the moon and the tides, it is cold. I see its superiority, its subtle millimetres of movement, and its savage beauty. The troubles and complications … I see them all now. I see numb bleakness and I try to understand its difficulty and the damage it will inflict – already *has* inflicted – on me, but I am mesmerised by beauty and sadness – by pain and difficulty.

The next day, I walked the steep grass until at the foot of Dinas Mot and I entered and shared myself. I nearly backed off – maybe I should have – maybe I should have run scared and saved myself the heartbreak. But I wanted the experience, the feeling of becoming one. And for a while, we moved together.

Leaving the shady side of the pass, Lee Robertson and I entered into the warmth and sat on the steep grassy hill beneath Scimitar. I looked below. Twisting through the boggy valley base, the stream of clear mountain water slowly flowed. It flowed the same as before and the same as the time Jenny and I were here together, that first time, that second time, and that final traumatic and devastating third time.

The sun and the mountains were reflected in the surface of the slow-moving water. The stream was as a glittering artery feeding the dark boggy earth – earth made up of lives blown on the wind of years, of desiccated skin, bone and sinew. Our lives, our lives apart, our life together and our lives apart once again. Scimitar holds so many memories; nearly all are good.

Jagged ramparts – overhanging calf cutters made from ripped aluminium

– undercut razor edges, melted crystallised quartz tacked to the smooth rhyolite surface. Generally, there is no one here on Scimitar, apart from my climbing partner and me. But now I have the memories and the blood in the grass.

'Low tide is at seven; we should be able to get on the climb at five.'

Will Sim and I followed the worn zigzag in the steep hillside and stopped at the rocky edge overlooking the Wen. Wen Zawn, the welt cut into the wrist of Craig Gogarth. Greedy, invisible wind-fingers pinched and pulled and snaffled. Grit was angrily thrown into our faces. The gulls circled and screamed. A layer of paste-white cloud covered the sun. Pink thrift lollipops headbanged on fragile necks. The mood was as murky as the rock.

'It looks a little dark. The rock needs sun.'

With time and the gravitational pull of the moon, the sea drained and the boulders in the base of the zawn revealed their damp, barnacle faces.

'Well, if you don't shoot ... ' I thought this was becoming my motto for life, but I wasn't sure if I was strong enough any more to live by this philosophy.

Will climbed the first pitch of *Mister Softy*. I belayed and stared at the arch of *Conan* and its massive orange mullion crossing the sea to meet the corner of *The Unrideable Donkey*. A grey seal popped up its shiny head from the green pool and stared with sad, unfathomable eyes. She must have been reading my mind.

The cobbled back-wall madness of *The Mad Brown*. The ready-mix of *Rubble* – I stood on my own and felt almost at peace and at home in the quartzite cathedral. The wind pulled the ropes as a peel of seawater dinged the overhanging walls. A shaft of evening sun broke the cloud. People, voices, images, flooded my mind.

> Paul Pritchard stretches thin Lycra legs across the rotting corner, but
> just as quick he is lying broken among boulders with the sea on the turn.
> Johnny Dawes repeatedly throws himself at *Hardback Thesaurus*.
> Adam Wainwright and Big George Smith wrestle with the back-wall
> craziness. Jimmy Jewell solos the greasy offwidth of *T-Rex*.

The zawn was a cacophony of bird cries, crashing sea, wind and, on occasion, the deep engine thrum from the Irish ferry. I imagined couples in the ferry bar, laughing and drinking beer. And there I was, feeding out the rope as Will climbed the first pitch of *Mister Softy*, standing on my own, surrounded by walls and water with old conversation for company.

'Let's bail, and get out on *T-Rex*,' I shouted in an attempt to be heard above the wind and the rain, and to slam the door on our *Mister Softy* attempt.

But wearing the rack, I knew the first pitch of *T-Rex*, the slippery unprotected offwidth pitch, waited for me. Maybe I deserved it?

What seemed like a long time later, following the final traverse of *A Dream of White Horses*, the blue rope – not clipped to any runners – arced above me. Obviously, it had had enough and wanted out more than me. But I didn't want out, I really didn't, but the wind played tricks and for a second it let go of the rope and it dropped into the Wen's vacuum, snatching at my waist before rising once again.

At 10 p.m. in the dark, with salt-smeared glasses pushed into a pocket and a skunk's white stripe of chalk running the length of my back, I pulled into that final chimney and then out, out on to the grass, out into the angry night, dodging bullets of rain.

Back at the hut, it was almost midnight. I made a sandwich and stood on my own and ate on my own, while all the time the bright strip lights illuminated the red tiles beneath my feet.

Avoiding sheep shit while walking to my van with no name, I breathed and sucked in the light from the moon, hoping the glowing radiance would act like an anaesthetic.

33
the mountain soundtrack

September 2014
Mount Alberta, Canada

The underground train rumbles through the night. This is the soundtrack of the mountains.

I lie awake, stretching my frame the length of the thin mattress on a bunk inside Mount Alberta. The hut is not really a hut, it's a small tin shed balancing on a deserted and lonely spur. I lie and listen and think, listen and think, and in my mind, I follow the silver mountain blur, I watch the stars leave a trace of their lives in a disintegrating trail. I imagine the Black Hole, the dark vacuum beneath North Twin, the largest vertical face in the Rockies. I imagine the Columbia Icefield, inching in time, ice blocks crashing to earth. I imagine the loneliness after abseiling beneath Mount Alberta's north face. Life-lived, love-found, new-life, love-lost, intimacy-lost, friendship-lost. Emptiness and vacuum. The Black Hole. The fear ...

The mountain soundtrack is a comfort.

The underground runs to a timetable. Echoes from crumbling brick walls, scrawled with nature's graffiti, topped with turrets, boom with precise regularity. Will Sim and I are trapped between the before and hopefully the after. Will, lying in the opposite bunk, is exactly half my age. He has his lifetime to live again before he catches me, and at this very moment, lying here in this tin shed, I'm intrigued – maybe even a little jealous – of his simple, uncluttered drive. The glacier above and below the hut creaks, stretching my overactive imagination like ready-to-rip polythene. Sleep–awake sleep–awake sleep–awake ... life's rattle.

The alarm rings, although it is not needed, and as I stir, pricked eyes see the underground train passing behind paved backyards. The train passes sagging lines of wet clothes, overgrown gardens, spray-paint fences that separate lives. It passes beneath windows that reflect flickering television screens, below roads and solitary people. I sit up, throwing the sleeping bag to one side, and the mountain passes through the rubble of my mind's moraine, through my fears, my separation, my guilt, my weaknesses.

Sim and I are here in Canada to attempt Mount Alberta's north face. This mythical mountain, the highest point in the Winston Churchill Range, cannot be seen from any road and has had more failures than successes. The north face has four established climbs, three of which still remain unrepeated including the House-Anderson route that we hope to climb. At the moment, in Europe, queues form on perfectly plastic north faces. Some people run to the hills where you are virtually assured of the outcome. But I value quiet and uncertain above crowds and guaranteed success. I'm glad climbers are different from each other: the speed we move in the mountains, the mountains we choose to climb and how we choose to climb them; this is individual choice, but at times the pressure to conform, perform, it can be oppressive. There is too much jealousy, too many people living in fear. Day-in, day-out, day-in, day-out, day-in, day-out ... The engine turns.

Sim and I leave the hut at 3.30 a.m. and walk uphill, crossing glacier and scree for an hour before committing to five abseils. We rig each abseil station because we have not found the 'correct' place. Sim has lost his belay plate and I take a lot of convincing to continue. The older I get the more I pay attention to superstition.

It's a matter of percentages, Nick.

The train rattles in the back of my mind; this climb will be difficult enough without stacking the odds against us. The omnipresent feeling of the walls closing in around us, around me, is almost suffocating.

Canada is a developed country and because of this it is difficult to appreciate that alpine climbing can be more intimidating and committing here than in the Himalaya. But as we successfully land on the glacier below Alberta's north face in the red dawn, ear-swishing silence and emptiness engulf us. With only one night of food, a few bars, no sleeping bags or mats and absolutely no way to contact anyone, the 1,000-metre north face of Mount Alberta feels like the moon, except the moon has had more people set foot upon it.

Crossing the bergschrund roped together, we pitch out green glacial ice before untying and soloing 550 metres of snow slope. At 10 a.m. we stand with bent necks beneath the 400-metre headwall. Spindrift closes a curtain across the shadowed face. The soundtrack had been put on hold as we dropped into the void, but it has started back up again now. Snow whispers all around me, and as I look up I wonder what it would be like to fall. Like stepping in front of a train, I suppose, and for some, that final step could signal relief, but not for me. Up here, up amongst the ice and overhangs is my relief. It is difficult to imagine life without some form of suffering to make me appreciate the good times, or maybe it makes some of the difficulty of the *bad* times less fraught. A friend recently told me she thought I would make a good monk, the type who self-flagellates. I'm not so sure. The mountains have never torn me apart, but the loss of love has.

A pick penetrating snow-ice, the wind rubbing a rock edge, icicles dripping – this is the soundtrack Jenny and I had once shared together, but we will never enjoy it together again. My heart still aches. And as I stand and look, I sense this mountain is class A: this mountain will anaesthetise.

I begin the first thigh-eating overhanging flake pitch and all my experience of Rockies limestone climbing comes back in an instant. Insecure, loose, little in the way of footholds; my mind steels.

Hanging from an old peg and nut Barry Blanchard placed and abseiled from when he went off-line making the third ascent of the Lowe-Glidden route – the first climb on the face – I watch Sim above climbing a similar scratty, steep, strenuous pitch. Crampons – steel wheels braking on the tracks – screech. A leg is thrown to nothing on the right wall. He shunts, kicks. Snow hisses – whispering emptiness. It whispers solitude, fear. A river thundering and dropping into a deep gorge somewhere, somewhere in amongst the silence of a million trees below, roars unrelentingly. Climbing out of sight into a steep corner, spindrift pours.

'SAFE.'

But already I have begun to imagine scenarios and actions should one of us fall and become seriously injured. And no matter how hard my imagination works, the scenarios are helpless and the outcome never good.

We meet and I cross to the left until stopped by a dry overhang. Above the overhang I can see thick ice in the deep fault that marks our line and leads to the cave and tunnel Sim has been speaking about for months. The icefall is easily visible from pictures and it makes this line and the climbing what it is: natural, aesthetically pleasing. But the voice in my head shouts: *shutdown*. But there is a chance to pass this barrier with cunning.

Sim works resourcefully and after a few falls, a pull on a cam or two and some free climbing of thin crud, it eventually happens: he is above, then so am I; we are established in the deep cleft. Cunning has taken it out of Sim – neither of us is adept at cunning – although one or two moves to keep us on a 1,000-metre track are well worth the feelings of inadequacy.

We left the Mount Alberta Hut at 3.30 a.m. Neither of us has a watch or a phone but the sun setting signals it must be approximately 8 p.m. After nearly seventeen hours, glittering crimson icicles are above me, as hard as topaz. I climb the right side of the ice while bridging a foot on the limestone wall. One, two, three blows for the foot – one, two, three swings for each pick placement. Thuds of effort echo within the chamber and the coarse air grates. Into the dark – three blows, three kicks, three blows, three kicks – echoes, ice splinters – my sweating face machine-gunned by shards of ice. The angle eases and I belay. Sim reaches me and says he feels knackered.

'Do you mind leading the next pitch as you are better at that stuff than me.'

I'm not sure I am better at 'stuff', but his strategy, if it is a strategy, plays to my ego and it works. After all of these years climbing I still feel like a freeloader or a fraud if, like on this climb earlier in the day, I stop below difficulties and allow my climbing partner to go ahead.

The second ice pitch, the thing I attempted to ignore while belaying, is a compressed glacial ice-organ, a massive creaking, beating, frozen heart blocking the wide fault. It is pitch-black, not even the light from the moon shines.

Make or break. Although this is the third time it has been make or break on this route, but up here, just above this black heart, is the cave and tunnel. Jason Kruk and Joshua Lavigne discovered it after repeating this first half of the climb before continuing direct and making their new route. I wonder how many more 'make or breaks' there are to come before we find the cave – if we find it at all. House and Anderson didn't, after all.

Entering a vertical chimney flowing with dark brown ice, bridging, kicking, flicking the head torch beam from white flock wall to white flock wall – embedded gravel locked in the frozen brown. Tap, tap, tap. Fabric snagging the rock, ragged breaths, all this intimacy. Large rocks balanced one on top of the other, like clots blocking a vein, are ready for me to set them free like a hit of warfarin. Sim is belayed in the fall line with his rucksack over his head. Squeezing past the rocks, hanging from axes planted in the apex of the overhanging heart, I discover the whole structure is made from layers.

Between each layer is the stench of rotten air and gangrenous snow. Climbing the outside to the right, my original plan, would mean treading water up a thin skin. Should the structure collapse, it would kill us both. I dither and procrastinate and eventually climb direct into the centre. The ice here is less layered and more solid, maybe even trustworthy. Chopping, balancing, bridging, pushing, manteling – I am transported into the left atrium. The floor is aerated. The walls are weak and thin. I shine my head torch and there appears no way out. I am an embolism caught inside the frozen heart of the mountain. I look at the floor; reversing is not something I want to do, and if I did, *what then?*

Breath escapes my mouth and catches on the surrounding ice before disappearing into the darkness. At this moment, I long to be vapour. Tentatively I swing an axe. The pick thunks into the outer wall. A few more swings and a small hole appears. The floor hasn't collapsed and the structure is still fast in Alberta's chest. More swings, the pulse of the pick repeatedly planting echoes around the atrium and the hole becomes bigger and bigger … until eventually the hole is large enough and I squeeze through and escape, reborn into the fresh air above.

Attached to an ice screw and axes, I look in front at the large floe of ice that should have been the sanctuary of the cave.

'It's going to be an uncomfortable night,' I shout to Sim, who is seconding. In delivering this message I accept and mentally prepare, but as Sim's thumps rebound from the walls, I shine my torch beam higher, and above an overhanging chimney, I see the white of a ledge and realise that the cave is actually up there.

Flat rock and sand provide comfort. Roll and turn, roll and burn, roll and turn, roll and pain … I climb the overhanging chimney directly into the mouth of the cave. Sim joins me and following the tunnel we find a flat spot, remove our harnesses and eat our one meal. I lie in the foetal position. Deep inside this tunnel, deep inside my body and my mind, I shiver. Recollections and cramps wrack my body.

The anaesthetic for this first day has run thin – the mountain and its difficulties are hidden. I lie in the sand, shrouded in the limestone tomb. At one time I would have said climbing is everything, but I'm not so sure any more. I imagine *her* face staring from a moving window of an empty carriage … the carriage is speeding away … speeding out of the tunnel. It takes with it dreams and hopes, fantasies, laughter, love and heartfelt emotions, away into the Canadian wilderness, away forever.

Stretching down into the tunnel, dusty vapours catch in the filtered light of morning. The wheels scream as the hour comes close. The stove chugs. Quartz ignites. Strata lines covered in ice run silently into the middle of the mountain. And outside, into the open space of the world, a life away from here, away from this tunnel, away from me, a life goes on.

In the fresh air, out of the tunnel, Sim shuffles; teetering into biting reality, he slowly slides along a snowy siding. I join him at his belay station and he points. There is a steep exfoliating crack at the end of his finger. The white of the snow does not disguise its difficulty or looseness, but after a short distance I lose the way and belay below a shallow groove, feeling disappointed there are yet more difficulties. Sim studies descriptions and pictures on his camera, he recalls accounts and eventually he decides the way. He continues through some of the steepest, most technical terrain we have so far encountered. Sim's drive, his determination and skill impress me, and in other ways depress me. Eventually I decide it must be a skill to climb with someone twenty-four years your junior and *not* feel inadequate, although I'm not sure I possess that skill yet.

For the first time, cracks in the rock are friendly, almost solid. Front-point placements become precise. The difficulty gradually eases and gently runs into being almost enjoyable. I try to absorb it, to catch a screen grab to draw upon in later life, but the train speeds forward and the mountain imagery blurs. Blanket clouds on cruel winds sweep and separate the barren ice slope. Sim and I have felt estranged from the world since leaving the road three days ago, but I have felt separated for much longer. Snowfall smatters my face and sprinkles down the ice sheet we are kicking and kicking and kicking.

Pulling over the corniced ridge, I lean over and shake Sim's hand. Mount Alberta's north face is below, a memory, but in no way crushed. This mountain does not get crushed by anyone. It allows passage.

In reaching this secluded and seldom-stood-upon place, the Japanese route has to be descended, which involves traversing Alberta's one-kilometre-long knife-edge, several abseils and finding our way through cliff bands, tile-strewn slopes and pockets of slab. Sim and I both know that Steve House and Vince Anderson had trouble finding the correct way and their descent turned into a long drawn-out affair, including a bivvy. Even Jon Walsh and Chris Brazeau, Rockies experts, had taken nine hours to descend in perfect weather after their single push of a new route on the north face.

Climbing up here, up on to this ridge, certainly does not spell success, and as the gloom and the snow come down, I stand and balance, listening to the wind and the familiar rumble of séracs breaking and falling into the Black Hole beneath North Twin. It must nearly be time to catch a new train, but I am not sure of the direction, the final stop. But this is it, isn't it? This is the soundtrack of life.

34
please queue here

December 2014
Stoke Bruerne, England

At the beginning of December, I had driven from Llanberis to Chamonix and on the way, I called to see Mum and Dad on their boat. *Jasper* was still moored at Stoke Bruerne, near Northampton. After a couple of hours, as I stood to leave, Mum handed me a Waitrose shopping bag of Christmas gifts: mint chocolates, dried dates, a Christmas cake she knew I liked to eat on bivouacs, a good bottle of South African Shiraz and a birthday card containing cash she could not afford to give. Dad was in his chair smoking and drinking tea. I took the hessian bag – a bag for life – from Mum's painfully thin and arthritic hand, and after a gentle hug, left the boat.

The week after New Year 2015
Chamonix, France

Tim Neill was up front; on occasion I saw his head torch shine in my direction. We had left the Rifugio Torino at 6.30 a.m. and headed into Cirque Maudit with the intention to climb *Fantasia*, an enclosed ice line I had climbed a few years before. My lungs crackled with infection, my breathing was laboured and I wondered if this was the same strain of infection that Mum caught soon after I had seen her, the same strain that she died from a week ago. I had been climbing up here with Tim that day also – the day Mum had been rushed to hospital – but I didn't receive the text from Lesley until the following morning when I got up in preparation to climb again.

I pictured Mum then, the same as I pictured her now, lying on a trolley in a hospital corridor, tended by ambulance men. Lesley had been with her; she said they were in the corridor for three hours before being taken to the intensive care unit. Following Tim, my skis cut the snow and my breathing burnt, and in the dark, all around, I could see Mum lying on a trolley in a long, brightly lit corridor.

When it became light, I could see jagged mountains on the distilled red-striped horizon. There had been so many mountains. Choughs circled, their wings spread wide to catch the breeze. The choughs reminded me of starlings, the birds from my childhood. As a teenager, to feed my ferrets I would shoot starlings with an air rifle. As a fourteen-year-old, starlings were scrawny scavengers: they had nothing to offer, no beautiful song, no beautiful plumage, no grace. Starlings were ferret food.

Tim and I geared up, the same as I had geared up a million times, the same as I had geared up beneath this climb a few years earlier with Steve Ashworth, a time when Mum was still alive.

I sat on my rucksack, fitting crampons to my orange ski boots.

Mum was tall and slim with dark Mediterranean features, but in that frame was strength and determination. I could see the deep scar in Mum's leg where, as a child, I had opened all of the drawers of a steel filing cabinet, and as the cabinet toppled forward with the weight, she had jumped in front, taking the force of the fall and supporting it as it pinned her to the floor with me underneath her. Someone eventually found us and lifted the cabinet away.

SNAP. My crampon locked to my orange boot and the holes in the snow at my feet filled with powder.

Arriving home from school once, I found Mum covered in oil underneath her blue Hillman Minx, changing the starter motor. It was a time when cars with diesel engines were rare, another of Dad's car experiments, and this engine had been taken from a large van; it was old and the starter motor was big and heavy.

'Pass me that spanner, love; I'll get some tea on in a bit … '

Tim set off, wading deep snow and crossing the bergschrund beneath the stream of ice that clung to corners and flowed over rock overhangs until it hit the col beneath the summit of Mont Maudit. I followed, clipping to a belay by the side of the first steepening.

There were many times I thought I would not outlive Mum; I thought she would be in that unenviable situation which, I'm sure, most parents dread, of outliving one of their children. I was wrong, and as Tim and I climbed higher and the wind on the col increased, this time, for the first time, the situation felt different. I realised that if I died, there of course would be upset and sadness from friends and family, but the one person who would have been really truly devastated was now gone. This was how it felt, but was there more?

Since staying in Ynys Ettws I had become friends with Dave Astbury. He is a member of the Climbers' Club and also an engineer who used to know Mum and Dad through servicing their printing press when they had their computer stationery business. Dave told me how Dad had offered to pay him to take me out rock climbing and learn how to climb and use ropes safely – or at least how to use ropes, as I would just go out and solo.

'Your dad used to come up to me all the time,' Dave said, in his thick Potteries accent, something like a more refined Birmingham accent, 'and he would beg me to go out climbing with you before you killed yourself.'

Dad's interest on the surface had never appeared deep, but Mum always took a delight in whatever activities my sister and I were involved in, to the point that when I became interested in mountaineering and climbing, within months she could name mountains, mountaineers, Scottish winter climbs, summer rock climbs, alpine climbs, Himalayan climbs, South American climbs – the lot; she could enter into conversation about the subject with confidence. This of course was not always the best, because pulling the wool over her eyes became impossible.

Leaving the sun and climbing into the shadow, into the confined icy corner, images and memories flowed with every drag of the pick, every kick and swing and pull. I could see Mum totally worn out, falling asleep in a high-backed chair with a half-filled mug of strong instant coffee balanced by her side. Sometimes, so tired, the mug fell from her hand. Strong coffee was certainly a big part of Mum's life and she was seldom without one, and it was generally partnered with a super-long cigarette. It says something about her determination, that after nearly fifty years of smoking, one day she decided to give up.

... Up ... up, up above, the spindrift ripped into the blue sky and swirled.

It swirled like steam from a mug, like starling murmuration, like smoke. Like ashes. On either side of this slender ice formation, the granite mullions hemmed us in. I was reminded of the strong yet skeletal oaks that stood on either side of the wooden church gates as we waited for the hearse that carried Mum to arrive. In the topmost branches, the starlings had waited with us.

March 2015
Chamonix, France

Another winter season in Chamonix was drawing to an end. I sat on a stone wall and soaked up the afternoon sun. The newly constructed entrance of the Midi téléphérique station was in front of me: glass, metal, stone, wood – the structure proudly shone. How many times in my life had I sat and waited like this? How many nervous and excited minutes, hours ... days even? But like a stone rubbed smooth, I could not help but think, some of the innocent mountain magic had been lost with the passing of almost twenty-two years of my climbing life.

Jack Geldard, my climbing partner for our attempt on a climb called *Stupenda,* had still not returned from the boulangerie, and as I sat and waited – waited with the Chamonix hubbub happening behind me – I watched two workers dressed in blue boiler suits chipping and spreading salt on a patch of ice that looked like the outline of an island. Pocked brown and jagged, water ran from the disintegrating edge of the ice island. The slow brown flow trickled and finally disappeared into a deep crack between paving slabs. Above, starlings looked down from where they were perched on the sparkling steel frame of the Midi station ...

Heavy breathing and the rumble of rocks loosened by the late afternoon sun were the only sounds now. Jack and I had skied down the Vallée Blanche. On my left, a single old ski tip was pointing from the glacier. I checked to see if it was an Atomic, one of the set I lost when airlifted with my broken ankle from the Petites Jorasses. It wasn't, and with a dull ache in my right foot, I continued toward the Leschaux Hut.

I had stayed in the Leschaux many times and with many different partners: Jules, Jon Bracey, Rich Lucas, Stu McAleese and Tim Neill. So many people, so many days and nights.

Jack and I left the hut at 5 a.m. We had crossed the glacier and climbed the approach slope beneath *Stupenda,* an overhanging and direct crackline in the Aiguille du Tacul. I was deep inside a chimney at the beginning of the third pitch and I struggled to remove the gloves I had stuffed down my front. The food in my chest pockets, and the bundles of blue four-millimetre tat still bulged in front of me like a beer drinker's paunch. The styrofoam conditions Jack and I had read about in the Philippe Batoux book, *Mont Blanc: The Finest Routes,* were nowhere to be found. Instead, stuck to the dark, beneath the numerous overhangs, was meringue.

Stupenda is given a grade: III 6 M6 A2. I'm not sure what this means; grades in the mountains can often be superfluous. I climbed higher, squeezing deeper, deeper into overhanging granite, deeper into the mountain, to finally reach the pitch three belay. Jack seconded the pitch and I set off on pitch four. I swung through the overhangs directly above the belay. Certain I had just free-climbed the crux, I shouted to Jack, 'Hashtag, first free ascent!' But as I pulled through another overhang and into another crack, I looked up to see a flared and overhanging offwidth. My hashtag hubris smacked back at me and I made a pact with myself to try and be more humble.

On the smooth wall to the right were two spaced bolts. I realised this must be the A2 section and the bolts had been placed for upward progression. I squirmed and arm-barred and leg-barred and body-barred until I felt drunk and I could bar no more. My stomach felt punched. My torso was above the highest bolt. I attempted to swing a pick into a clear sliver of ice glued to the back of the crack, but each time only a single tooth caught. I could not swing the axe properly because of the restricting crack and because my body was balanced precariously – taut, extended. I needed to escape these constricting granite chains. My left foot, shin, knee, thigh, failed to purchase and repeatedly I slithered back to the one foothold inside the crack.

Suddenly I realised how important free-climbing this stupid *Stupenda* had become and my younger determination kicked in, shocking my older self. Knee-bar, arm-bar, squirming, battling …

First free ascent.

… millimetres … arm-bar …

Look at me.

I took hold of the axe jabbed into the drool of ice. Thrutching. Sweating. A millimetre, a centimetre.

Still clean.

Hunting. Hanging. Wedged.

Still clean.

Held in place by a twisted thigh, body tension.

Still clean.

Level with my right foot was the higher of the two bolts which had a karabiner clipped to it. I stared. It was tempting for a front point. *Who would know?* But I couldn't, I just couldn't, because of course, I would know.

Some of the less honest things I have said or done, of which I am less than proud, still haunt me, and I have learnt that my life is more healthy with honesty. I have stripped myself to skin, bone and sinew to make myself light. Ego and the fear of failure could, at one time, weigh me down, but fortunately not that often any more. So what if I fall and the free ascent is lost? So what if I don't clamour to update my status? This fight is my fight and my fight alone.

I matched the axe with both hands – pulled and squirmed. Millimetres. Millimetres. My right leg flapped and scraped. Millimetres. Squirming… but the ice grew tired and the axe ripped and ice shards exploded, hitting me in the face, and I fell. I fell like a starling shot with a lump of lead, fired from a teenager's air rifle. And as I fell, being scared hardly entered my mind. But for a second, just one plummeting second, being disappointed and even being angry did. But the disappointment and anger was only for a second, and by the time eight metres had passed, I was happy and in some way content.

'Are you OK?' Jack shouted.

'Yep, I'm good, ta.'

I pulled myself up the rope and this time, using a front point neatly placed into the karabiner clipped to the high bolt, I managed to find a hook. Once more, I began to squirm and thrash until I eventually reached the belay.

Three bold and technically demanding pitches followed, but finally I was standing in the brèche at the top of the climb. Exhausted and enshrouded by dark, I had taken a claw hammer to my brain; in fact, my life was taking a claw hammer to my brain. But Mum would have been proud, right? And Dad also?

I lay on a wooden bench looking at the stars. Jack lay on a second bench doing the same. There were millions of them, a starling's chest of iridescence – black plumes smattered with silver flecks amongst an oil slick of green, blue, purple and red. It was half past midnight. Jack and I had skied the bottom section of the Vallée Blanche and walked the steep snow slope leading through the woods to the small wooden hut at the start of the narrow and zigzagged James Bond track. The track would eventually lead us back to Chamonix. I sat up and looked across the orange glow of town, across the moving white headlights, the dogs and cats, the parties, the blue shutters, the frosted cobbles, the cafes, the silver icicles hanging from gutters, the stationary lorries with smoking chimneys and beyond. My eyes moved on to the snow slopes of the Brévent and Flégère and the piste bashers out on the hillsides, moving around like a War of the Worlds invasion: flashing yellow lights, powerful white beams, smoothing and grooming.

'How you feeling?' Jack asked.

'I'm totally knackered,' I replied without taking my eyes from the moving lights of the piste bashers that were now blurred by the cloud of condensation rising from my mouth.

'Bloody love this feeling, never want it to end.'

And then it hit me, because of course, it *will* end. I had lost Mum and I had already crossed the halfway point in my own life and as I lay on the bench looking at the stars, I knew this queue was the same queue that we all stood in. Realising this almost made me weep, but it also made this life time-expanding, and the sacrifice to live it, even more worthwhile. And as I lay in the chill, with thick steam rising from my clothing, I realised that I still clung to the alpine innocence, but with growing older, it needed more of a jolt. But with this growing older, other facets had also become more important: the shared experience, the connection to the surroundings, the friends and of course the memories.

And in the branches of the trees surrounding Jack and myself, I imagined starlings, such gregarious and beautiful survivors.

35
dawn to dusk to dawn

October 2015
Canmore, Canada

Two years after the successful trip with Greg, I visited Canada for an eighth time. It was half past midnight when I arrived in Banff, the last person on the white shuttle bus that had carried five passengers from Calgary airport. I sat in the back of the bus in the dark. A freight train bullied its way through the centre of town. Red lights flashed and an X between barriers marked the spot. The deep bass of the train horn blew. A grey cat with white stripes skittered across the tracks. It was almost twelve years to the day that I had walked from the door of Leicester Prison for the final time and fifteen years since my first visit to Canada.

I spent a month at the Banff Centre writing this book before moving to the Alpine Club of Canada's clubhouse, where, aged forty-seven, I waited for my climbing partner Greg Boswell. Greg is from Scotland and is half my age, but unlike some of my other, older Scottish friends, he doesn't appear to have that aggressive Scottish nationalism. I don't mean to belittle this fierce nationalistic pride, but Greg appears to place all of his fierceness into his climbing and when he is not climbing he is generally relaxed and good fun to be around.

The temperatures dropped and a metre of snow fell with Greg's arrival. Winter was again with us. Our first climb had been one of those long-lusted-for climbs, *The Real Big Drip* set in the heart of the Ghost. After this climb, we made a return to the Stanley Headwall climbing *Dawn of the Dead* and *Nightmare on Wolf Street*, two big mixed classics. We thought we would try going even bigger after these routes and attempt the second ascent of a climb called *Dirty Love*.

Dirty Love is a 500-metre, twelve-pitch alpine climb, high on Mount Wilson, which is situated off the Icefields Parkway, the road that runs from Lake Louise to Jasper. No coffee shops, no people, just wilderness, emptiness, deserted, alone ... almost ...

Jon Walsh and Raphael Slawinski had climbed the first ascent of *Dirty Love* in April 2008, grading the climbing M7. The climb had taken them twenty-three hours from the car to the summit of Wilson and another eight hours to descend. The trouble is, there is a very technical approach, which includes several mixed pitches and approximately four hours of slog through trees and alpine terrain before the bottom of the huge gash, which looks something like *Cenotaph Corner* on steroids, is reached.

Greg and I aimed to put a track to the base of the climb to become knowledgeable about the approach, before retracing our steps back down to the valley and returning in two days' time to attempt the second ascent. Everything was going well, although the three loose and difficult mixed pitches after half an hour's walk didn't really match Jon's description, and took us longer than we had hoped. We assumed there should have been ice on the approach, but after the days of snow and the subsequent days of minus twenty, it had been warm and we guessed that the sun had melted any exposed ice.

At the top of these initial pitches, we slogged snow for an hour before climbing an M5 mixed pitch in the dark. Engulfed now by the last of the forest on the highest level of Mount Wilson, we checked Jon's description: 'two hours forty-five of snow slope to reach the climb'. We had come this far, so felt it would be pointless not to now put in a track, even though we were in the dark and the wilderness.

We left ropes and some gear at the top of the mixed pitch and after five minutes we also dumped axes and anything heavy before attaching snowshoes and bushwhacking through thick forest. Eventually we escaped the trees and found the snow gully that led to the foot of the climb and at seven thirty, really high and near the foot of the climb, we decided we had done enough to establish a track so we could return in two days and follow it without too much bother. Retracing our steps without snowshoes to consolidate the track, I walked in front with Greg behind, until the edge of the forest was reached.

The moon had yet to rise and darkness enveloped the both of us. We followed a glittering track in the light of our headlamps. I kicked as the snow clung to my knees. Small spruce lined the edge of the forest and all I thought about was how, in two days' time, we would return, fresh from rest, to attempt the stunning-looking line we had taken photographs of earlier. Having the time to search out the unusual made my roving and sometimes lonely existence bright and fulfilling.

Greg was behind, and then I heard something that took over my reflexes …

I spun. My headlamp caught blue as Greg flailed past, all arms and legs. Snow splattered everywhere. Just behind Greg, but moving quicker than him and with much bigger arms and legs, was a grizzly bear.

Ink-black, bottomless, unfathomable eyes turned and focused on my prone form. Erect ears, a broad industrial snout and an open mouth full of brown teeth were attached to a beautiful head etched with pale flecks. His bounding body was muscular, seemingly propelled by pistons. The snow lapped at the bruin's belly, which didn't appear to slow it. Frozen, terrified, my torch lit the snorting, hungry freight train that was now rattling by inches away from me and dusting me with spindrift.

I just stood. I was frozen. Terrified. Incapacitated. For a second, the bear looked right at me, for just one second, and for that one second I thought *this is it, this is really it.* Or, more like, I *would* have thought that if I could have formed thoughts, but I couldn't; my mind was white noise, it was a TV screen in the times before twenty-four-hour programmes, when the screen became horizontal bars and the sound was a constant *beeeeeeeeeeee.*

All in that exact same second, the bear had seen Greg fall and it flew past me, close enough to run a hand along its fur. Immediately I ran away. I ran as fast as I could, I ran uphill, in the opposite direction, as fast as the deep snow would allow. And my now functioning mind had capacity to scream, and alongside that scream was another scream. Greg had fallen on his back and I could only watch as the bear bounded towards him. Screaming and shouting, Greg kicked at *Ursus arctos horribilis,* and it bit straight through his boot as if it were just a sock. It pounced again and crunched into his shin, while placing a paw around his other leg before lifting him clean off the ground.

'Nick! Nick! Help, it's got me ARGHHHHH, HELP NICK, NICK HELP …'

I stopped running then, and hearing my friend and his high-pitched pleading, my mind insisted: *the bear has got Greg, let it eat him, run, run as fast as you can, save yourself.*

But on hearing the chilling, terrified scream, my survival instinct subsided. I stopped and turned. But I'll tell the truth, the thought of running back to face the bear armed with only a ski pole slowed me. My limbs and mind were unravelling but Greg was shouting my name, I couldn't just stand there. I couldn't just stand and listen to my friend as he was torn apart. I began walking towards the bear and Greg, thinking *this is it: I am about to die*. After fifty years I was about to return to the stomach of another living creature.

Suddenly, out of the dark, a shape came hurtling toward me. I screamed so loud the skin at the back of my throat tore. But the shape coming at me was Greg. My torch shone into his ashen face, and in that face I saw something I had never seen before.

We both yelled, attempting to sound big, but feeling insignificant with primeval urges coursing through our veins. Feeling helpless, feeling very much a part of the food chain, we ran into the woods following our tracks. The trees and branches closed in, caught and ripped and tore as we crawled, clawed and stumbled.

'Watch me, stay with me, watch me … ' were Greg's distraught cries.

I had a plastic, orange-coloured knife that I used for cutting tat and the like. I held the knife, ready to plunge the two-inch blade, if need be.

After what felt like hours of waiting for the dark to ambush, we found our crampons and axes, which meant the ropes and the tree from which we could abseil and escape this ledge and the bear were just five minutes away.

'Keep a look out,' said Greg, packing gear into his bag. I stood, shining my headlamp while brandishing axes.

'If it comes, no running, no running, we stand together, we're in this together, side by side, no running. Hit the bastard,' said Greg urgently.

'Yeah, we're in this together, hit the bastard, hit it as hard as fucking possible, in the head, in the eye.'

In my mind we were now starring in the film *Alien*, and I daydreamed watching the bear shrug off an axe as easily as a bullet bounces from that slippery black alien skin. *They mostly come at night … mostly*. And in my mind I knew, I just knew that if the bear attacked again we would be torn apart; we wouldn't stand a chance, the creature was so powerful and wild and inhuman. It was a beast that survived in order to eat food and raise young; it couldn't be talked down, controlled or compromised with.

We launched again into the woods, sweating, swearing and shouting and banging axes, following our trail. But after an hour, we discovered it wasn't our trail we had been following. No. It was the bear's trail, and we had become hopelessly lost. We crawled beneath a massive tree. It was an anomaly as all of the other trees were big with wispy branches; this tree was enormous and with thick branches.

'Let's climb the tree and wait for the morning and daylight?' suggested Greg.

I looked into the branches and imagined being sat in minus sixteen with Greg bleeding and suffering hypothermia.

'No, we need to find the ropes and get out of here.'

'Let's head for the clifftop,' Greg said, before throwing himself over snowed-up rock shelves that were just above the cliff face.

Down, down and down. Greg tomahawked over small cliffs. Powder exploded. We were about to launch over the main cliff if we weren't careful, and a small part of me hoped we did.

Greg shone his torch. I kept watch. We stood on the edge of the cliff looking down, peering into dark space. Quiet.

'Can you hear that? It's the bear, it's coming, it's coming for us.'

I attempted to calm Greg. 'It's OK, it's just running water.'

We had come too far right. We had to retrace our steps and head back, back into the woods, back towards the bear. I knew I had to be forceful because Greg – normally very sure – was losing blood. He was going into shock and his thinking was not to be trusted. A part of me felt we were never going to find the ropes, we were going to be stuck up here, stuck up here in this nightmare, with the bear, and even if we weren't attacked again and stayed up here for the night, Greg would surely bleed out.

'We have to retrace our steps, Greg.'

Another hour, crawling, bushwhacking, following our steps, until we at last discovered where we had gone wrong. Within minutes we found the ropes and the place to abseil. Greg abseiled first. I sat on the clifftop brandishing both axes, looking into the dark, looking into the trees while all the time expecting them to explode with a freight train of growling fury. I hadn't clipped in to stop me falling, because I had thought that if the bear came, I would jump. Eventually Greg shouted and I followed, and after reaching the snow, the two of us waded the middle shelf between the two sections of a climb called *Shooting Star*.

We screamed and shouted, making as much noise as possible, and in the distance wolves howled in reply.

'Nick, stop howling, the wolves will get us.' Greg's boot was full of blood, which was squirting from the tooth holes every time he stepped. I followed, wondering from what distance bears could smell blood.

Reaching the bolted anchor above the first section of *Shooting Star*, Greg rigged the abseil, and again, I looked into the dark holding my axes. The abseil was from a single twisted bolt. My mind was calming and I thought how ironic it would be to die of an abseil anchor failure.

Three abseils later we landed. We waded our tracks for another thirty minutes until reaching the road and the hire car – it was 12.45 a.m. At 2.30 a.m. Greg and I entered Banff emergency hospital. The friendly nurse asked me if I wanted a drink. There was no wine on offer so I had ginger beer. Greg couldn't drink anything as the five huge holes in his shin – which was now so swollen it resembled his thigh – might need surgery.

I savoured my ginger beer and told Greg it tasted good.

36
threshold shift

October 2016
Stoke Bruerne, England

Paul Ramsden and I left Tibet and flew back to Britain nine days ago, and already Tibet feels like a country someone else visited. Standing on the canal towpath in the grey Northamptonshire morning, I am about to embark on a journey with Dad to move *Jasper*. I left home at age sixteen, thirty-four years ago, and the thought of spending so much time with Dad scares me. *What will it reveal? When will it end?*

Stoke Bruerne to Apsley Marina near Hemel Hempstead in Hertfordshire. Fifty miles and fifty lock gates. *Jasper* hasn't moved for years. A parrot and a Jack Russell terrier. An eighty-three-year-old man who wants to stay where he is. Stoke Bruerne has become the place he calls home. Dad won't help.

'I'm going to sit in my chair drinking tea and smoking,' he says.

He prefers to shut himself away. I have no experience of controlling a notoriously unreliable boat. I'm a fifty-year-old man, I can feed myself and keep myself clean, but I've made climbing into my comfort blanket, the intermediate between me and the world. Are we so different?

Mum was always friendlier, more tolerant, more adapted to life and its people than Dad. Dad is insular, a smouldering ash. The woman who owns the mooring wants rid of him. She has also recently lost her partner of many years, and she doesn't want the hassle of a disagreeable tenant. Dad pees into a bucket at night, and in the morning he throws the contents into the canal. All his life, Dad has taken pride in being stand-alone, antisocial. But even the most driven individual needs a final destination.

I understand both sides, though to me, the eviction feels cruel. Imagine being eighty-three and having your home moved overnight. You wake in the morning and look out the same window, but there's a new, unfamiliar view, with unfamiliar people and pavements and streets you don't know your way around.

My close friends Mark Goodwin and Nikki Clayton are due to arrive soon to help me. Mark is a poet – eccentric and creative – and Nikki has a unique, gentle way of viewing the world and its complications. Mark and Nikki have lived together on a narrowboat for fifteen years. For three days, they will teach me how to handle the boat, and perhaps how to handle my lack of understanding for Dad. But my mind screams, *the journey could last for five days …*

By 15 September 2016, Paul Ramsden and I had been in Tibet for six days, and the orange tent with its blue-striped tarpaulin had become our home. We sat at our base camp near the river. Several miles up valley, the water sprinted from the snout of the glacier, which inched from the foot of the mountains we hoped to climb. In the morning the current was subdued; still noisy, but the day's sun hadn't yet warmed the ice, and the volume was less. Later in the day as the grey water rushed, polishing the rocks, the sound increased. After a day or so, the noise became less invasive. Our minds decided it wasn't important any more. Threshold shift.

We were there to attempt a new route on the north side of the Nyainqentangla West range. To our knowledge, we were the first Westerners to explore this valley.

'No, that's not the side to climb from. It's too steep, no one has climbed from that side,' local residents told Paul. Truth be told, hardly anyone had climbed from either side. This small sub-range was something of an enigma, a very-difficult-to-get-permission-for, a magician's trick.

I followed Paul into the unknown above Base Camp to begin our acclimatisation. Walking into ever-thinner air, walking ever farther from news reports of Brexit and Trump and Aleppo. When the clouds parted the sun felt warm, as if its protection would last forever. But the sun was burning and ageing, and at some point, it would die. The river, milky grey, grew shallow. Yaks lifted their heads and watched us for a second, before resuming their grazing. Boulders rubbed smooth by glaciation and rumbled by water were scattered along the wide valley base. Redstarts, feathers the colour of paprika, perched atop large, snow-covered rocks. I imagined there were still birds thriving among the rubble in Syria, but my numb brain was crammed with a glut of images and information and distance, and my privilege made a comprehension of other people's plights more unobtainable.

The mountains, their danger and noise, were similar to the noise of the river. There, always there, always roaring, much as it had been for over twenty years of my life now. But my mind, my energy and exuberance had dumbed-down the risk. It's the same as when you are young and you see an older person push their glasses from their eyes before sitting them on the top of their head. *That will never happen to me, the short-sighted glasses thing,* you think. But of course it does, and as I read the newspaper these days with my glasses propped on the top of my head, I can clearly see the mountain's print and the text reads 'Loss'.

The red cushion where Mum once sat has a small hollow. The nearby shelf is full of bits and bobs: a small camera, a phone, a picture of me in the snow on Ben Nevis, a dictionary that she used for reference while completing her puzzles. It's 24 October 2016. Nearly two years have passed since she died, leaving behind Dad, her partner for fifty-four years. Everything is covered in a thick layer of dust. I move a photograph that lies flat on the shelf. The wood beneath is bright and sharp; there is a picture shape in the dust.

Dad sits close by smoking his roll-up and drinking tea while reading an Inspector Morse story. Barney the parrot stands on her perch inside the cage on the old oak table. Empty sunflower seed husks lie scattered. Paddy the Jack Russell claws at my legs. Dad's jeans are unwashed and dirty; his flat cap is greasy. His chin full of grey whiskers, his mouth full of yellow stumps. The boat is quiet apart from the creaking and when Barney talks. Dad appears not to notice, but Barney calls in Mum's voice.

The year 2003, the same year I resigned from my job as a prison service PE instructor to become a nomadic writer and full-time climber, was the same time Mum and Dad sold their house and almost all their belongings to live in a narrowboat and explore the waterways. I now stand in the gloom of their kitchen looking into a dirty sink. Butter and bacon grease smear the draining board. Granules of white sugar are stuck to brown stains of black tea on the spoons scattered in the sink. Mugs, swinging on hooks, are covered in tar. The fridge is leaking water. A pan on the hob is half full of congealed fat. Avoiding a pool of water on the floor formed by the leaking sink in the bathroom I look down on a bunch of Mum's silk roses in a round container at the bottom of the dirty bath. Faded, withered white petals with black edges, the whole bloom is dishevelled, covered in tangles of a spider's web. In another room, the double bed where she last slept is still made with her bedclothes. The floral duvet is brown and damp with nearly two years of waiting. The flower print is almost invisible beneath the coat of dirt. The boat – the dream – is unloved.

When Mum died, she left behind an on-the-wagon alcoholic who was used to hiding behind her sociability, her care. Dad has not cooked, shopped for food, tidied or washed clothes at any point in his life. *How is this possible?* I want to run as far away as I can, as fast as I can.

I climb through the small double doors and step on to land. The canal is a gash cut through the earth and filled with dirty brown water. Straight, like the cleft in Cirque Maudit that I climbed on the day that Mum died. Unforgiving. Compulsive.

I am afraid. I know I'm wrapped in the same skin, blood, bones as the man who sits inside the boat.

On day two of our acclimatisation, Paul and I walked around a corner, and from nowhere, a towering north face appeared. Instantly I was beguiled. I felt a deep longing, an ache. I wanted that drunken euphoria that almost nothing else in my life provides. This buttress was a rabbit from the hat, unseen by the mountaineering world. I wanted to down this hill in one swig and revel in its headiness.

'I don't need to look any further for an objective,' I said.

And Paul said, 'If we don't do it, you can't publish a picture anywhere because I will come back.'

But we had to do it. In an instant, my mind had gone from a successful climb, to published articles, to awards, and then, just as quickly, to failure. *So much failure. So many dreams, so much ambition, so much time. So much life.* And in another second, I was already plotting a return. I was like Dad – in fact, worse – in that I had fallen from the wagon even before Paul and I had put the wagon into gear.

In late August, Kyle Dempster and Scott Adamson went missing on the north face of Ogre II in Pakistan. I'd socialised with Kyle in the USA and Canada and rock climbed with him in Italy, and I couldn't get the image of him out of my mind, or at least the image of where he once was; those broad, strong shoulders that rose and fell every time he laughed. As I'd caught the plane to Tibet, I still clung to the belief that he and Scott would stagger into their base camp with another story. But I was wrong.

It snowed all through the first night that Paul and I camped beneath the buttress, so we returned to the river. Three days later, we headed back to the start of our route. Lying in the little tent below the buttress, I came clean with myself – possibly for the first time in more than twenty years. *Life affirmation, the challenge, live life to the full …* It was true at some point, I suppose, and still is for some, but now it all felt clichéd. It felt like marketing consumeristic bullshit. The most honest statement I could conjure up was: know what you are and what you have to do when you wake in the morning.

Today I will walk to the foot of something that intimidates me, and I will begin to climb.

… But even this statement was untrue, even this was my mind's marketing, because the real reason was for the after, for the adulation and acceptance and the slap on the back. It was all just a big erect middle finger. *I'm getting mine, how about you?* But at least I was being honest, and possibly that is my answer, that is why I do it. Honesty is easy. Honesty is open. Honesty is a weight off. Honesty is no secrets, and once discovered, honesty is peace. *Maybe I'm getting old?* I am old. Trying to set the record straight.

Maybe it was that picture that got me thinking this way. Luca Signorelli took the photo seven years ago at the 2009 Piolets d'Or outside Le Majestic Hotel, Chamonix. Andy Houseman laughs while placing a flower into Kei Taniguchi's hair. I stand on the other side with one arm around Kei and one arm around Kyle Dempster. Alexander Ruchkin and Vitaly Gorelik crouch at the front. Everyone is smiling.

Now, Kei, Kyle, Alexander and Vitaly are all dead.

Heavy snow covered the cliffs before me. I felt as if I were breathing through plastic stretched over my mouth. At altitude, my lungs crackled; at altitude I had Mum's physiology, not Dad's. Mum was tough, but her body was frail, though she always battled and rarely complained. Mum's mind was tough also, I'm sure of it; she had put up with Dad for fifty-four years, after all.

At times, the drifts were waist deep. Inauspicious. Spiralling above us were 1,600 metres of unknown ice and rock. The summit had a reported elevation of 7,046 metres. I plunged and waded remembering the butterfly. One day, at Base Camp, a red admiral with slightly dried and faded sections of wing stumbled into the tent. I cupped the butterfly in both hands and returned it to the outside, but as it took off, a gust of wind pushed it into the snow. I offered the back of one hand. The butterfly, with damp wings, crawled aboard. I placed it atop a brown boulder in the sun. Half an hour later, I watched the butterfly take to the air.

'I can get down from any mountain in any condition.' That was how Paul had put it. I didn't doubt Paul was strong; it was obvious from his big legs. Paul told me he had run the Bob Graham Round, one of the three classic mountain challenges in the UK – forty-two Lakeland peaks within a twenty-four-hour period – when he was seventeen. Paul reminded me of the Shar Pei dog I had photographed in Lhasa: friendly, but bred for fighting.

That evening, we squeezed on to a tiny snow step for an open bivvy. Through the night, I looked at the stars and thought about friends burnt out by brightness of living. So many dead. Friends. Friends of friends. Family. I'd like to say they are always with me, every day, every night, locked inside some vault inside my mind. But the days and the nights and the weeks, the months and years … All the time I've spent in the mountains, all that self-satisfying and goal-driven time, rubs smooth the edge like the grey, numbing water rushing from the glacier, until it is only on occasion that the shocking drops of cold, clear revelation remind me they have gone, gone forever, and at some point, I will go also.

Two parent swans and an almost-mature, grey-feathered cygnet run the surface of the brown canal before take-off. Wings chop the air with a powerful swishing noise. Mark is at the tiller. He could stretch out an arm to shake hands with them. The swans are a family, but instead of closeness and unity I see Vulcan bombers, planes designed to kill. War is in the news: Syria, Afghanistan, Iraq. As we leave the mooring that was Dad's home, no one comes to say goodbye and Dad stays inside the boat, sitting in the gloom.

The noise of the engine is as loud as the river in Tibet. My mind vibrates, listening, willing it to stay alive. At twenty-one metres, *Jasper* is the longest length of boat able to navigate the canal system with its many lock gates. Instead of a simple standard throttle and gear shift, a long rod of steel gets pushed forward to engage the forward gears and pulled back to engage reverse. The throttle is a small bronze wheel, turned clockwise to increase the revs. It soon becomes apparent how physical it is to jump on and off the boat to prepare the lock gates. No wonder Mum always looked so thin and worn out.

Beneath the shredded grey and black thistling of his unruly hair, Mark's face turns serious with concentration. At first, I think he is hamming it up; Mark has a creative, almost over-the-top exuberance. Later, I find out exactly how much I need to focus just to keep the boat straight. As we pass through narrow bridges, around bends, meeting other boats travelling in the opposite direction or stopping, I begin to feel as if rock climbing, in comparison, is almost uncomplicated. Rock climbing is concentration and forethought, but this is like rock climbing with someone else's body. Nikki reminds me how to operate the lock gates. She explains with such careful and intricate detail that I tell her to simplify her instructions. I then immediately feel guilty for being so blunt.

A year ago, I decided I had done enough. 2012 was my last expedition to the greater ranges, and I was finished. *Nada mas.* The toll over the years had been paid ...

Then Paul showed me a picture. Maybe one more time? Go out with style? Finish with something people would remember me for? *Ego*. People ask why I think younger climbers aren't going on expeditions. The reason is easy for me to see. Expedition success is like crack cocaine, but in the hands of an addict, more dangerous and expensive. I was a pusher. I wrote about what I found: the high, the release, the escape. But as I pushed the glasses to the top of my head, at last I could see. At last I could write with honesty. I thought myself a modern man, but in reality, I was a throwback. Almost extinct.

Threshold shift. Western society, or maybe society as a whole, doesn't seem to want to wait any more. The instant is in vogue: instant gratification, instant pictures, instant food, instant fame and instant fortune. Before he met Mum, Dad was drafted into the Korean War. Later, after I was born, he worked a string of jobs to pay the bills: bricklayer, insurance salesman, brewer, social worker, machinery operator for cotton weaving and printing presses. Dad would get home almost every evening and hardly move from his chair in front of the fire while watching TV. He didn't have a credit card. Enduring hardship over an extended timeframe is something I appear to have inherited. I battle against my intolerance, something I have also inherited from Dad. On occasion, I lose that battle. And at times the failure is difficult to accept. I never asked for intolerance. As for platitudes, I didn't want those either. I don't ever want 'he died doing what he loved'. Dying young or even dying old but still healthy is desperately sad and heartbreaking and overrated and should not be celebrated. It should be seen for what it is: a terrible waste. Life is a gift. Living more so.

Paul and I christened day two the crux day. Runnels of creaking ice. Arêtes of snow sculpted by the wind. Bulging rock with grains of orange and yellow stripes. The whole face twisted in some warped, massive monster Matterhorn way. Day two was the test … but of course it wasn't really. The real test is always continuing.

'It's never as bad as people think,' Paul had said. 'They always think their situation is much worse than it actually is and come down. You just have to wait it out and carry on up. Don't come down; take the rough with the smooth.'

But if it got bad, I really wanted to come down, instead of hanging in for the good of the overall outcome. I gave up easily. Many better climbers stayed up. Many died because they did. Staying up was not something I wanted. Dad didn't come down. He stuck at it, committing to a life that I suspect was not of his complete choosing, one that he accepted because of the expectations of his society and for the company of the woman he loved. He quenched his aching with alcohol, only to be left alone to grieve.

On the way to Nyainqentangla, we stopped in the tiny hamlet of Badigog at the village leader's home; a block fortress perched high on the windy plain above the straight road where he conducted his business of Tibetan trinkets, yak rides and blessings. We never did get the village leader's name, but he was generous. He was tall and thin and wrapped in a fur-lined, wine-red-coloured coat that touched the back of his knees. His eyes were bloodshot and glassy. I liked him, although I'm not sure the feeling was mutual. Paul and I were on our own. Tashi, our liaison officer, knew we had a permit for the range, but he had no idea where we planned to climb. No one did. Paul's wife Mary wasn't fooled. Before we'd left, I could see it in her eyes. Paul himself appeared to have bought into the story that he had told Mary and his daughter Katy, a story of safety. Denial. But then again maybe it wasn't? Paul was obviously very good. He seemed, almost, to believe in all he said, and his track record was exemplary.

I've told myself that if I die on a mountain, it's going to be the unsuspecting thing that ends it all. But of course, this isn't true. It will be one of the obvious. It will be storms and a slab avalanche, or I'll be pinned down by bad weather until exhaustion gets the better of me.

The final runnel of creaking ice was overhanging and enclosed, a frozen gullet that released me at last. Side by side, Paul and I dug a ledge for the small tent. The blue of Namtso Lake disappeared behind a bank of cloud.

This was not one of those wait-for-a-perfect-five-day-forecast climbs, which was OK. We had absolutely no way to get one.

Standing in the deep drifts on the morning of day three, we hoped the most technical climbing was below us. We didn't want much more uncertainty. We felt we had earned an easy completion to our climb, and we chose a wide snow ledge that led directly to the central crest, which we hoped then led directly to the summit.

I've been climbing and writing full-time with no fixed abode now for thirteen years. I say this as a fact, not a challenge or a boast. I have witnessed so many people rush and push and strain, attempting to wring the essence from their short period of time away. They appear to cram – or at least try to cram – a lifetime into a weekend, and who can blame them, as the existence they are returning to on a Sunday evening might be difficult or disliked, or even hated. Have you ever stood back and watched? Have you ever separated yourself and really watched? It soon becomes clear there are a lot of good people surviving.

After Paul and I had climbed for a total of four and a half days, the central crest led with an almost monotonous and uniform regularity to the summit: a windblown sculpture that didn't mean anything to anyone, but on this occasion it meant everything to me. That place was years of training and dedication and loss and loneliness, and after twenty minutes, we said our goodbyes. As if the curtains were being drawn, the clear lake with its lithe sparking blue and warm comforting sand disappeared again. The clouds closed in, and once again separated us. The view had gone.

I don't know how, but like a homing pigeon Paul led across ridges and down and around unstable snow slopes. We hoped to descend the East Ridge to its lowest point, where we would turn left to walk down a gentle snow slope back into our valley. But the cloud, as if it knew our fear, became thicker, and the snow became whiter, and the angle and the many-corniced ridgeline became even more dangerous as they all blended into one. And after Paul had fallen into three bergschrunds, we pitched the tent in one of the holes that Paul had found with his body.

A few years ago, I bumped into Scottish alpinist Rab Carrington in the old chapel on Llanberis High Street that was now a gear shop. Around us, climbers pulled on new rock shoes smelling of glue and rubber. Couples wearing new and crunchy vibrant-coloured jackets looked at each other and themselves in mirrors. The coffee machine gurgled to the smell of espresso.

I asked Rab why he had given up mountaineering at a time when he was still in such good form.

'I wanted to continue living,' he said.

I decide at the end of the first day's travel with Dad, Mark and Nikki that I'll run back to collect my van and park it somewhere nearby to sleep because there's no way I will sleep on board. But finding the boat again isn't simple. The canal quietly runs behind gardens and hedgerows and fences and walls. The canal swirls beneath roads. It splices farmland and industrial land alike and passes through the hearts of towns and cities. The canal and its deep swirling brown is surrounded, and yet separated. But at last, with a combination of satnav and walking in circles, I arrive back at the boat.

In the morning, the journey resumes. The water is low, starved by drought. If *Jasper* veers from the middle ground, she bottoms out, and all three of us have to push and pole to get her moving again. On one occasion, Dad leaves the gloom and steps to the towpath to join Mark and me on the rope as we attempt to pull *Jasper*'s bow to the bank. Mark compliments Dad on his strength and tenacity. Dad registers this compliment with an 'Aye', as if this was simply what was expected.

Twice I have to disappear, shoulder-deep, into a small hole in the back of the boat. I turn my head and hold my breath to try to stop the brown water from entering my mouth. I explore with invisible fingers until I discover the propeller and the clothes and plastic bags wrapped around it. I lie on my stomach against *Jasper*'s hard steel, and I rip and slice and pull at the rubbish with bear-like hands, and once again I am a twelve-year-old attempting to help.

The drains leading from the toilet in 6 Brookhouse Road, the house where I grew up, had blocked. Dad rodded the drains, but they refused to clear. After measuring, Dad guessed the obstruction was directly under the *Echinops* thistles with their spiky globes of electric blue. For a time, Dad had tended and maintained his garden with love. In the evenings, he would stand with a mug of tea and a cigarette while taking it in. Often he chose unusual plants, for he had an exploring, creative imagination, albeit trapped inside what seemed like a narrow existence. *Echinops* radiate a strong scent, similar to buddleia, and like buddleia they attract butterflies.

In the summers I used to sit on the paving stones next to the small pond.

I leant against the wall that Dad had built with old red bricks before I was born. Already the bricks were crumbling, showing their age. Red admiral butterflies, bumblebees and sparrows orbited the spiky blue globes as they swayed in the wind. A honeysuckle bush cascaded over the wall. The scent from its flowers mixed with the fragrance of the *Echinops* and the flowering lilac. Pond skaters slid on the water's surface. Occasionally a flash of gold erupted, and a goldfish disturbed the quiet with a pop and a gulping mouth.

The bed of *Echinops* had to be dug up to get to the drains. Dad grasped the wooden handle of a spade tightly as he raised it. He hesitated for a few seconds before driving and chopping into the roots. Eventually the *Echinops* were just a pile of leaves and stalks and fading blue globes thrown over the wall. He and I took turns, continuing down into the dark, damp earth. By evening, I had hit a brown-coloured pipe made from clay. Whoever had installed the drains had bungled the job. The small, cemented-together sections had fallen apart, causing the sewage to leak into the flowerbed. Dad decided we had done enough for one day, and in the dusk, we walked back to the house together. Perched in the top branches of the lilac tree, a blackbird sang. That night I lay in bed excited to see what tomorrow would bring.

The next day Dad and I dug out the old pipes, and he inserted new ones that would last longer. He lay awake for most of that night with severe stomach pains and vomiting and diarrhoea, so in the morning, I went to the garden by myself and filled the hole. After finishing the job, I went to the house. Dad was in bed where the doctor had told him to stay. I told Dad I had finished the job, and he looked pale, almost embarrassed, before he nodded. Later, Mum let me know that Dad had told her he was proud I had worked so hard. I felt happy to have pleased Dad, but I also felt guilt at the sight of the dark empty space in the ground where once there was so much colourful fragrance and life.

I rip the last of the rubbish from around *Jasper*'s propeller. Dad has left to take Paddy for a walk along the towpath. He expresses surprise at the rubbish around the propeller, but no particular encouragement or thanks, not that I expected or wanted any. The sooner we can move again, the sooner I can escape.

The scent of the summit and success vanished with my memory of the *Echinops*. Where once there was blue there was a space. And where once there were butterflies, there was empty air. Darkness fell, and the empty air filled with snow. It snowed all night long, and all through the night I lay awake, admonishing myself for not insisting on abseiling the way we came up, because now we were somewhere teetering on a ridge above 6,500 metres in a storm with limited food and limited knowledge of how to get off. Paul and I had climbed the line. This was just the way off. It didn't matter. It was just a dumping ground over the wall. And we were going to die and the memory of us would fade ...

The morning. Still snowing. Still white-out. We knew we would have to stay put. But by 9 a.m. the winds abated, the blizzard stopped, and we decided we had to take this opportunity. I couldn't help voicing my concerns about the amount of snow that had accumulated, but what were we to do? Sit there and hope for some kind of miracle? Paul said only two inches had fallen. Had he expected me to believe that? Maybe he had said it more for himself.

Once more, with incredible accuracy, Paul found the exit gully to the lower ridge. Snow crystals blown upwards turned into rainbows. And through the rainbows appeared the blurred blue of Namtso Lake. Paul's route-finding ability, from years of alpine climbing, was something I greatly respected. But as I led across large pockets of windblown slab, I still imagined myself swept and buried amid a chaos of crevasses and séracs. A mess of glacial holes and overhangs blocked the designated left turn to our valley, so we turned right into the south valley, where we spent a sixth night. *Almost safe.* A mile below, I could see the green of shrubbery. *When did Dad give up his garden?* It must have been when Mum and he retired to the boat. I suppose in order to follow a dream there must be a sacrifice.

I have been on the boat for almost three days. Autumnal sunshine coppers the fields. At last I understand *Jasper*'s idiosyncrasies. I am beginning to relax, although the thought of Mark and Nikki's departure is terrifying. We pass a field of fading sunflowers. Wood pigeons, plump and silver, sit on sorrowful seed heads. Mark and Nikki's opinion of Dad has mellowed. I didn't hear Dad say thanks when Nikki shared the large tub of curry she had made for our journey, but both she and Mark insist that he did. After a full seventy-two hours in Dad's company, they see an old, formerly strong man left behind by time; they see the empty spaces where he once had Mum, a strong and forthright stare, a firm grip and the ability to engage in conversation. They see a man who dotes on his dog and his parrot. They see a lost and lonely man who for so long only needed Mum, but now has to rely on others.

Maybe I need to lift my glasses, to sharpen the view that has dimmed through the passing of the years? For a second, I feel betrayed by my friends' understanding. But I try to throw these thoughts away. If I let the intolerance fester, it will drown me.

A heron, bolt upright, proud and grey, stands among green reeds, missing nothing. A cormorant with wings spread balances in the top branches of a skeletal oak. Dad sits inside, in the dark. The tiller judders in my hand. The hawthorn bordering the canal is tangled with decaying fruits. Goldfinches fill themselves on past-their-best berries, flitting between sharp thorns as if understanding the danger but revelling in the risk. Autumn is nearly gone, and the cold will soon be upon us.

On the morning of day eight, Paul and I followed a jumble of moraine and river, back to the grass and the grazing yaks and the deeper currents. Strings of colourful prayer flags streamed the hillside, and we eventually popped from our self-imposed isolation into some form of reality near Badigog, the village we had started out from nearly a month before, and the house where Tashi was staying. There was no one home.

I collapsed amid the concrete blocks and sand piles before crawling inside my sleeping bag. Paul sat, leaning against a pile of rubble. An old woman from a nearby house walked over. She smiled and spoke. Although we couldn't understand, she held out a flask and offered hot water. I joked with Paul, 'What do you think would happen in Britain at the moment, if people from another country were to appear and lie down outside a house?'

The inlet to Apsley Marina is narrow and at a right angle to the main canal. I shudder at the thought of turning *Jasper* in this confined space. New and expensive flats surround what was once a thriving and active working marina where people mucked in, but now it is a floating housing estate where a few are friends or at least know their neighbours, but many who live here are distant, and the people who live in the flats, looking down on the boats, are more separated. Electronic locks and signs forbid entrance to non-residents. Teenagers with skateboards stand looking at mobile phones. Mark and Nikki left last night, but my nephew Jake had arrived earlier that morning to help, and together we successfully reach our final port of call. Dad stays inside the boat looking out through the glass doors, almost as if he's scared to encounter this new place. Dave, the marina warden, shouts instructions. His face appears friendly, unconcerned. And with some controlled manoeuvring, *Jasper* slides through the entrance without bumping against other boats. Dad's final journey is almost at an end.

postscript

As I drive west, leaving Hemel Hempstead, on my way back to Llanberis, I look through the windscreen of my red van, a van still without a name. Out into the dark, out over the cold brown water of the canal and beyond the bright lights of cities. Britain at the moment feels like a land that has forgotten how to care, especially for people with little in their lives. The gap between those with and those without grows. A self-proclaimed xenophobe has recently become president of the USA. The conflict in Syria continues with the death toll and displacement of thousands.

Mountains once seemed to protect me from such realities. There was always some part of me that wanted to be a hero; I suppose I did want to try and be an inspiration for the underdog, and I used to believe that climbing could be the way. But there was also a part of me that wanted to be absorbed in something bigger, something better. I never much thought of the danger when I started out all those years ago. I never imagined the pain, the grief. Heroic ... I was young and indestructible ... I saw myself breaking shackles, ripping free ... But I was naive. In my defence, it's difficult to see the downsides when you don't really value what you have at the time. It's easy to make light of it. When you are young, life is cheap, time a giveaway. But of course, life is never cheap, and time goes one way only. Entropy.

And now, like Dad after he lost Mum, I'm more aware of all I refused to see in the past. The world is changing. I'm changing. People, or at least many of them, appear to be more out for themselves, and the louder an individual can shout on social media the better they are thought of. And what of solidarity? What of the feeling of community, of loyalty and friendship?

But what do I know of loyalty? Because as I drive, my dad is sitting on his boat, alone, listening to Barney the parrot speaking in Mum's voice.

acknowledgements

In the acknowledgements section of *Echoes*, I wanted to thank as many people as I could in the space provided: friends, climbing partners, house owners, cat owners – because they have all helped and been with me for much of the time. For *Tides* the original list still stands, and to reiterate, without the help of my friends I would not be able to do what I do and for this I cannot thank you enough.

There are certain people who have gone a little above, or above and beyond. In no order of preference, below is a list of these people.

Nikki Clayton, Mark Goodwin, Jo Croston, Katie Ives.

The Paul D. Fleck Fellowship and the Banff Centre. I can't express my thanks enough. What a wonderful place and what great support you give.

Dr Zylo Zylinski for putting up with me and being a great sounding platform for much of what I write.

Tessa Lyons for her wonderful cover artwork.

Ben Silvestre. Graham Desroy (The Hippy). Rich Kirby and Helen. Tim and Lou Neill. Ray Wood. Bayard Russell Jnr and Anne Skidmore. Katie Moore. Andy Houseman. Paul Ramsden. Lindsay Griffin. Naomi Risch. Kev Mahoney. Kenton Cool. Lukasz Warzecha. Ulrika Larsson, Wojtek Kozakiewicz. Neil Brodie. Matt Helliker and Zoe Valérian. Matt McCormick. Doug Madara. Claire Carter. Jon Popowich. Ryan Lang. Stephen Jones. Andrew Denton. Robert Macfarlane. Joe Simpson. Duncan Machin. Matt, Emma, Adrian, Matt and everyone at Coldhouse Collective.

Mountain Equipment, DMM, and Boreal: my sponsors who help me live this life.

Alpinist magazine and everyone who works for the magazine. Your support and encouragement and confidence in me over the years has been invaluable, and your support of mountain writing and writers second to none.

Vertebrate Publishing and everyone who works for the company, especially Jon Barton, John Coefield and Camilla Barnard. Without Vertebrate, their imagination, vision and courage, many writers including myself would have nowhere and would not be published. I feel privileged and fortunate to have your support.

Alison Osius and *Rock and Ice* magazine. Ian Parnell at the now defunct *Climb* magazine. David Simmonite and *Climber* magazine. Natalie Berry, Rob Greenwood, Alan James, Nick Brown at UKClimbing. Alex Messenger at *Summit*. Dougal MacDonald, David Lintern, Jack Geldard and all the other editors from magazines around the world who have given me a chance.

My sister, Lesley Stone, and her partner David. Cloe and Kyle, Jake and Fiona. Keith and Rachel Ball. Chrissy and Nigel Shepherd. Raphael Slawinski. Ian Welstead. Jon Walsh. Michelle Kadatz. Guy Robertson. Greg Boswell. Will Sim.

The Alpine Club of Canada, especially everyone at the Canmore Clubhouse. The BMC, especially Nick Colton, Becky McGovern and Dave Turnbull. The Mount Everest Foundation, the Alpine Club, the Nick Estcourt Award, the Chris Walker Award and any other grant bodies I have forgotten who make it possible to attempt things that are at times almost impossible. The Climbers' Club.